Pr

"It takes considerable courage to le.. . .. .ui., and even more to speak out about such an experience."
RICK ALAN ROSS, CULT EDUCATION INSTITUTE

"Beth Granger shows how much emotional damage a cult can cause, and how difficult it is to overcome the experience."
NORI MUSTER, *BETRAYAL OF THE SPIRIT: MY LIFE BEHIND THE HEADLINES OF THE HARE KRISHNA MOVEMENT*

"Beth Granger provides readers with an insightful and self-reflective journey into, then eventually out of, a debilitating cultic environment ..."
STEPHEN A. KENT

"... a stunning contribution to the growing recognition of the impact and trauma of growing up in a cult."
JANJA LALICH, *TAKE BACK YOUR LIFE: RECOVERING FROM CULTS AND ABUSIVE RELATIONSHIPS*

"This well-written, explosive Canadian memoir will have you on the edge of your seat."
JANICE SELBIE, RPC, *DIVORCING RELIGION: A MEMOIR AND SURVIVAL HANDBOOK*

"You'll cringe, cry, and cheer for Granger as you read her compelling story. I did."
CHARLENE L. EDGE, *UNDERTOW: MY ESCAPE FROM THE FUNDAMENTALISM AND CULT CONTROL OF THE WAY INTERNATIONAL*

"Beth Granger's beautifully written, searingly honest and heartrending account ... is a must read."
GILLIE JENKINSON, PhD, *WALKING FREE FROM THE TRAUMA OF COERCIVE, CULTIC AND SPIRITUAL ABUSE: A WORKBOOK FOR RECOVERY AND GROWTH*

"Born and Razed is a haunting memoir ... shining a powerful spotlight on institutional spiritual abuse. It left me enraged—and in awe of her fight for justice and recovery."
ANKE RICHTER, *CULT TRIP: INSIDE THE WORLD OF COERCION AND CONTROL*

Beth Granger

BORN
AND
RAZED

Surviving the Cult
was Only
Half the Battle

Published by Ingenium Books Publishing Inc.
Toronto, Ontario, Canada M6P 1Z2
www.ingeniumbooks.com

International Standard Book Numbers (ISBNs):
Paperback: 978-1-990688-32-4
Ebook: 978-1-990688-33-1
Audiobook: 978-1-990688-34-8

Cover Design by Jessica Bell Design via Ingenium Books

For everyone whose life was razed in the name of God.

Contents

Prologue: My Turn 9

PART ONE 13

Chapter 1 In the Beginning 15

Chapter 2 Invasion 19

Chapter 3 Let There Be Light 28

Chapter 4 My Sin 35

Chapter 5 Bereft 42

Chapter 6 Road Trip to Headquarters 48

Chapter 7 The Good, the Bad, and the Ugly 59

Chapter 8 Damned if You Do, Damned if You Don't 65

Chapter 9 On D 72

Chapter 10 Glory Days 76

Chapter 11 Tightrope Walker 81

Chapter 12 Under Threat 90

Chapter 13 To Eat, or Not to Eat? 102

Chapter 14 Scarlet Letter 114

Chapter 15 Banished 132

Chapter 16 Probation 145

Chapter 17 Boiling the Frog 155
Chapter 18 Getting Fired and Other News 165
Chapter 19 Boot Camp 173
Chapter 20 The Last Straw 181

PART TWO 195
Chapter 21 Freedom? 197
Chapter 22 Shit Hits the Fan 208
Chapter 23 Edge of Sanity 223
Chapter 24 The Wheels of Justice Turn Slowly 231
Chapter 25 Breakdown 242
Chapter 26 The Reckoning 256
Chapter 27 The Aftermath 285
Chapter 28 Revelations While Writing 294
Chapter 29 Victory (with a Side of Loss) 307
Chapter 30 Hope 319

Epilogue 324
Bibliography 326
Acknowledgements 328
About the Author 331
You Might Also Enjoy 332

Author's Note

This book was written from my point of view, with my memories. When trauma causes dissociation, we sometimes experience gaps in memory. (Which is probably a good thing, or this book could have been three times longer.) In cases when I couldn't recall dates or details, I relied on yearbooks, historic documents, court records, journals, and people from my past to help me fill in the gaps.

Some of the names in this book are real, others aren't. If you know, you know.

Prologue: My Turn

I hurried along the streets of downtown Toronto, feeling nauseous as I tried to keep pace with Jacqueline and Lisa. *Are we really doing this?* I could barely comprehend our audacity.

Shivering, I looked up at the cloudy sky, typical for a Canadian November day. The skyscrapers reached towards the heavens as if mocking my insignificance. My mind filled with doubt as I walked. The city was so overwhelming and unfamiliar to me. *Am I on a fool's errand? Or is this actually God's will?*

That last question caught me off-balance. I had been so trained to consider God's will for everything, that I had trouble knowing where my own began. This, among many things, was a work in progress. After all, I'd only been out of the cult for seven years.

Just breathe, Beth. You've got this.

I inhaled deeply and took it all in. The city, the emotions, the looming meeting. And the uncertain outcome.

We found the imposing high-rise office building on Bay Street. In the lobby, we met two other representative plaintiffs, Tim and Richard. My stomach was doing backflips. *This is really happening.*

As the elevator lifted us toward the eighteenth floor, I could tell that the others were just as nervous. This was uncharted territory, to put it mildly.

We were about to present our case to the Ontario Class Proceedings Committee. If successful, they would agree to cover litigation costs should we lose in court. Without this backing, there was no way we could shoulder the burden of pursuing a multi-million-dollar class action lawsuit. Only five plaintiffs had been selected to represent a class of nearly 1,400 members. It was too great a risk for all involved.

As usual, I was full of doubts and fears. Only now, my thoughts seemed to be broadcasting on loudspeakers: *Who do you think you are? Launching a class action lawsuit! Grenville wasn't that bad! And they aren't going to listen to someone who looks like you. Why haven't you lost all the baby weight yet?*

I struggled to focus on the matter at hand. Stuffing down my self-doubt was a futile, full-time job. Like shoving Hydra's nine writhing heads into a box.

Outside the elevators, we met our lawyers. Taking the lead that day was Loretta Merritt, a partner at her firm, whose serious eyes twinkled whenever justice was served. I was grateful for her kind, reassuring demeanor. She explained the proceedings to us and checked to see if we had prepared statements. Three of us had, including me. My stomach churned again. Even though I was ready on paper, I didn't feel that way at all inside.

We entered an impressive boardroom. The huge oval table was surrounded by large expensive leather office chairs. Soon, the five committee members entered, all of whom had been appointed by the attorney general and the Law Foundation of Ontario. To say I was intimidated was the understatement of the year.

I coached myself to breathe through my rising panic. *Our lawyers know what they're doing. They wouldn't be here if they didn't think we had a good case.* Russel Raikes in particular had represented thousands of Indigenous Residential School survivors in the Cloud class action. We were in good hands.

Introductions were made. I struggled to hear what was being said over the noise of my pounding heart and blood rushing in my ears. Before I knew it, the time had come for Loretta to present our case.

I'm glad she's going first, I thought as all eyes turned towards our lawyer. She looked poised and self assured, so I resolved to adopt some of her confidence.

But as soon as Loretta started to tell our story, I burst into tears. Not subtle, quiet tears, but an eruption like a volcano, taking me by surprise. Emotions that had fermented from being bottled up for thirty-eight years burst forth in an ugly cry that couldn't be silenced. Using my new burgundy blouse to mop my face, I tried desperately to pull myself together. The last thing I wanted to do was distract anyone from our lawyer's opening remarks.

It would be years before I understood my emotional response. All I knew at the time was that the minute I heard a lawyer speaking on our behalf, it was like a dam broke. I'd been holding a massive reservoir of pain for so long, and the magnitude of the moment was more than I could hold.

Finally, we're being heard. We're being taken seriously.

For some reason, there were no Kleenex boxes in that boardroom. I vaguely recall several lawyers searching their briefcases before one woman graciously handed me a crumpled tissue. Gradually, my sobs stopped, but tears still streamed silently down my cheeks.

I was scheduled to speak to the group after Loretta. When she finished, she turned to me and whispered, "You don't have to. It's OK."

I shook my head, rubbing my face with my palms. "No, I want to. I have to."

With that, I unfolded my notes, took a shuddering breath, and apologized for my outburst.

The members of the committee nodded in understanding and encouragement.

After another deep breath, I began. It was finally my turn to speak.

PART ONE

"The Devil can cite Scripture for his purpose."
William Shakespeare, The Merchant of Venice

Chapter 1
In the Beginning

Being born and raised at Grenville Christian College had its perks. My mind can conjure up many good memories, especially from the earliest years, before everything changed.

A rare photo from my childhood transports me to one of those good moments. I'm surrounded by ten happy people all squished around our only couch. My dad looks like a thirty-something version of Buddy Holly and next to him is my loving mom, her trademark dimples lighting up her face. My older brothers look equally cheerful. Danny with his gleaming blond hair—that I already envied—and brown-haired Garth with his freckles and a precocious gleam in his eye. The rest of the faces belong to contented-looking teenagers from around the world, all of them assigned to be part of our family.

I am the three-year-old in the middle of the bunch. Perched on the laps of both parents, I'm clutching my Raggedy Ann doll while my dad's arms encircle me and our dog Linus in one cozy hug. I treasured those family nights, when teenagers from mysterious places like Bermuda, Hong Kong, or Venezuela would gather in our trailer for an evening of fun. They called me their little sister, and I soaked up the attention. "Do you know I was the first baby born here?" I'd announce triumphantly. That was my claim to fame. I was so proud to be the first staff kid born on campus.

I was even more proud of my family. My dad had many important jobs on the campus: high school principal, English and music teacher, and director of the Visionaires. I was in awe of his choir. Back then, I didn't know they were the school's PR machine. They performed all over Ontario, Quebec, and New York state, successfully recruiting students everywhere they went. All I knew at the time was that I loved their music and their matching seventies outfits. I listened to their albums on repeat and was determined to be one of their singers someday.

My parents made a home for us kids that was full of music, laughter, games, and bedtime stories. Sometimes my dad read novels aloud to us. The Narnia series was a favourite, but my dad was on a mission to educate us, reading us books like *The Hiding Place* by Corrie Ten Boom, and *The Diary of a Young Girl* by Anne Frank. Stories that equally fascinated and scared three-year-old me.

My mom, who taught high-school French, was warm and dedicated. Even though we had almost no money, I rarely felt the lack. Mom would sew and knit our clothes or take us to the school's basement Blessing Room for hand-me-downs. Every Saturday night, she'd curl my short brown hair with pink foam rollers. "You look like Shirley Temple!" people would often say at church the next day. I couldn't tell if this was a compliment, so I remained embarrassed.

In truth, the one thing I wanted most was to have long hair, like the girls in the Visionaires.

"Look what I drew!" I'd announce to anyone who would listen. "This is my mommy, my daddy, my brother Dan, my brother Garth, my dog Linus with his blanket, and me. See, that's me when my hair is long! My mom says I can grow it when I'm five." As soon as I could hold a crayon, I'd draw pictures of my family this way, almost willing my future hair into existence. I couldn't wait to be older.

Above all, I was proud of our school. I was raised to believe that it was God's kingdom on Earth.

The main building commanded attention. You couldn't drive past it without being struck by its imposing presence. It was like a grandiose Gothic stone fortress looming large over the landscape that seemed to announce its holy destiny to the majestic St. Lawrence River and the country across its waters.

The campus held endless fascination for me. In the fall, we would rake fiery red and orange leaves that had fallen from the sugar maples that lined the long driveway, creating enormous piles. Dozens of us staff kids would hurl ourselves onto our leaf mountains, revelling in the joy.

Out in the barns, where the school raised pigs, cows, and horses, we would play hide-and-go-seek in the haylofts. Bales of hay, stacked to infinity, provided endless delight. If we were lucky, we'd get to ride the Shetland pony or the donkey. I lived for my turn, even though both Dusty and Joshua loved to buck us off. The horse barn became my happy place. To this day, the smell of horses makes me smile.

I learned to swim in the St. Lawrence River's freezing waters. We would spend hours in the river on the rare weekends when staff paused from their ceaseless work. "Jump in!" we'd call to the adults sitting on the huge dock. "The water's boiling!" (It wasn't.)

Behind the school were hundreds of acres of beautiful, forested land and trails for horseback riding, hiking, snowmobiling, and cross-country skiing. Winters on campus provided nonstop fun. Every day we would hurtle down Murray Hill on our sleds. "Look out below!" we'd shout, as if our warnings would matter to passing cars.

When I was almost two, a pair of three-acre lagoons were dug at the edge of the forest as part of a sewage treatment process. Our leaders often preached about how those lagoons were built: "If God hadn't performed His miracles, the Ministry of the Environment would have closed our school down!" Even better, we got to skate on the lagoons in the winter, and hike around them in the summer.

I also loved being a staff kid. I relished the chance to live on campus, where there was never a dull moment. When we weren't in school or doing chores, we got to share our lives with paying students: at meals, church, performances, picnics, sports, talent shows, plays, banquets, camping trips, and family nights. Something exciting was always around the corner.

Best of all, we were taught that we were special. Chosen by God for a unique mission. We were in training to be God's little Christian soldiers. Our school would be a Heaven on Earth where the lives of countless students would be saved. And staff kids, we were told, had a very important part to play. I liked the sound of that.

Chapter 2
Invasion

Before I started kindergarten, life as I knew it ended.

Of course, I was too little to understand all the upheaval. I didn't fully comprehend that our school was in danger of closing. That bankruptcy loomed, leadership wasn't cohesive, and the overworked staff were becoming disillusioned. I didn't know that my parents only made $7 per week.

I had only known about the miracles.

Before everything changed, I had loved listening to our leaders tell us how our school began the year I was born. How God had led the Haigs to find our campus and then orchestrated the deal of the century. For the current price of one small modest home, they had acquired the entire 260 acres of riverfront property, including the main building, a new gymnasium, chapel, and dormitory—all fully equipped.

Our leaders constantly preached how God was in charge, even though Satan was intent on our demise. I hung onto their every word as they proclaimed God's goodness. He turned our financial crisis around and saved us from contaminated well water, our school's boiler breaking down, and the sewage system giving out. *God must think we're very special,* I'd think proudly.

These six leaders—the Haigs, the Farnsworths, and the Snures—liked to preach a lot. Our church services sometimes lasted for hours. I didn't mind them so much unless the leaders were singing in tongues. That terrified me. I'd look up, bewildered, and see adults with their eyes closed, rapturously singing in gibberish, waving their hands around. *What's happening? Am I expected to join in?* I wanted to hide under the pews.

Christian leaders from the outside often visited our school to preach. Pastor Haig and his wife Mary seemed to have contacts everywhere. Among them were Cay Anderson and Judy Sorensen, leaders of the Community of Jesus, a Christian commune in Cape Cod, Massachusetts. Their followers addressed them as the Mothers.

When the Haigs drove down to visit the Mothers on the Cape the first time, they were extremely impressed. They brought back stories about this mysterious place that was so full of peace, order, beauty, and love.

Soon our leaders became convinced that these Mothers could be the key to our school's success. They invited Cay and Judy to offer spiritual guidance here. On April 28, 1973, the Mothers arrived on our campus to lead a retreat. None of us could have foreseen the drastic changes that were in store.

†

Their planned two-day visit stretched into two weeks. I wasn't privy to their staff meetings, but I was there when the Mothers preached to the entire school. In a low, almost menacing voice, Mother Judy shared a scripture verse she had received from God; "The axe is laid to the root of the tree." Apparently, God told her that our school was like a twisted tree that needed to be hewn down to its very roots before He could bless it.

I was trying to picture them taking an axe to our school when Mother Cay took over in her strange New England accent. She started by quoting her favourite verse from the Bible: "Except a grain of wheat fall into the earth and die, it abideth by itself alone; but if it die, it beareth much fruit." Then, she added, "Pride, jealousy, disobedience, self-centredness, self-satisfaction, willfulness—all these are enemies of God and stop His life from flowing here on this campus." After a long pause, she continued, emphasizing every word, "The key is death to self."

I gulped, taken aback.

Everything about them scared me. For starters, they each took up more space than any other adults I knew. Sometimes they laughed heartily but I never mistook them for jolly fat women. Apart from their imposing statures, it was their ominous voices and stern expressions that really unnerved me.

And yet these two women were treated with reverence, almost as if they were royalty or deities. Adults would speak of them in hushed tones, reminding each other of their teachings. People started telling my mom to say prayers like, "Lord, make me a real person." Whatever that even meant.

There was also a sort of fanaticism to adopt their philosophies. The Mothers, we were told, had received a vision for our school directly from God. It was destined to be an extension of their Cape Cod community. If the staff were obedient, God would work miracles in our school and in its students.

Al Haig would soon write about their visit and its impact:

> Then the day came that heralded the most important miracle in all the history of Grenville Christian College. The two directors of the beautifully run Community of Jesus, located in Cape Cod, came to visit our college. They told us we were too permissive, too soft, where we had failed to take our place of authority as the leadership of the college. It hurt. Every word they spoke cut deeply within me and all of us. The truth often hurts, but the truth also heals, and this truth set us free. The miraculous part is that our community, all sixty of us, listened and learned and accepted what they said to us.
>
> Cay and Judy said, "If you're willing to pay the price, if you're willing to sacrifice, then you will see the results. Your school will change. Your direction will change. This school, instead of being a hundred and fifty thousand

dollars in debt, will have its financial needs met. Furthermore, you will have more students knocking on your
door than you can possibly handle." (Haig 1977, 8)

What I didn't know was that the staff were being moulded into one
single-minded sacrificial unit that was being challenged to adopt an
entirely new way of thinking. According to the Mothers, they were
a repository of rebellion, and repentance needed to be their full-time
preoccupation. Buzzwords like *stay low*, *stay open*, *be needy*, and *be
wrong* quickly became part of their vernacular. Any staff choosing to
stay on for the cause was obliged to commit for life. In addition, one
by one, staff were required to make lifetime confessions to the Mothers.
What they didn't know was that these declarations of guilt would be
used against them for years to come.

Once the Mothers returned to Cape Cod, the Haigs and Farnsworths
were appointed as their official spokespeople. Pastor Haig was chosen
to be headmaster, while Mrs. Haig, Pastor Farnsworth, and his wife
Betty were named directors. Whatever they said became law. Staff were
commanded to respect their authority, without question.

I began to fear all four leaders. They each seemed to project a new air
of importance. Pastor Haig, a former halfback for the Toronto Argo-
nauts, loomed larger than ever. What his sidekick, Pastor Farnsworth,
lacked in stature he compensated with his cutting remarks, smug smirk,
and penetrating gaze. Mrs. Farnsworth seemed timid until she injected
her stinging two cents in a Southern drawl that did little to soften the
blow. But Mrs. Haig terrified me the most. I'd watch in horror as she
publicly shamed people time and again. Her dark, piercing eyes were
like sin-seeking lasers. She seemed to enjoy everyone's discomfort as
much as she relished her own exalted power.

Eventually, the adults started conducting secret group meetings.
These would happen anywhere: around dining room tables, in hallways,
in offices, or in the living rooms of our trailers. I could tell from their
faces that these were deadly serious affairs. We staff kids weren't allowed
to interrupt our parents during those gatherings. I didn't have to be told
twice. I hated hearing all the yelling.

One day, however, I burst into a session.

I had had no choice. I'd been whacked across the top of my head with a broken hockey stick. The girl who had wielded the weapon was furious because I didn't want to play with her. (I guess I had good instincts.) The blow knocked me to the ground, and stars clouded my vision. All I could think of was wanting my mommy. Once I pushed myself upright and stood on shaking legs, I touched my wound. My fingers felt something sticky; they came away covered in blood.

I heard myself scream. The other kids looked on in shock. Then I took off across the trailer park towards the help I so badly needed.

When I entered my family's trailer, the adults were engaged in a secret meeting. Before I could open my mouth, one of them sternly told me to leave. I felt their scorn like a force field. Normally, that would have been enough to make me hightail it. But not this time.

"My head is broken!" I wailed. "There's blood!"

As if needing permission, my mom looked to her peers before timidly leaving her chair. It seemed to take an eternity for her to come to my aid. Of course, once she saw the damage, it was obvious I needed a hospital.

Reluctantly, the adults released my parents from the meeting, and I was whisked off to the ER for stitches.

†

Following the Mothers' first visit, every aspect of life at the school subsequently changed. Families were moved around. Jobs were switched. Uniforms were altered. Dress codes were revamped. Long hair was cut. Policies and practises were reinvented. Staff kids were instructed to address all staff members as our aunts and uncles—except for the four leaders. Worship services were reformed. The pastors started wearing long robes and we began using Anglican prayer books. Pastors Haig and Farnsworth began their training to be officially ordained as Anglican priests. Soon we'd be calling them our Fathers.

Even my parents changed. There was an air of heaviness about them, as if they were wilting, their confidence and vitality diminishing with each passing group session. My mom went from being a cheerful, kind, confident woman to someone I didn't recognize. She became timid and serious, like she was putting on an act. Her attempts at harsh discipline were confusing to me.

Much worse was the edict that my dad would lose his job. "I was the high school principal in the morning," he told me once, "and was digging ditches around the new tennis court in the afternoon." To add insult to injury, the Visionaires were subjected to endless harsh criticism by the Mothers. They disbanded soon after that first retreat.

I could tell my dad wasn't happy. He'd try to contain his rage by retreating inside himself. His frustration and anger vibrated around him like an energy field.

Staff meetings would terrify me. Whenever one was called, high school students would arrive at our trailer to babysit. Then the fear would set in. It got to the point where I couldn't sleep. Instead, I'd stand up in bed, craning my neck to look outside my window, waiting until both my parents returned. I was afraid. I didn't know why, but I sensed that bad things were happening.

It turns out that I was right to have been scared.

A few months after the Mothers' first visit, my family was torn apart. We were moved out of our staff trailer and into the student dorms. My parents were assigned a single room. They lost their private kitchen, living room, laundry, and bathroom. Even worse, they lost their children.

Each of us was assigned other families to live with. I was placed with Aunt Katie and Uncle Bill and moved into a dorm room with their two daughters. At the time, I was five years old, implanted between four-year-old Julie and six-year-old Karen. Though my parents lived one floor below, I was instructed not to seek them out, rely on them for my needs, or even talk to them. I was told that this was my new family. For now.

At least Aunt Katie and her husband didn't scare me. She was a short firecracker while he was a tall, silent type. They had recently completed a missionary trip in Africa and I marvelled at the stories of their adventures. Every night Uncle Bill would read stories to us from a children's

Bible. I didn't mind their bedtime rituals but they didn't measure up to mine. The fact was, I missed my family desperately. The ache was constant. *Why can't I live with my parents?* I'd wonder. *And why do Karen and Julie get to stay with theirs?* The unfairness was maddening.

We weren't the only family to be split apart. Several staff children were removed from their parents and assigned to live elsewhere. Apparently, the Mothers were trying to root out idolatrous parental love, which made parents blind to their children's transgressions. Gone were the days when my parents could show love and affection to us. The Mothers even preached that all human love was sin. I had questions about that, but instinct told me to keep my mouth shut.

As the months passed, I became increasingly aware of the concept of sin. I also learned the name for those ominous secret meetings: *light sessions*, because they helped us live in the light. The Mothers were teaching the staff that to be in the Spirit they had to be convicted of sin regularly. Everyone was subjected to light sessions, in which adults were expected to publicly berate and humiliate each other. They would gang up on a person in the hot seat and torment them until that person broke down. If someone resisted or refused to agree with the condemnation, the heat would be turned up. Being yelled at was a best-case scenario. Sometimes glasses of water were thrown in faces, or people were slapped or even spanked in front of the others.

My parents were loyal to a fault. Like their colleagues, they believed the Mothers' teachings and were determined to endure the harsh light sessions. My dad thought of them as a necessary evil and spent most of the time in his own head, concocting responses that might get him off the inevitable hot seat.

†

All staff were required to spend the next summer at the Community of Jesus on Cape Cod. Young staff kids were farmed out to relatives so our parents could focus on their indoctrination. My brothers and I were sent to our grandparents near Toronto.

During their time at the Community, when my parents and the other staff members weren't gardening, cleaning, building, or ironing, they were at church. Or enduring light sessions at meals. They were schooled in the art of public humiliation and shaming one another about any and all sins, real or imagined. At one group light session, all the men and women were forced to have their long hair cut short—right then and there, on the lawn outside the chapel. They all returned to Canada with a new commitment to a life of service, correction, and personal sacrifice.

I, for one, was alarmed by their makeovers. *How could they possibly give up their beautiful long hair?*

The following summer my father was sent to the Community to be mentored by the music directors. We heard all about their thriving music program, complete with a marching band, choir, and orchestra, and annual Gilbert and Sullivan (G&S) productions that were a hit. What my dad didn't tell us was that he wasn't allowed to do anything involving music that entire summer. Instead, he did hard manual labour and endured unending light sessions. He was repeatedly told how haughty he was. And that if he didn't repent and change, God would have no use for his musical talents.

I asked my parents once why they put up with the torment. Here's how my dad responded:

> "I was so afraid the school was going to close before the Mothers came. What they offered was hope. They inspired us with their high standards. We could see that their community was thriving, so they must have been doing something right. Finally, at the school, there was no more infighting. Academic programs improved. The school got cleaned up. There was strong leadership. Staff were challenged to do better in every area. So, I made up my mind to endure. No matter what."

My mom's take was slightly different but just as determined:

> "By the time the Mothers came, I felt the school was my home, my security, my calling. I used to tell myself that they could do whatever they wanted to me—I wasn't leaving."

Chapter 3
Let There Be Light

It wasn't long before I was exposed to light sessions.

What started behind closed doors soon became public shaming sessions that unfolded in front of everyone. We'd all be gathering in the chapel for worship or eating in the communal dining room when the Holy Spirit would strike, prompting the leaders to attack sins and sinners.

I attended so many of these sessions that all the memories blurred together, creating one infinite highlight reel that would plague my dreams for decades. Still, there are a few that stand out in my memory. One such meeting, so typical of the rest, was prompted by an alarming event that took place when I was in kindergarten.

The light session happened during a school break, when only staff and their children remained on campus. Everyone was gathered in the dining room, making conversation over the loud clatter of silverware and dishes. I was gobbling a grilled cheese sandwich as fast as I could, hoping for seconds before they were gone.

Tap! Tap! Tap!

Mid-bite, I swiveled my head toward the microphone. So did everyone else. *Here we go again,* I groaned inwardly once I noticed who was preparing to speak. Our leaders sat at a head table mounted with personal mics.

It was Pastor Haig who began. "Charles and I meet on my front porch for early morning devotions. We pray, read scripture, and wait for the Lord to speak to us. He never fails. Today, we received a very serious message from our Heavenly Father. We feel you all need to hear this, so let's pray together. Charles, would you lead us?"

Pastor Farnsworth leaned into his mic and began. "Dear Lord, we are gathered in your name, asking that you make your truth known to every person here. Open our hearts and minds. Help us to see our sin, and reject it with a holy hatred, so we can repent and move forward in the light of your truth. In Jesus's name, we pray."

"Amen," we gravely responded. By then my sandwich tasted like leather, and I couldn't eat another bite. I knew that nothing good was about to happen.

"As you all know," Pastor Haig continued, "a two-headed calf was born in our barn. This alarming event certainly got our attention. We felt it was a sign from God, and prayed fervently, asking the Lord for discernment. We met with the entire student body and watched God work miracles in the hearts of our students. Still, we sensed that God wasn't finished. So, we kept praying, and He answered. God sent us a prophecy. It is vital that you all take heed."

Mrs. Haig took her turn to speak. "As I deliver God's revelation, search your hearts and pray to be convicted by His words." With an ominous tone, she continued, "Double-minded. Double-hearted. Ease, comfort, and satisfaction; that is what you desire."

The dining hall went silent. Except for the ticking clock on the wall.

After what seemed like forever, Mrs. Haig asked, "Are you letting those words sink in? Do you realize how far from God some of you must be? For Him to have sent us a sign like a two-headed calf? God is surely trying to wake you up! And if you don't take this seriously, the next sign will be even more shocking.

"How many of you have double minds? How many of you have double hearts? With your words, you say you love God and want to devote your life to His service. But in your minds, you hold on to your sinful desires. In your hearts, you feed your ego, your lust, your greed.

"We are deeply concerned about many of you. And we feel your sin needs to be rooted out. Some of you are hosting Satan in your minds and hearts. If you continue, the entire community will suffer."

By then, I was almost afraid to breathe and dreading what might come next.

Sure enough, Pastor Farnsworth ordered someone to stand up. It was Uncle Ted, at the other end of the dining hall. He stood up alone and looked worried.

"Ted, where are you double-minded?" Pastor Farnsworth asked.

Uncle Ted bowed his head, trying to form an appropriate answer. Not an easy task, in front of such a crowd. "Well," he said eventually, "sometimes I struggle with accepting my job in the kitchen."

"You have a will of your own, Ted," Pastor Farnsworth replied. "And until you let the Lord break your will, you will be miserable. Your real problem is your ego. You think that with your university education, kitchen work is beneath you."

"Ted, what you need is to find your worth in God," Pastor Haig added. "Not in positions with so-called status. You need to become single-minded in your love for the Lord. Then it won't matter to you where you work. You'll even be happy shovelling pig manure."

Mrs. Haig interjected, "That's a good idea! I think Ted needs to join the early morning barn crew. Ted, it's working in a lowly job that will help you get closer to Jesus."

Uncle Ted looked stricken. "I already get up at 5:30 a.m. for breakfast prep every school day."

Mrs. Haig shrugged. "I'm sure you can fit in an hour of barn duty before breakfast prep."

She turned to address everyone then. "You see, God is requiring sacrifice from all of you. If you want to continue a life of ease, comfort, and satisfaction, then you don't belong here. You can leave and join a regular church. One where so-called 'Christians' profess to love God only when it suits them."

Pastor Farnsworth piped up, "So, Ted, what are you going to choose? A life of ease, or a life of service?"

Uncle Ted looked anxious now. "I can see now where I've been double-minded. I have been doubting God's will for me." With his gaze lowered, he added, "I guess I do need to change."

What followed was a prayer, with Uncle Ted repeating after Pastor Haig, phrase by phrase. We all joined in, our eyes closed, seeking the Lord on Ted's behalf.

During the prayer, I snuck a look around. My friends all had their eyes squeezed shut. *Who will be next?* I wondered. Instead of praying for Uncle Ted, I prayed it wouldn't be my parents.

Next, the leaders called on Aunt Alice. As she stood up, I could sense her fear. I liked Aunt Alice. She was cheerful and pretty, and never scared me.

"Alice, why do you think we called on you?" Mrs. Haig asked.

Aunt Alice couldn't seem to find her words.

"Alice, you know that the devil lives within you when you choose to remain hidden," Mrs. Haig went on. "Now is the time to be open and honest. Where are you double-minded?"

Alice remained silent, frozen in fear.

"Alice, you must be so steeped in rebellion that you can't see the reality of your situation," Mrs. Haig continued. "You know very well that in your heart, you still pull on your family. You refuse to cut ties completely. We hear that you've agreed to be a bridesmaid at your sister's wedding. Yet you never asked for our permission! We've been over and over this. You're refusing to let them go."

Alice started to cry. "I know God wants me to choose Him over my family," she explained. "It's so hard. They don't understand."

"Of course they don't understand, Alice," Pastor Haig replied. "They are not part of God's elite. They are content to live in a wicked world, full of temptation. They are happy, living a life of ease. Remember the scripture tells us, 'Many are called, but few are chosen.' Alice, you have been specially chosen by God. The rest of your family is choosing their own path. And if you want to follow your calling, then you can't be part of their lives."

Mrs. Haig added, "Let me make myself clear. You had better not expect to be involved in your sister's wedding. God has other plans for you. I think He is testing you right now. How long are you going to continue walking this path of double-mindedness?"

Alice didn't defend herself. Quietly, she answered, "I do see that I've been torn between my family and God's will for my life."

"I think you need to repent of your jealousy of your sister," Mrs. Haig went on. "All you seem to want is to get married. But I think you know God has more important plans for you." Her dark eyes appeared to pierce Aunt Alice. "What's really happening is that you're in rebellion. You're refusing to accept your true calling. Surely you know what I mean."

Alice's eyes widened. "Not really …" she stammered.

Mrs. Haig started whispering with her husband and the Farnsworths. After a few minutes, she leaned back into the microphone. "We think you need to spend the next week in silence. During that time, you need to pray about testing your call to become a sister at the Community of Jesus. We strongly feel that's the Lord's will for you."

Alice nodded, looking ready to collapse.

I looked at her in sympathy. *I hope I'm never in her shoes.*

While I suspected the light session was just beginning, I already knew I couldn't take much more. I looked dejectedly at the flies circling my unfinished sandwich. *So much for getting seconds.*

As the session continued, I only paid attention to snippets of the scrutiny.

Some staff were striving too much for the students' approval. Others weren't honest enough in their confessional notes.

I didn't understand what they were telling Aunt Donna. Something about having a seductive walk? And a seductive voice when she made announcements? *What does that mean?*

But what Mrs. Haig said next really got my attention.

"Donna, you love food more than you love God. The fact that you haven't lost weight since the last retreat is shameful. In fact, we think you should no longer be in the school choir. No one wants to see you performing up there, looking like that!"

That is so mean! I couldn't help thinking. *Also, is Aunt Donna even fat?* I wrapped my arms around my own little pudgy belly, slumped even lower in my seat, and felt my fear growing.

Just when I thought I couldn't stand it anymore, I heard them call my parents' names.

My stomach twisted. Trying not to cry, I watched as my parents reluctantly rose to their feet. I searched my mom's face, but her anxious expression didn't reassure me. Neither did my dad's, which looked stoic and resigned.

"Malcolm and Pat," Mrs. Haig said. "Of all the staff members here, you two are probably the most double-minded. Neither one of you has fully gotten on board. You both keep trying to do your own thing.

"Pat, you refuse to live in reality. You constantly seem 'out of it.' It's like there's no one there. We are told that, during light sessions, you contribute almost nothing. You are passive, and you never speak truth to anyone else. There is definitely something off with you."

My mom looked stricken. *Please, Mom, make them stop*, I thought, feeling nauseous.

Father Haig took over then. "Malcolm, you only care about your music and teaching. You think you're so talented, like you're God's gift to this school. Well, let me assure you, that is not true. Time and time again, it is painfully obvious just how much you are out of the spirit. Your refusal to rely on Jesus is infecting the entire music program. In fact, the whole school suffers because of your pride and haughtiness."

My dad was having trouble hiding his anger. Before he could respond, Mrs. Haig jumped back in. "And the real problem is that both of you are so idolatrous with your children that we can't even trust you to raise them. You are always too soft on your kids. They are turning into brats! Haughty, rebellious, and self-centred, just like the two of you."

I clenched the wooden seat of my chair, willing myself to bear the onslaught of shame. Mrs. Haig's hateful words struck me like a physical blow, and I desperately wanted to escape.

"Your idolatry is keeping you from growing in the spirit," she went on. "You both seem to be stuck in your sin, like pigs wallowing in the mud. When are you finally going to get out of yourselves? The truth is that you are the worst examples to your children. They would be better off living with any other adult on campus than with the two of you. And what's worse is, all the adults here are willing to raise your kids for you. But you refuse to do your part. You can't be trusted with any children here. We know you'd be too easy on them. You'd refuse to stand up against their sin."

I stopped listening then. It was as if my senses had shut down, or the room had gone silent and the lights had turned off. I had no idea if my parents responded because I couldn't bear to pay attention anymore. All I thought about was how worthless the leaders said my parents were. And, therefore, how hopeless, wrong, and sinful I was. The shame was almost unbearable.

I felt more alone than ever.

Chapter 4
My Sin

I soon learned that I was full of sin. During my light sessions, I was constantly told I needed to change. For starters, when I was five, Mrs. Haig decided I was too fat.

The details of how she orchestrated my first diet are hazy. Some memories are still too painful to recall. But I do remember her declaring that I was a sinful glutton. The shame of having an unacceptable body was almost unbearable.

As much as she scared me, Mrs. Haig also fascinated me. She was like a middle-aged Barbie with the blonde permed hair of a Mrs. Beasley doll. You could smell her pungent perfume all the way down the school hallways. She always looked so put together. Her colourful dresses even had matching shoes.

I desperately wanted to gain her approval. *Maybe if I lose weight, she'll let me live with my parents.*

Desserts were my favourite part of meals. I lived for the sweet taste of ice cream or brownies that provided instant comfort. Whenever they were served in the dining room, I'd fight my tablemates for seconds. But now that I was on a diet, desserts were literally off the table for me. I remember being offered an orange while everyone else indulged. I can still feel my bitter frustration as I peeled that hateful fruit.

Over time, my diet became my identity. During holiday meals, when I'd actually get to eat with my family, my brothers would catch me sneaking a second helping and gleefully remind me, "Aren't you on a diet?" Then they would laugh and swipe away the treat I'd been considering.

Aunt Katie also reminded me regularly of my body's flaws. She'd bend down and push my stomach, urging me to suck it in, while doing the same thing to my butt with her other hand. *Make up your mind,* I thought defiantly. *I can't push my butt in without my tummy sticking out. Or the other way around.*

Losing weight was a lot more difficult than I expected. Especially when all I wanted was comfort. I always felt like I was being watched, evaluated, or criticized. Also, I longed for food. I fantasized about food. I thought about it constantly and started sneaking it. Then every time I cheated, I felt more sinful. *No wonder they put you on a diet, Beth!* I'd think. *You're such a glutton!*

One day, during kindergarten, I was seated at a dining-room table with at least ten other girls, celebrating my new friend Jacqueline's fifth birthday. I'd never been invited to a party off campus before. Jacqueline was a day student at Grenville who lived in Brockville and her house was fancy. I was awed by its beauty. It reminded me of my grandma's house in Ohio, which I longed to revisit, but had only actually seen once.

After polishing off a small piece of birthday cake, all I could think about was having more. *The adults here don't know about my diet. If I'm lucky, they'll offer seconds!* I could hardly wait for another slice.

When Jacqueline's mom offered second helpings, however, the girls seated farthest from me said, "No thank you." To my mounting horror, all the other girls politely declined, one by one. I stared at them, silently willing at least one to say, "Yes please." *What's wrong with these girls?* I screamed silently. *Why are they pretending not to want more?*

With growing dread, I realized I couldn't risk the shame of being the only girl to accept a second piece. I'd have to choose between my cravings and the humiliation of being the only glutton in the room. Finally, after the girl before me declined a second piece, I had no choice but to say, "No thank you."

Sighing, I tried to accept that maybe it wasn't God's will for me to eat that second piece of cake. *Beth, you shouldn't have had any in the first place*, the voice in my head said. Somehow, I'd have to stop being such a sinful, greedy glutton.

After months of restriction, the scales finally showed some weight loss. I later sought out my dad for some much-needed validation. "Daddy! I lost five pounds!" I announced, hoping for praise.

Ever distant, my dad muttered a cautious, "Good for you."

My dismay at his reaction was profound. *Why isn't he proud of me? Am I doomed to diet forever? Will I ever be thin enough?* With my sin on display, I realized I'd never feel safe. Unless I found a way to get skinny.

†

Being labelled a glutton felt like the worst kind of sin. But what truly confounded me were the times when I was accused of sins I didn't understand, or was asked to confess to being wicked when I didn't know what I'd done wrong.

Once, Uncle Bill walked into our room and looked horrified to see me and his oldest daughter in bed together, giggling and tickling each other in a rare act of defiance over an early bedtime. I understood why he was angry about us being loud. But the lecture that came next stumped me: "You girls should be in your own beds! What were you doing in there? Being in the same bed is a sin. Don't let me catch you ever doing that again!"

As a six-year-old, I had no idea what he was talking about. *I must be a terrible sinner*, I thought.

Before long, I was moved to another family. In fact, over the next seven years, I'd be passed around like some unwanted pet. Parented by everyone and no one. I never felt safe. Or loved.

At one point, I was placed with two single women. Aunt Yvonne was fairly harmless, but Aunt Judy, so tall and grumpy, with a glare that could curdle milk, would frighten me with her frequent light sessions. One time, right before lunch on a Saturday, she cornered me in the red lounge, which was the only room on campus with a TV for the students. After having spent all morning cleaning the school, a bunch of us were watching *Fat Albert* during our fifteen minutes of free time.

Aunt Judy's loud voice mortified me. "You're not being honest!" she accused. "I can tell you're determined to stay hidden, wallowing in your rebellion. I warned you that the next time I saw you, I'd expect a confession. You've had all morning to think about your sins."

I looked down, willing the ground to swallow me whole. *Why does she have to embarrass me here, in front of so many high school students?* The fact that I was only seven didn't help matters. *What sin should I confess this time? What dirty thought, jealousy, or wrong deed can I share that would satisfy?* My mind was blank, though, and I panicked. If I didn't make an acceptable confession of my sins, I'd be in even more hot water.

Finally, I stammered, "I've been jealous of my brothers, since they get to live together."

"OK, what else?" Aunt Judy demanded.

"Well … I guess I'm angry because I don't get to live with my parents."

"Well, that's a start. But I know you're hiding more. Tonight, at bedtime I'm going to expect the rest. And then we will pray to God to cleanse you from your jealousy, anger, hiddenness, and whatever else comes up. I knew things have been off with you this week."

As Aunt Judy strode away, I felt shaken. That exchange might have been over, but I was already dreading the next one. *Beth, you had better come up with some sins by bedtime, or else.*

†

When I lived with the Steinbachs, I couldn't quite put my finger on what scared me about Aunt Wanece. I would tell other kids that I was afraid of her height. But I knew it was more than that. She was so stern about my mistakes. It didn't help that I started wetting my bed after moving into her trailer, and I lived in fear of the backlash. Aunt Wanece would get so angry about it, and who could blame her? I always felt like such a disgrace. Especially since her daughter never wet the bed, and I was six months older than her.

One time I snuck my sheets into the washing machine. I didn't know how to use it, though, so Aunt Wanece still found out. I got in huge trouble, not just for the sin of bed-wetting but also for being deceitful. Which, she said, was far worse. Afterward, I could barely sleep at night for fear of having another accident.

I also eavesdropped a lot while living with the Steinbachs. During Lent, I'd hear Uncle Ron and Aunt Wanece complain about the Grape Fast. They were nothing if not loyal to the Mothers' decrees. For several years in a row, all staff were ordered to eat nothing but grapes during Lent. For some sort of variety, Aunt Wanece would roast the grapes in the oven with salt and pepper. The entire trailer would be full of smoke, since Uncle Ron liked all his food on the burnt side. There is nothing quite like the smell of burning grapes. Uncle Ron hated the fast so much that he talked of little else. I didn't blame him. I couldn't fathom how the staff survived the torment of those forty days.

Many nights, I'd lie in bed, wide awake, while light sessions were brewing down the trailer hallway. Adults would be yelling, condemning one another of all kinds of sin. The accused would cry as they defended themselves. Eventually, they'd beg for forgiveness. I heard laughter, too, once each sinner had finally broken down, repented, and begged God for mercy. Then the adults seemed to become friendly again, hugging and reassuring the sinner of God's forgiveness.

I also overheard the Steinbachs yelling at—or about—their eldest son. Tom, who was fifteen at the time, was always in trouble for his rebellion. No amount of discipline seemed to break his defiance. I secretly admired Tom. His quiet confidence amazed me. He ran away from the school more than once. Each time, the police would apprehend him and bring him back. Then he'd be in terrible trouble, enduring harsh discipline and endless reprimands from his parents, other staff, and the leaders.

Once Tom turned sixteen, he ran away for good. His parents were told never to speak of him again. I could tell they were worried about him, but they obeyed orders. Tom, like any other staff kid or staff member who left, was to be shunned by the faithful community. So, that's what his parents did.

In the late seventies, the school acquired land for staff vacations and school camping trips on White Fish Lake. My first trip there occurred when I was about eight. I went with the Ortolani family for some reason I cannot recall. I didn't even live with them. We staff kids were always being shuffled around.

Being an early bird, I enjoyed waking up before everyone else during camping trips. I loved watching the mist creep over the water as the sun rose across the lake. One morning, I invited the Ortolanis' six-year-old daughter Elisa to go for a walk. She eagerly agreed.

We set off down the road that led from our campsite to the neighbouring cottages. Eventually, we rounded a bend and noticed a man pushing a lawn mower, his back to us. Something didn't seem right. *Where are his clothes? Is that really his naked bum?* I stared in disbelief. Belatedly, Elisa realized what she was seeing. We looked at each other, our eyes as wide as saucers, and covered our mouths with our hands as we tried not to laugh. Then we bolted from our hiding place behind a bush and ran back to the campsite.

I was too mortified to tell an adult what we'd seen. Elisa felt the same. We agreed to keep it to ourselves.

A week passed, and life resumed as usual at the school. Or so I thought.

Before long, I was summoned to a light session. The Ortolanis were there, along with other colleagues. They wanted to know what I'd been hiding. At first, I wasn't sure what they were hinting at. So, I played dumb, hoping they weren't fishing for the naked man story. Of course, they eventually pulled it out of me. And as I told the tale, I felt their disapproval and condemnation growing.

Instead of an innocent sighting, the event became a cause for infinite shame. "Why were you out walking by yourselves?" the adults demanded. "Did you get permission? When you saw the man wasn't dressed, why did you keep looking at him? Were you excited to see a naked man? Do you fantasize about what men look like under their clothes? What about women? Do you imagine naked women? Do you know what lust is? Do you know your lustful thoughts come from the devil?"

I bore the onslaught of their questions with mortified confusion. *Why am I being accused of such dirty thoughts?* I hadn't liked seeing that man naked. Rather, I'd been disgusted, alarmed, and afraid that he'd turn the corner and show us a front view. *How could I put that into words?*

Things went from bad to worse after I attempted to defend myself. "What concerns us the most is your deception," the adults went on. "The fact that you chose not to tell an adult what you saw shows that you are in league with Satan. Even worse, you were a terrible influence on Elisa by teaching her to lie. She has felt so guilty, trying to keep your secret. Why didn't you confess? We are very worried about you, Beth. We don't think you can be trusted around our little ones."

Deeply disgraced, I considered the truth of their accusations. *Why didn't I tell an adult? What was I trying to hide? Am I really full of lust?*

That last thought made my skin crawl. I felt such shame I could barely breathe. *I must be a horrible, hopeless sinner.*

Chapter 5
Bereft

I spent my childhood in a perpetual state of longing, keeping my desires to myself. It soon became easier not to hope for anything.

My dreams of growing my hair were dashed by the time I was five. After the Mothers invaded, having long hair was a sin, though I never understood why. I resigned myself to my cringy boyish haircut and shifted my attention to wanting new clothes. Not secondhand clothing from the school's musty Blessing Room. I wanted items bought just for me.

It didn't escape my notice that things weren't exactly equal. While my parents couldn't afford new clothes, for some reason, others could. One family I lived with would regularly order clothes for their daughter, who was my age, from the Sears catalogue. I'd watch, silently simmering, as she opened the bulging packages and modelled each outfit in the living room. On the verge of tears, I'd bite my lip, trying to swallow the lump of despair in my throat. I felt desperate for new clothes of my own. And for my own parents.

Once in a blue moon, my Canadian grandparents would make the trip from Toronto to Brockville to visit. I couldn't wait for their visits; I was starved for love and affection, which they freely gave. Grandma Gillis always wore the latest styles. Occasionally, she'd bring me new clothes, but to my despair, they rarely fit. I didn't blame my grandma. How could she have known? Unfortunately, the fact that she always guessed a size too small reinforced my growing self-hatred.

Greed was one of my worst sins, and it mortified me. Still, I let desire get the better of me when I got my hands on a copy of a Sears Christmas *Wish Book* one year. There was a caramel-coloured Barbie horse with a white blaze on its face and a fancy rubber saddle, and I wanted it more than life itself. We weren't allowed to have Barbies, but I figured, *horses aren't sinful, right?* So I wrote Santa a letter, even though I didn't believe he was real. Then I tried to make my request clear to my parents. This was tricky, since I wasn't living with them.

When Christmas came, though, there was no toy horse for me under their tree. It was a hard pill to swallow.

Maybe I didn't make my wish crystal clear, I reasoned. So a year later, as Christmas approached, I took every opportunity to mention my request for the horse whenever the topic arose. If I visited my parents' table in the dining room, and older students asked me what I wanted for Christmas, I'd repeat myself, thinking there was no way my parents wouldn't get the message. In fact, I mentioned the toy so often that I hoped they'd buy it to shut me up. But my hopes were dashed again. For the second year in a row, I didn't receive the only toy I'd requested.

I received the message loud and clear. *I'm too sinful to earn my parents' love.*

Still, the disappointment cut deep. I dealt with it by scolding myself: *Beth, stop wanting things! Your greediness ruins everything!*

Above all else, I simply desired to live with my parents. While I tried to endure the separations without complaint, I desperately missed my family. Even though my mom and dad were trying not to show outward affection, I knew they cared about me. I craved their love and attention. And frankly, I liked them better than the other adults at Grenville.

When I was seven, my parents invited me, Dan, and Garth to their dorm room for an announcement. Excitedly, we tried to guess the big news. *Were we going to live together? Were we going on a trip? Were Grandma and Grandpa coming to visit?* Try as we might, we didn't guess correctly.

"We are going to have a baby!" my mom declared.

43

I was shocked. And delighted. And as always, afraid to get my hopes up. *Will I get to live with our new baby?*

Just before the baby was born, my wish came true. I was moved next door to my parents' dorm room where I'd share a room with my new sibling. I was beyond excited. I was going to be a big sister!

The day the baby was born, I got the news when I was in a lounge full of boarding students. "It's a boy!" someone announced from the hallway. "His name is Robert Andrew Gillis!"

I was crushed. I'd been hoping for a sister. *Why doesn't anything ever go my way? The last thing I need is another brother!*

But over the next few months, Robby taught me how wrong I'd been.

From the start, I claimed him as my responsibility. I was nearly eight, after all, so I took on the role of big sister with gusto. I learned how to change his diapers while his umbilical cord was still attached to his stomach, and how to hold him carefully so that his head didn't flop around. I was protective of the soft spot on the top of his head, covered in downy blond fuzz, where the bones hadn't formed. I thought Robby was the sweetest baby ever.

At night, Robby's relentless screams woke me repeatedly. For some reason, our mom never heard him. So I'd drag myself out of bed, stumble over to his crib, and rub his back to soothe him. Eventually, he'd calm down, either because his crying had exhausted him or my comforting had done the trick. Regardless, it was a trying time for both of us.

Then, when Robby was about six months old, he and our mom were sent to the Community on Cape Cod.

I was never sure why. Something about my mom needing to repent and change. No one knew how long they would be away. I was moved back to the Steinbachs' trailer and my older brothers were assigned to other families. I don't know where my dad lived. All I remember is that I felt devastated.

Months passed. I never stopped thinking about Robby and longing for his return. I had so many questions. *How big is he now? Can he say any words? Does he eat baby food yet?* Missing him and my mom was agony. Now I was the one crying myself to sleep.

When Robby and our mom finally came home, he was barely recognizable. His pudgy cheeks were adorable, and his chocolate brown eyes twinkled like he was hiding a secret. I showered him with hugs and jumped back into big sister mode, taking over his feeding and happily turning food into baby mush with a hand grinder. Robby would move food he didn't like from his tray onto the plate of the person next to him without them even noticing. He was hilarious.

When Robby was learning to stand up on shaky, pudgy legs, my worst fear repeated itself: I was called to the headmaster's table. All four leaders were seated there, and I was terrified.

"Beth," Mrs. Haig began. "Can you guess why we called you up here?"

I was afraid to look at them, but I tried to be brave. "Not really," I managed, scouring my memory for sins I might have committed.

"We called you up here to tell you that your mother needs to go back down to the Community of Jesus," Mrs. Haig continued. "She will be taking your brother Robby with her."

Tears threatened in my eyes as a huge lump formed in my throat.

"No matter how much help she gets, your mother is refusing to change. She is rebellious and is determined to live in unreality. We cannot have her on staff, being such a bad example to students and her own children. Do you know that your mom lives in a fantasy world? We think you're turning out to be just like her. What do you fantasize about, Beth?"

Mrs. Haig's words stung as usual. But this time I couldn't bear to answer her. My chest felt like it was being squeezed. I could barely breathe as I tried to hide my face, my tears, and my emotions behind a soaked Kleenex.

I couldn't tune in to the rest of what was said. Something about my mom being full of sins that she was passing on to me. And that the longer she was kept away from me, the better. She was going to live on Cape Cod for as long as it took for her to change.

I can't endure this again. I can't live without my baby brother again. I can't live without my mom again.

The other leaders joined in and talked about how sinful my mom was. I'm sure they told me how sinful I was, too. But by that time, I wasn't listening.

How come my friends get to keep their moms? Do they have any idea how much I'll miss my baby brother?

I knew better than to voice my real feelings. Instead, I spent the following year in a perpetual state of despair, trying not to think about missing them. I'd painstakingly write letters to my mom but continually felt overwhelmed. I had so much I wanted to tell her and writing it all down felt like a chore. Still, I did my best.

Occasionally, my mom would write to me about life on Cape Cod. I hung on to every word. At one point, she shared a story where, during an especially long sermon, Robby shouted "Amen!" to put a stop to the minister's preaching. I would have burst out laughing if I'd been there.

Once my mom sent me a care package that contained the most delicious squares. They tasted like a mix between pecan pie and chocolate chip cookies. *Heaven.* But Aunt Lillian scolded me for trying to eat my fill. "What are you doing?" she said. "Your mom did not make those just for you! Do you want to get fatter? Don't you think you should share?"

I reluctantly agreed. The squares disappeared much faster than I'd hoped.

When I was living with the next family, my mom sent me a bright yellow square dance outfit with red flowers. When I twirled, the skirt billowed around me like a spinning top. I was delighted! On the first Saturday after receiving it, I proudly donned the outfit and was about to head out of the trailer to breakfast in the dining room.

"What do you think you're doing?" Aunt Rachel demanded.

"What do you mean?" I asked, stumped.

"You aren't wearing *that*!"

I looked down at my outfit, feeling dread. "What's wrong with it?"

"That is a square dance dress! You can't wear it on a Saturday!" Aunt Rachel sounded exasperated, as if speaking to an idiot.

I was desperate for her to change her mind. "I know it's for square dancing. But we only have square dances twice a year! I don't want to wait that long. What if I grow out of it?"

"You'll have to wait for the next dance. That is not appropriate for wearing on Saturday. You'll only attract attention. Is that what you want? To show off?"

Yes! I can't wait to show off this dress! I wanted to say. But being honest was out of the question. I'd only get in more trouble.

Against my will, I removed my square dance outfit, hung it up, and put on my boring turtleneck and corduroy skirt.

Sighing, I tried to accept my fate. But missing my family had become a permanent painful ache in my chest. *Will my mom ever come home? What if she never sees me wear my new dress?*

In the end, she never did get the chance. It was just another bitter pill to swallow in a childhood that was a blur of confusion and disappointment. I kept trying to curb my selfish, sinful desires. But my efforts to do so proved futile. What I really needed was to feel loved.

Chapter 6
Road Trip to Headquarters

I was about ten when I first visited the Community.

It was the first time all the staff and their kids went to Cape Cod. We filled two school buses and a few vans for the ten-hour drive. The plan was to be live-in members for a week.

I was apprehensive yet excited about the trip. My mom had been living down there with my baby brother, and I was dying to see them. Plus, I wanted to see what all the fuss was about.

We loaded the buses at 5:00 a.m. for a ride that seemed to take forever. But I revelled in the endless hours of having nothing scheduled. As we finally approached the Sagamore Bridge to the Cape, I felt a growing tension in the bus. The chatter died down; the games stopped. We kids were nervous, but it was clear that the adults were even more so.

As the buses headed down Route 6 towards Orleans, everyone looked out the windows to take it all in. It was a blur of pitch pine trees, quaint Cape Cod architecture, and glimpses of the ocean.

I can't wait to see my mom and Robby! I thought, the anticipation calming my nerves.

Soon enough, the bus slowed down as we approached a harbour. I craned my neck to get a better view of the ocean. Where was it? All I could see was sand dotted with shallow pools, almost to the horizon.

Through some nearby trees I glimpsed a long, white wooden structure festooned with black shuttered windows and a set of red doors overlooking the harbour. A short bell tower was perched on top.

Is that it? It's not nearly as grand as our school's main building.

We were told to stay in our bus seats and await instructions. Everyone was quiet and uneasy. A few women emerged from a white house with a covered porch, gabled roof and shutters that matched the chapel. I heard some adults calling it Zion. The women wore matching light beige dresses (if you could call them dresses) that looked like calf-length tunics with hoods attached and white ropes around their waists. *I'd hate to wear those.*

"That's Sister Christine with Sister Susanna," an adult said. "They'll probably tell us where we'll be sleeping and living."

I knew a little about what to expect, thanks to my mom's letters. Apparently, the thirty-plus houses in the Community were named after locations in the Bible. Three families usually lived together in each dwelling. When visitors came to stay, they were assigned to live in one of these households but to sleep in a dormitory elsewhere. *Please, let me be sent to my mom's house!* I pleaded silently.

We were told to exit the bus and gather around the sisters silently. One by one, the sisters announced our fates, starting with the adults.

"Dave Poth, you're living at Gennesaret; Lyn Poth, you're living at Cana. Dave, you're sleeping at Olivia Henry dorm, bed eleven, and Lyn, you're sleeping at Estelle Carver dorm, bed three."

"Geoff Henderson, you're living at the Ark, and sleeping at Emmaus."

"Julie Case, you're living at Olivet, and sleeping at Nineveh in the basement."

Soon enough, they got to the children. As the reading of names continued, I noticed family members being split apart and was slowly losing faith that I'd be placed with my mom. Still, I dared to hope. *Please let me be at Judea! Please let me stay with my mom and Robby!*

Finally, my name was called. "Beth Gillis, you'll be living at Jericho and sleeping at Sarah Rowe, bed twelve."

My last shred of optimism rushed out of me like air escaping a balloon. *Why had I allowed myself to hope again?* Then, new worries rushed in. *Who lives in Jericho? Will they be friendly? Are any other staff kids going to be there?*

In the end, none of my family members were assigned the same homes. I was partially relieved to be placed in the same house as my friend Cindy. But apart from that, everything was unknown.

Fear crept in and made itself comfortable, like a familiar but unwelcome guest.

The dorms weren't at all like the ones at Grenville. They reminded me of army barracks from the movies, only more posh. My dorm was packed with ten wooden bunks, the beds perfectly made. Typed note cards issuing instructions were lying everywhere, reminding us to turn off the lights, use as little water as possible, remake beds perfectly, and clean the bathrooms with certain products. It looked so official. I'd never been in a hotel, and I wondered if this was what they were like.

At least I'll be sleeping in the same dorm as the other staff girls. Maybe this will be fun after all!

After unpacking, we were told to report to our houses. It was late afternoon, and everyone was expected to eat dinner in their assigned homes.

Cindy and I were given directions to walk to Jericho, passing several dormitories and extensive communal gardens on the way. Each house was unique, though they were all built in the Cape Cod style with shutters, gabled dormers, and shingle siding. We passed the Ark, Damascus, Olivet, and Cana before being told that Jericho was next.

I wondered which door to use, since it wasn't at all clear. Eventually, Cindy and I chose the front door. My nerves jittered as we carefully walked up the path and rang the doorbell. Then we waited, worrying whether we'd made a mistake.

Eventually, a middle-aged woman opened the door, looking flustered. "Hello?"

"Hello," I said. "We were told this is the house where we'll be living. I'm Beth and this is Cindy."

"Right," the woman said, looking mildly annoyed. "First things first. We don't use this front door. So, in the future, use the side door by the cars. I'm surprised you didn't notice it."

"Sorry. We weren't sure which one to use." I laughed uncomfortably.

She let us inside, and it was clear by the freshly vacuumed plush carpet that indeed no one used that entrance. We followed her through a spacious living room and past a large dining room into an even bigger kitchen.

"I'm Aunt Janet," she informed us over her shoulder. "Dinner will be in forty-five minutes and there is still plenty to be done. Why don't you two go and wash your hands in the sink over there? Then I'll put you both to work."

Everything was so unfamiliar, but I tried to think of this as an opportunity. *If I work hard, maybe I'll make a good impression. Cindy will be fine. She's so cute and little. Everyone likes her.*

My job was to make a tossed salad with lettuce, cucumbers, tomatoes, and carrots that Aunt Janet had placed on the counter. Looking at everything, I had several questions but was afraid to speak up.

"Do I cut all of these things and mix them together?" I whispered to Cindy. She shrugged, and I felt stupid asking her, since how would she know?

Once Cindy was sent to the dining room to set the table, I prepared the lettuce. I didn't know what I was doing, though. At Grenville, lettuce was shredded in a large machine before we mixed it together.

Eventually, I asked, "Aunt Janet, how do you want me to prepare the lettuce?"

"You look old enough to know how to make a salad!" she answered. "Just take out the centre of the head and wash it well. I don't want to find any dirt in my salad."

I searched the kitchen for a large knife. Tentatively, I cut into the head of the lettuce.

"No! Not like that!" Aunt Janet exclaimed. Frustrated, she pushed me aside and showed me how to bang the head on the counter to loosen it and then pull out the centre.

"Wow! I didn't know how to do that."

Aunt Janet humphed. "Don't you make salad at Grenville?"

"Well yes, but I've never made one by myself before."

"Well, it's about time you learned!"

I set about preparing the salad with a lump in my throat. With each step, I had questions I was too afraid to ask. *But what if I make a mistake and get reprimanded?* I constantly agonized about what to do next. In the end, I arranged the tomatoes, cucumbers, and carrots in a pattern on top of the lettuce. *I hope this is OK.*

"Did you toss the salad with some of the toppings before you made it into an art project?" Aunt Janet asked.

"N-n-no," I stammered.

"I told you to make a tossed salad! My instructions couldn't have been more clear. Obviously, you are off in a dream world, fantasizing about who knows what."

My hopes of impressing Aunt Janet evaporated. By then, other members of the household were buzzing around the kitchen, helping to put the meal on the table. Embarrassment took its familiar hold as I carefully tossed the salad with a big spoon, dismantling my vegetable design.

Soon, we headed to the dining room. I was directed to one of the fourteen seats at the huge table and shyly looked around. There were three married couples, a young single woman, three teenage boys who weren't related to any of the adults, one toddler, and one baby, plus Cindy and me. And I knew no one except Cindy, who was seated several chairs away from me on the same side of the table. I couldn't even make eye contact with her.

Introductions were made; I tried to memorize everyone's names. Then we closed our eyes as one of the men prayed. "Dear Lord, we thank you for this bounty and the hands that prepared it. We ask you, Father, to make us receptive to your will and help us to live in your light as we eat."

We passed food around the table and helped ourselves. I should have been starving. But for some reason, I felt queasy. *Live in your light as we eat?* I didn't like the sound of that.

I poked at the unfamiliar tuna cheese casserole on my plate before figuring out how to open the salad dressing bottle. *What is Ranch flavour?* At home, we never bought food from a regular grocery store.

As I lost myself in the wonderful taste of Ranch salad dressing, the light session began.

First, one of the adults criticized Aunt Kathy for her fussing baby: "Every dinner it's the same! You tolerate her bad behaviour. You need to stand against your baby's rebellion!"

Aunt Kathy seemed torn between her baby's cries and the advice she was given.

"Don't you give your baby one more minute of your attention! When she cries, you need to wheel her out into the kitchen and give her what she really needs: a time-out!"

I couldn't help but think of Robby. He was somewhere nearby, sitting in a highchair at a large table like this one. Was he crying? Was my mom being told to discipline him? With tears threatening, I swallowed hard and tried to stop them in their tracks.

Once the baby was left in the kitchen, the crying got louder. One of the adults closed the dining-room door to muffle the noise.

Please let Robby be OK, I silently pleaded. It was all I could do to tune in to the chastisement of Aunt Kathy. I'd heard it all before. She was being scolded for her idolatry. For being too soft on her baby. For trying to be in control and refusing to submit.

Then someone started in on Aunt Kathy's husband. "Don't think you're blameless in all of this, John. You consistently refuse to stand against your wife. When was the last time you confronted Kathy about her sins? No wonder your children are in rebellion!"

I felt so uncomfortable witnessing the humiliation of these strangers. But none of it surprised me. If I could stand it at Grenville, I could stand it here too.

As other people were urged to confess their latest sins, a fresh worry rose from the pit of my stomach. *What if they target me? Do they care that I'm still a kid?* I couldn't shake that terror as one by one, each household member was convicted by the Holy Spirit. Uncle Tony was full of anger and needed to pray about its root cause. Aunt Betsy was plagued by jealousy. Uncle Ben was too haughty and full of pride. Aunt Janet was too controlling and resentful.

I tried to tune it all out. But how could I while being tormented with fear that I'd be next? All my senses were on high alert.

"What do you think God wants to teach you while you're here, Beth?"

My heart rate doubled at the sound of my name. "I'm not sure?" I hesitated, stupidly caught off guard.

"That's not going to fly here. You need to plead with Jesus to convict you of your sin. Anyone looking at you could tell you're trying to remain hidden."

I swallowed the lump in my throat. "I think I'm angry," I offered eventually, though what I really felt was terror. But I wasn't going to admit that.

"About what?"

"I'm angry that I didn't get placed at Judea. That's where my mom and baby brother are staying. They've been down here for a long time." In a smaller voice, I added, "I miss them."

It was almost a relief to be so honest. But then Aunt Janet pounced. "I could tell there was something off with you from the moment you arrived. Who do you think you are? Do you think you know better than the Holy Spirit?"

I felt like cowering in a corner. But Aunt Janet wasn't finished. "Your anger tells me how haughty you are. You think you should be able to dictate what's best. Well, you are going to learn how far that is from the truth."

"Beth, don't you realize that Judea is the last place you should be?" Aunt Betsy added. "Your mother would only ruin you with her idolatry, and you wouldn't make any progress while you're here."

I sat there speechless, feeling gutted and pinned to the chair. Any hopes of receiving compassion from the adults were long gone. *Why did I tell them the truth? I should have confessed a different sin.*

Another part of me considered the truth of their message. *Maybe my mom really is a terrible influence on me. Maybe it's time I quit missing her. I don't want my parents to ruin me.*

Someone pulled me out of my reverie then. "Beth, are you ready to confess your anger and ask the Holy Spirit for His blood washing?"

"Yes!" I complied, wanting to add, *Let's get this over with!*

Aunt Janet led me in prayer. I did my best to mean what I was saying. When everyone said "Amen," all I felt was numb relief. I'd survived my first meal.

The rest of the evening was a blur of washing dishes, cleaning the kitchen, doing meal prep, and going to church. At 9:00 p.m., the community gathered for compline. After that, we headed to our dorms. Later, as I lay in bed, I tried to ignore my hunger pains while calculating how many hours remained in the rest of the week.

†

The remainder of our stay was a blur of new experiences.

We spent a lot of time in church, but that was nothing new. The only difference was, the Community's church was packed with unfamiliar faces. Many were sisters and brothers wearing their awful habits. They filled several rows of the church and sat apart from us.

Living in those dorms wasn't as much fun as I'd hoped. There were rules about everything. No talking was allowed once we arrived to get ready for bed. In the morning, we'd rush to get ready and clean the dorms. Our beds had to be made perfectly, which was impossible. I could barely reach my bunk while standing on the floor. And we had to clean the bathrooms every morning before breakfast.

On Wednesdays, the households did their grocery shopping. Cindy and I accompanied Aunt Janet to Stop & Shop and it was a wonder. I'd never been grocery shopping before. We filled three shopping carts to overflowing. There was a whole aisle for drinks, and brands I'd only seen on a TV we rarely watched. The entire process fascinated me. The only downside was being surrounded by so much tempting food. I'd think about the cookies, chips, and ice cream we bought. *Will they let us eat some of this bounty? Maybe I could sneak some? Beth, are you insane? What if you got caught?*

I also saw a lot of the Community's grounds while doing kids' group chores. At one point during work crew, I was walking down one of the roads to weed the next garden, when I spotted my mom and Robby.

My heart leapt with excitement. I had the urge to sprint towards them, but something stopped me. I'd learned better than to demonstrate love for my family.

As I approached my mom and my baby brother, I lectured myself. *Keep calm, Beth. Walk normally. Rein in your enthusiasm.*

When I finally hugged them both, the reunion was bittersweet. Little Robby looked so different, and I marvelled at the changes in his appearance. He'd transformed from a baby into a toddler who didn't seem to know me. That stung bitterly. My mom was friendly, but wary and distant.

All too soon, I was summoned away by my supervisor. I reluctantly left my mom and Robby on the road, and we headed our separate ways, emptiness escorting me as I walked.

†

When we weren't doing group chores or at meals or church, we'd clean our assigned homes, fold laundry, iron, or help in the kitchens. All day long, we were given job after job. "You finished the upstairs bathrooms? Did you scrub the showers like I instructed? Well, I'll be checking. Let's see: next, I'll have you vacuum while Cindy dusts. Don't forget to do the stairs by hand like I showed you yesterday."

The Community's cleaning products also took some getting used to. *What's this stuff called Vim supposed to do? And this 409 spray? What is it for?*

The worst part was, we had to listen to tapes of the Mothers' preaching while doing chores. Their voices alone put me on edge. My instinct was to tune them out and think about anything else.

†

I suppose we had some opportunities for fun. Once or twice, Cindy and I were invited to walk the dog down to the beach. I learned about low and high tides. Cape Cod Bay looked different every time I saw it. I can still feel the goopy sand between my toes while walking on the beach at low tide. The tidal pools were full of weird-looking plants, razor clams, and creepy-crawly things. Thick salty air swirled around me, its residue clinging to my skin.

Even if we'd been taken to amusement parks that week, I wouldn't have relaxed and enjoyed myself. Fear loomed like a spectre over every waking minute. What had happened at the first meal continued throughout the week. And not just around the table. The adults would discuss sins at any point in the day. We'd be doing the dishes, making lunch, or walking to church, and someone would want to know what we were thinking about and whether we were steeped in sin.

Meals were the worst, though. I had to brace myself for each one. At dinner especially, the discussions always veered into light sessions. I wasn't always targeted, but that didn't lessen my dread. I'd constantly wrack my brain for possible reactions, sins, or thoughts I could confess if the need arose. Something I could offer that wouldn't land me in too much trouble but appease their desire to expose my wickedness.

Finally, the last day arrived. I was more excited to go home than I was about Christmas. The best thing I did that week was pack my lunch for the bus ride home.

The silver lining was that I developed a new appreciation for life at Grenville. From the moment I arrived at the Community, I longed to return to Canada. I missed everything about my home. The routine, the normalcy, the students, the activities. Even living with random families at Grenville seemed tolerable compared to the Community, where I felt completely unsafe and exposed.

To my chagrin, our trips to the Cape became routine. We'd go there for a week every summer and March break. The adults—and sometimes teenagers—also had to attend intensive weekend retreats once or twice a year.

I dreaded every trip to the Community. Most of all, the retreats scared me. *Please don't make me go to a retreat before I'm an adult!* I'd silently beg the heavens. (Spoiler alert: God wouldn't honour that request.)

†

A few months after that first trip to the Community, my greatest wish was granted.

My mom finally returned home with Robby when he was three. For one glorious year, our family was allowed to live together in a trailer. It was thrilling. I loved singing to the music my dad blasted from his record player. I loved learning to sew and cook with my mom. I loved hosting family nights, playing board games, and going on outdoor excursions with my real brothers and adopted student siblings. I loved chopping down our first real Christmas tree together.

I especially loved being a big sister to Robby and watching him grow. I read him stories, kept him laughing in the bathtub, and was his potty training cheerleader. When he got the measles, I was so afraid. Luckily, he recovered in time for Christmas when he received a plastic British police helmet. Robby and his best friend Michael would don their matching helmets and expertly re-enact scenes from *The Pirates of Penzance*. "That's my baby brother!" I'd proudly inform any student within earshot.

That was the first and last time we'd all live together. After that year, Dan, Garth, and I were moved away again. We'd only see Robby in passing at school. Over the years, we'd steal moments to visit him, but they were never enough.

Chapter 7
The Good, the Bad, and the Ugly

Growing up in a boarding school was never dull. There was so much to experience that it was almost possible to forget about our sins, at least temporarily.

Our day-to-day schedule was jam-packed all year round. School days were scheduled from 6:30 a.m. until 10:30 p.m. with church, meals, chores, classes, study halls, and extracurricular activities crammed in.

There was never any free time. We staff kids never got to hang out or watch TV. When we weren't in class or at meals, we were supervised in a large group by older students. During kids' activity we'd play in the large gym or on the playground, or do group chores. I can picture us, spread out in a long line across the sprawling front lawns, looking for litter. We'd pick up random bottles, sticks, or cigarette butts, wondering aloud in horrified whispers, "Who was smoking?"

The chores seemed endless. But during the school year, we only had to clean the school for four hours every Saturday morning with the boarding students. In the summer, it was another story. We staff kids worked nonstop to prepare the school for September.

One time, I was perched on the top of a twelve-foot ladder, struggling to remove a curtain from a hook—and I noticed my fingers were one inch away from a sleeping bat! My scream pierced the air and probably gave the bat a heart attack. To this day, I don't know how I didn't fall off that ladder.

In August, a few weeks before the students arrived, the work would intensify. It wasn't unusual for us to have work parties in the evenings after a day of toiling. *Why do we call them parties?* I'd grumble inwardly.

We had good times too. Every Wednesday afternoon, over one hundred of us would travel by school bus to Brown's Bay Park for swimming, boating, playground fun, baseball games, barbeque, and campfire singing. I can imagine what a passerby might have thought when our barbeques turned into group light sessions. You never knew when the Holy Spirit would strike.

Sometimes we got a break from chores for group lessons. I was always keen to learn new things. My favourite lessons were on horseback. If it had been up to me, I would have spent my life in the barn or the saddle.

The music room was another happy place. When I was seven, staff kids chose instruments. I picked the violin and was instantly hooked.

All staff kids received swimming lessons in the river. Despite the cold water and my fear of biting fish, I thought we were quite lucky. It sure beat cleaning the school!

For a few summers, we also got sewing lessons. I made my first skirt when I was in grade four. That skill came in handy, as I sewed most of my own clothes in my teens and twenties.

Summers had their ups and downs. But during the school year, there was always more to anticipate.

Watching the older students was a constant source of inspiration. I'd scream from the sidelines of basketball or soccer games and jump in the stands at track meets. I'd sit transfixed as brave teenagers took part in public speaking competitions. I'd watch intently as students rode horses, cross-country skied, played hockey, and waterskied on the river.

Most of all, I was enchanted by the actors on stage. Grenville put on plays all year round, like an annual junior musical, a festival play for competition, and a G&S production every spring. Our school's drama program was well respected, and the shows always sold out.

Fun was scheduled at Grenville. (At least, I thought it was fun at the time). Friday night activities were mandatory. Students would play volleyball, watch G-rated movies, play bingo, compete in scavenger or treasure hunts, go skating, or play simulated game shows like *Let's Make a Deal*. And during Saturday family nights, there'd be board games, hikes, picnics, sledding, skiing, or movies—always with delicious snacks.

Several times a year, the school held lavish banquets. Thanksgiving, Christmas, Chinese New Year, and graduation were the biggest occasions. The dining room would be transformed with candlelit centrepieces, crisp linen tablecloths, intricately folded napkins nestled in glasses, and flowers galore. The food was always delicious and plentiful, with mouthwatering desserts. There was also live music, performed by the school's most proficient musicians. Best of all, I'd get to see all the girls showcasing their beautiful long gowns. To me, it was like a live beauty pageant.

Every single day there was some type of church service. I was in the chapel so often that it almost felt like our living room. When I was little we had Sunday night sings and I'd lie on the pews in my fuzzy feet pyjamas. All the staff, most of whom weren't musically trained, would gather to sing the classics like "Messiah." My dad was tasked with directing these sessions, and I was so proud of him. I'd close my eyes and let the loud music swirl around me. (My dad remembers these events as his personal purgatory. After directing each one, he was treated to a harsh light session.)

After the Mothers arrived, we adopted the Anglican order of worship. During the first new service, our pastors showed up in long white robes. *What is going on?* I wondered as I gazed around, confused. An altar was covered in embroidered cloths, candles, and silver chalices with wafers and wine. We were given prayer books and followed along with the order of services for communion.

Over time, even the singing changed; we started using 1940 Episcopal hymnals instead of the gospel choruses we knew by heart. If the leaders didn't think the students were singing with enough enthusiasm, they would make us repeat hymns over and over. *Let's get this over with!* I wanted to shout. *My stomach is rumbling!*

Grenville advertised itself as an Anglican school, but what really went on in the chapel was a different story. Sure, we had regular Anglican services, with communion, morning prayer, and compline right before bed. Some days we had praise singing sessions or Bible studies led by the Haigs and Farnsworths. What made a lasting impression, however, were the mass light sessions held in the chapel. I witnessed so many of these that they almost became commonplace. Students would be singled out, forced to stand in front of the entire student body, and publicly humiliated. I hated the feeling of fear that permeated the chapel. I'd sit there numbly, watching students being shamed, degraded, and reduced to tears. They were accused of all kinds of sin. If they dared speak up for themselves, they got in even worse trouble.

I despised these sessions. The leaders were so mean. *What if this makes the students hate it here?* I'd worry. *What if they run away?*

Another practise that continued to make me wildly uncomfortable was when the leaders would sing in tongues. Even after we became an Anglican school, one of the Fathers would start singing or speaking gibberish, and the other would speak in English, like an interpreter. Soon, all the staff would join in, hands raised, singing nonsense words. This always made my skin crawl. With one eye closed in prayer, I'd sneak peeks around me, nearly dying of embarrassment as I noticed the looks of bewilderment on the boarding students' faces.

I did like some things about church, though. One of my favourite parts about Sunday service was that it felt like a fashion show. I paid closer attention to style choices than I did to the sermons. I wanted so badly to someday dress like many of the teenagers I noticed. I also enjoyed listening to our choir perform. They sang so many of the greats. Mozart, Handel, Bach, Mendelssohn, Vivaldi: the list was endless. I was always so proud of my dad for his dedication and musical skill.

The Gilbert and Sullivan operettas were my annual highlight. I adored everything about those plays: the costumes, the music, the dialogue, the dancing, the orchestra, and the set design. My father was involved in directing these productions, so I was invested in their success. Even when I didn't get to live with my parents, I was hyper aware of their roles on campus. Whenever they shone, I took vicarious pride.

I loved watching the rehearsals almost as much as the actual performances. If I got the chance, I'd tip-toe up into the auditorium's balcony, lie down on my tummy under the pew, and prop my chin on the cold metal railing. Then I'd watch, enchanted, as students transformed into fairies, gondoliers, or pirates. The spectacle of a stage full of teenagers singing and dancing was thrilling. I memorized every song by the time each play wrapped up. As I grew older, my capability to understand the dialogue's humour increased, and I'd laugh constantly throughout the production. The plays had it all: hilarity, heartbreak, absurdity, adventure, and true love. I couldn't wait until I was old enough to audition.

One time when I was eleven, I snuck up the stairs to the loft in the music storage room. The sheer volume of scores beckoned to me. I poked around until I found the G&S section. *Goody! I can start practising!*

I found *The Yeomen of the Guard*, the school's most recent production. Unable to decide between the two female leads, I opted to try all of their solos. Phoebe's song "When Maiden Loves" opened the play, so I started there.

Seated cross-legged on the loft's wooden floor, I tentatively began singing. I was so lost in the wonder of the song that I didn't hear footsteps on the stairs. When Father Farnsworth's head appeared, I froze.

"What do you think you are doing up here?" he demanded.

"I'm ... *singing?*" I stammered.

"Who gave you permission to be up here?"

Fear squeezed my vocal cords, and I could barely speak. "No one. I thought it was OK."

"You know very well that this area is off-limits. Furthermore, what possessed you to come up here?"

Might as well tell the truth, I figured, seeing as I wasn't ashamed of it. "I'm practising these solos because I want to audition when I'm older."

Father Farnsworth frowned. "How old are you?"

"Eleven."

"Is there no limit to your haughtiness?" he shouted, startling me. "What makes you think you'll be given a lead role? The Gillis family is full of haughty, self-centred attention seekers! All you want is to be in the limelight. When will you people ever learn?"

I gulped as a wave of shame crashed over me. My desire to perform on stage suddenly felt sordid, like a dirty secret. *Who do you think you are? I scolded myself. You don't deserve to be a lead on stage.*

It was yet another lesson in the dangers of making my aspirations known. More importantly, I remembered that desire was itself the problem. *Beth, whatever you do, stop getting your hopes up!*

Chapter 8
Damned if You Do,
Damned if You Don't

In many ways, Father Haig's 1980 yearbook address accurately summed up life at Grenville. Boredom had no place there. In fact, the school was a breeding ground of great expectations:

Dear Graduates, Students, and Friends,

Grenville Christian College is dedicated to developing leaders by putting young people through a total training program specifically designed to sharpen them mentally, physically, and spiritually.

While most of the social structures of the western world are easing up, lowering standards, and softening demands, Grenville Christian College keeps on raising her standards, increasing the demands, requiring more and more from her students, and getting it.

Graduates of 1980, I know you are grateful to Grenville because you have discovered that you are capable of far more than you ever dreamed possible. Under the firm and steady hand of those who loved you, you pulled out of your lazy, self-centred ways and worked harder, concentrated longer, played, and served more unselfishly than ever before. All you needed was consistent, loving discipline, a firm push from behind, and you found that you could do it!

Each of you has become a fighter. Boredom has been left behind, and life has become an exciting adventure. Your inner enemies, such as jealousy, anger, desire for ease, and highmindedness, have been strongly dealt with at Grenville. You saw where you were wrong. With God's tremendous help, you did battle against yourself ... you persevered through, and won. You found freedom through discipline.

Keep it up! The world needs Christian warriors like you more than ever before. Mankind needs unashamed Christian leaders with high ideals and self-discipline who will stand in the front line of battle.

Your Alma Mater salutes you. Go in God's strength and peace.

Your Headmaster,

J. Alastair Haig (*Anno Domini* 1979/80, 2)

Staff and students were continually pushed to be the best they could be. Perfection was demanded and required in all areas of life, even the mundane parts. Demerits were handed out to students who were seconds late to meals or classes. If your dorm room wasn't spotless, your uniform had wrinkles, or your hair was out of place, you could expect at least a stern reprimand, at worst a light session and disciplinary action.

Outwardly, the school made a big deal of student achievements. The names of those on the honour roll were painted in gold on carved wooden panels outside the chapel. Prefects of the year, valedictorians, and salutatorians were memorialized on the atrium walls outside the front office. Newsletters were regularly sent home to parents, packed with photos and articles showcasing student success. During announcements at meals, students with notable accomplishments were publicly congratulated. Star athletes, academics, actors, singers, public speakers, debaters, artists, show jumpers, and musicians were celebrated.

As I grew older, I noticed all the ways these students got validation. *That's what I want. Someday, I'm going to be the one getting noticed.*

What I didn't know until later was that these achievements often came at a terrible price. Many who met the school's great expectations received far more criticism than praise. While Grenville expected and demanded excellence, the actual high achievers were continually told they were full of sin and needed to change. That without God, they were worthless and could accomplish nothing. That their inner enemies, like Father Haig said in the yearbook, needed to be dealt with strongly.

It's hard to explain how this worked. As a youngster, I discovered how talented people—like my dad—were constantly pushed to do better, train harder, and achieve more. Nothing was ever good enough. What I didn't realize was that these people were simultaneously confronted for their haughtiness or highmindedness, or reprimanded for being full of self-love or other sins.

I also didn't know that my dad dreaded every performance. After church services, he was cornered by certain staff members and leaders for a light session. He was told how out of the spirit he was, that the choir didn't have God's anointing, and that this was his fault. He was never allowed to forget how his haughtiness might be ruining the school's music program.

†

Since I didn't know how much pressure high achievers were under, I set my sights on being one myself. *How else will I get my parents' attention?*

I was acutely aware that my older brothers were garnering attention for their talents. During graduation ceremonies, I'd watch them win most of the awards for the highest marks in each subject. In middle school, they landed lead roles in junior musicals. Dan was a fantastic Tom Sawyer and Garth was a hilarious Huckleberry Finn. They were good athletes and dominated in basketball, cross-country skiing, and track and field. Dan was an excellent pianist, and Garth played the violin equally well. If all this weren't enough, they were allowed to join the boys' choir at a local Anglican church for a few years, becoming head choristers and even singing solos on recorded albums. We would attend their concerts, and I'd sit on the edge of the pew, bursting with pride as they performed. I admit that jealousy got the better of me when their choir travelled to England, San Francisco, and Washington, D.C.

Envy aside, I was proud of my brothers. They inspired me and I couldn't wait to prove myself.

By the time I was ten, I was an avid student, striving to get top grades, and getting upset whenever I made mistakes. I lived for the smelly stickers my teachers would attach to perfect math tests. *Ahhh, the delicious fruity smell of achievement!* I eagerly memorized and performed poems for our public speaking contests, revelling in the chance to make the crowd laugh. Though it scared me, I wrote and delivered speeches in front of our school and the local legions.

Like Dan and Garth, I was athletic, though I didn't realize it at first. In elementary school, I avidly competed in cross-country skiing races. I was fast and loved the thrill of competition. Little by little, I built up my own collection of medals.

In the warmer seasons, my single greatest desire was to ride horses. The barn felt like a getaway. Around the horses, I felt a kind of belonging that I sensed nowhere else. When I had spare time, I'd happily offer to muck the stalls or help lunge the horses. By the time I was in grade seven, I made it onto the riding team. It wasn't easy. My muscles would shake with the strenuous exercises as we prepared for jumping. But I was determined to become a good rider. No matter how much it pained me or scared me.

By the time I approached middle school, I was also good at the violin. The best part was playing in ensembles. I revelled in the sound of all the strings as we joined forces, making beautiful music. At some point, the school needed a viola player, so I volunteered to try it. I loved its rich, lower sounds and relished the opportunity to play for all kinds of occasions. The first time I played Bach's *Brandenburg Concerto* in a string quartet for the benefit of visiting dignitaries was a thrill.

In addition, I had a clear, strong soprano voice and loved to sing. Our elementary and middle schools put on musicals, and I adored these productions. Starting in grade four, I landed roles with solos and even got the female lead in middle school. While I was always self-conscious, I developed enough confidence year after year to enjoy myself on stage. Despite Father Farnsworth's dire warnings looming in the back of my mind, I still secretly harboured dreams of someday playing leads in the G&S operettas.

Any outsider would have assumed that I was happy, well-adjusted, smart, and confident. That my talents were being developed at Grenville and I was lucky to be a staff kid there. That's also how I tried to view myself. But as I think back to those years when I was trying to spread my wings, a few memories cloud over the good ones.

Despite all my accomplishments, I forever worried about my size. Ever since that first forced diet, I'd felt like my body was under a microscope. It didn't help that my ballet instructor kept telling me to lose weight. When I was in grade four, her explicit instructions were not to eat any pie at Thanksgiving dinner. "Suck, tuck, and squeeze," she'd yell repeatedly, walking along the barre, making disgruntled sounds in my general direction.

Eventually, in grade six, I declared to my roommates, "I'm never going to let myself weigh more than a hundred pounds! No matter what!" Even as I said those words, I felt a sinking feeling that I'd fail. By then, I was already sneaking food. I'd cut tiny slivers of cake, or pinch chunks of leftover cookie dough that Aunt Rachel had left in her fridge. Once I started, I couldn't stop. Even as I shovelled it in, I felt so ashamed and was terrified of being caught in the act. I did everything I could to cover my tracks. Much of the motivation to become good at sports had to do with my quest to look thin. And as I neared middle school, my despair and fear increased.

On top of all that, my parents seemed to be completely unaware of my achievements. They never mentioned my stellar report cards. They never cheered me on at ski races or watched me learn to navigate my first jumps on a horse. They might have been in the audience during a few of my stage performances, but I was never sure. It seemed that my parents were ignoring my accomplishments. This made me strive even harder. I was going to earn some attention, come hell or high water.

By grade six, I finally did get attention, but not the good kind.

†

I never understood why I landed on Discipline the first time. All I know is that I was an enthusiastic student, focusing on getting the best grades possible. Yet it was decided that I was a problem. I was pulled in for questioning by the elementary school principal, my teacher, and the adults I was living with. The episode was so shameful and confusing that I still can't recall which adult said what.

"Beth, you know that God called you to be a staff kid in this community, don't you?"

"Yes," I said.

"And that you are extremely fortunate to be receiving such a privileged education?"

"Yes."

"You also know that we expect you to conduct yourself with exemplary behaviour at all times?"

"Yes …" I repeated, wondering where this was going.

"Are you curious about why we are gathered here?"

I hesitated before answering, "Yes."

"Well, we have noticed your bad attitude is permeating the classroom and threatening to infect the spirit of our elementary school."

I was frozen with shock, even as my mind raced, trying to grasp what they were saying.

"Your haughtiness is growing like a weed. You act like you're someone special and that you think you're better than others."

"Next year, you're going to be in grade seven! You will be expected to set an example to all the boarding students in your grade. We cannot have a staff kid who is a negative influence! You need to cultivate a much better attitude. One without rebellion or disrespect. You need to stop trying to get approval from outside students. They cannot be your true friends."

"You staff kids have a critical role to play. Without your good example, many students will falter. Do you want to be responsible for the failure of others?"

"No," I murmured, trying to mentally recap what was being said. *I'm too haughty, rebellious, and disrespectful. And, I have a bad attitude— wait, what? I thought I had a good attitude. How am I supposed to fix that?*

I could hardly bear the shame of it all. But what came next caught me completely off guard.

"We have decided that you need to go on Discipline until your attitude changes. You will not attend school until we are satisfied that you've repented."

What? I'm being put on Discipline? My heart sped as objections surged into my brain. *Elementary students are* never *put on D! Now I'll be the first one ever. The whole school will think the worst of me. How will I bear the humiliation?*

Even though I hadn't been put on D before, I was afraid of it. What I didn't know was, this would be the first of countless times I'd be put on Discipline over the next two decades.

Looking back now, I can see how Father Haig's message was prophetic. He predicted that my inner enemies would be strongly dealt with. I would see where I was wrong and do battle against myself. With God's help, I would persevere, and win.

But try as I might, I never did find freedom through discipline, as he'd boldly promised in the yearbook.

Chapter 9
On D

I'd always been acutely aware of students who were on Discipline. In a sea of navy, white, and Gordon plaid uniforms, these kids stuck out like sore thumbs. They had to wear casual work clothes and were prohibited from interacting with anyone. Their faces were downcast, their demeanor resigned. Their silence was strictly enforced. Even making eye contact with other students was forbidden. They couldn't attend classes and rarely received study time. Prefects or staff would supervise them as they ate, hidden away from view. Kids on D worked from dawn till dusk, or longer, doing the dirty work around the school. Whenever I went into the kitchen, students on Discipline were always there, scrubbing burnt pans, cleaning the industrial ovens, or on their hands and knees, scouring the floor with toothbrushes.

I'm never going to end up like them! I'd tell myself. They were treated so harshly that I'd always assumed their punishment fit their crimes.

As far as I understood, students were put on D for breaking the rules. There were many strict policies at Grenville, and it was hard to follow them all. Especially for teenagers who were from the outside, wicked world. Naturally, some of them would rebel against the school's restrictions. Regardless, I'd figured most students deserved their punishment. I mean, how hard was it to follow the rules? Kids who were caught smoking were put on D immediately. I didn't have much sympathy for them. They'd been warned.

Rock music was forbidden at Grenville. Students couldn't have Walkmans, radios, cassette tapes or CDs, or even T-shirts depicting the names of rock bands. If these were found in a student's possession, they'd be put on D without question. Almost any music with a beat was considered the work of the devil. Boarding students complained about missing their music more than anything else. I figured giving up music was easier than being on D, so they'd better get used to going without.

The six-inch rule meant boy/girl relationships were forbidden. The staff were always on the lookout for developing crushes or romances amongst the boarders. If they discovered that two students liked each other, they'd watch the couple like hawks. By the time I was in grade six, I'd seen many students be accused in front of the entire school of tempting someone of the opposite sex. I didn't understand the terms that were used, but they sounded terribly sinful. Girls were often called whores, jezebels, or bitches in heat while being reprimanded for pulling on the boys, as it was called. Conversely, boys were yelled at for being weak enough to fall for a girl's seductive behaviour. Students learned to hide their attraction, or they paid a high price.

Whenever I saw students on D, I assumed they were in trouble for breaking an obvious rule. However, as the years went by, I realized that students were often in trouble for mysterious reasons. In fact, one major way to land in trouble was to have an undefined bad attitude.

Until grade six, I'd never considered what it was like for students whose only crime was being negative. I'd also never experienced the despair and confusion that came with being told I'd be on Discipline indefinitely until I had changed.

Upon being sentenced to Discipline, I was escorted to my trailer to change out of my uniform. I stared at my closet in misery, wondering which skirts I could afford to ruin. I was then escorted across campus to report to Mrs. Leitch.

Once I was put to work, I felt like I was on display. There was no way to hide. All I could do was focus on completing a never-ending list of unpleasant jobs, like scrubbing, scouring, scraping, and cleansing. I kept my head down, afraid to look at or speak to anyone. My lack of uniform felt like a glaring spotlight. Whenever I looked up, I'd see students glancing at me sideways, their expressions ranging from curious disbelief to cold condemnation. So I kept my head lowered, working with a constant lump in my throat as tears threatened to further expose my shame.

Students on D weren't allowed to eat in the dining room. Instead, we were escorted to nearby offices, closets, or storerooms. I dreaded meals because it was so humiliating to have an adult or prefect babysitting me as I ate in awkward silence. Even worse, sometimes I was forgotten. If no one showed up to relieve me from my duties, I'd miss the meal as I kept scrubbing, my stomach aching with hunger.

While I worked, I was consumed by fearful thoughts. *What is everyone saying about me? Why am I in trouble? How long will I be on Discipline? How do I prove that I've changed?* My mind would race as I tried to predict the answers. I thought that rumours were circulating about me, for sure. *"I heard she was caught* stealing!" I imagined kids saying. Or *"I bet she was cheating on her tests!"* I wanted to set the record straight. But what would I tell people? *"Calm down, everyone. I'm on D because I'm haughty and rebellious. And I have a* bad attitude. *Nothing to write home about."*

Day after day, I felt literally sick to my stomach with fear. I knew I was being watched. My daily private light sessions were proof enough. I'd be asked what God was teaching me. If I was being convicted of my sin. If I was learning humility. If I was grateful to be a staff kid and ready to lead by example with an excellent attitude.

I'd choose my words carefully, frantic to make a good impression. But what words would mollify them? *How can I appear sufficiently changed? Or repentant?*

My efforts to prove myself in light sessions failed repeatedly. Discipline lasted for five agonizing days before my final light session. I don't know if I appeared to be an improved version of myself. But somehow, that session ended with the words I'd been dreaming about all week: "Beth, we've decided that you can resume classes next Monday."

The intense relief almost made me dizzy.

"But we hope you've learned from this time of reflection. We will be keeping our eyes on you. Your attitude can make all the difference in a classroom. You need to take this responsibility very seriously."

I sincerely assured them that I had indeed learned my lesson.

When I re-entered normal life—or at least, normal within my frame of reference—it was with a great deal of trepidation. It was painfully clear to me that I'd been on Discipline not for what I'd done, but for who I was. That fact scared me to my core.

How will I make sure this never happens again? Should I pretend to be a bad student?

I didn't know how to answer my questions. But I did learn two lessons from that first time on D: I wasn't safe to be myself, and being a good staff kid was going to be a lot harder than I'd anticipated.

Chapter 10
Glory Days

Grenville prospered as the eighties approached. Each year, new facilities were built. As enrolment grew, so did the school's good reputation. I got caught up in the excitement of its expansion and growing prestige. The notion that I was being raised and groomed to be a staff member there gave me a real sense of pride.

I had a vested interest in Grenville's success. By the time I was a preteen, it had been drummed into my head that I was called to be a lifelong member of the Community, like all Grenville staff. I hoped to become a teacher at the school. So, naturally, I wanted the school to thrive.

In April 1979, when the new dining complex was completed, we had a grand ceremony to commemorate the new building. Dignitaries were invited, including the Honourable Pauline McGibbon, who was the guest of honour. I was fascinated with her title of Lieutenant Governor of Ontario. We were told about her impressive roles in Canada—Chancellor of the University of Toronto and Guelph University, Chair of the National Arts Centre in Ottawa, a director of Massey Hall and Roy Thompson Hall in Toronto—and how important her visit was to the success of our school.

The entire day of her visit was planned down to the minute. Every student played a role in welcoming, entertaining, and impressing our distinguished guest. We all lined the long driveway leading up to the school, freezing in our dress uniforms without coats, waving Ontario flags with frenzied enthusiasm as her car entered the campus. Later, the Honourable Pauline McGibbon declared that she'd never been welcomed so warmly anywhere.

Upon her arrival, a grand banquet was held in the new dining room. We pulled out all the stops to dazzle her with entertainment. After some speeches, the lieutenant governor was treated to a choir performance, a tour of the school, and a stage performance in our auditorium. By then, Grenville was boasting an excellent reputation for its drama program. What better person to impress than a famous patron of Canadian arts?

The visit was a rousing success. The Honourable Pauline McGibbon joined our board of patrons, serving in that capacity for over a decade. In June 1981, she returned as our honoured graduation speaker. Word got out that Grenville was an exceptional school. We attracted some successful and influential VIPs to our board over that decade, including the Honourable John Black Aird, who had served as a Canadian senator before being appointed Lieutenant Governor of Ontario in 1980; Senator J. Trevor Eyton, a chancellor at Dalhousie University and a recipient of the Order of Canada; Jean Casselman Wadds, a former Canadian high commissioner to Great Britain and the first woman to serve as parliamentary secretary in the Canadian government; and the Lord Bishop of Ontario, the Right Reverend Allan Read, who was our guest of honour at several important church services each school year.

Another of our patrons was Sir Arthur Chetwynd, president of Chetwynd Films and the 8th Baronet of Brocton Hall, Staffordshire. His additional roles as the president of the Empire Club of Toronto and the Canadian Club of Toronto meant that the Grenville choir was often invited to perform at the Royal York Hotel during his club's special events. I did this on a few occasions. As ambassadors for our school, our job was clear. We had to impress Chetwynd's rich, successful colleagues, who could spread the word about our school's excellence.

Thanks to our patrons, our choir got to perform at elite venues throughout the eighties and early nineties. On one occasion, we sang in the atrium of the parliament buildings in Ottawa. Father Farnsworth shook hands and chatted with Prime Minister Brian Mulroney afterward. In Toronto, we sang in Massey Hall and performed the national anthems at the SkyDome. Singing on the infield in 1989, I felt like I was one of God's chosen elite. And of course, we believed God helped the Blue Jays win the division championship that year.

†

Once the dining-room complex was finished, fundraising started for staff apartments. Construction began in 1982 and within a year, several staff families moved out of trailers into beautiful new apartments with river views. This continued for several years until three connected residences were completed. The apartments were spacious, with enough room in some for at least three staff families to live together.

My family was chosen to move into the first phase of these apartments. For a few glorious months, I could barely contain my excitement. *I am getting my own room in my parents' apartment! They even let me choose the paint colour!* Sadly, when it came time to move in, I was told I wouldn't be living with my parents after all. Instead, I was directed to move in with the Steinbachs and bunk with their daughter Amy. Though my disappointment was acute, I was getting used to it by then.

In 1985, another capital campaign was launched to raise money for a new boys' dorm. By 1987 the three-storey building was built with space for 125 boys—and twenty-four showers! The old dorm was then converted into ten brand-new carpeted classrooms. The next summer, a new IBM computer lab and network were installed in the school.

Also, flanking the new dormitory, a double-sized gymnasium was built (with bleachers!) and huge locker rooms (with more private showers!). It was massive, with an impressive GCC Lions logo painted on the gleaming wooden floor. There were tempered glass backboards that lowered with large hydraulic arms. The new giant digital scoreboard made me feel like we were at an NBA facility.

As soon as the boys' dorm was finished, an eight-lane rubberized track was constructed behind the school. What a huge improvement from training on the school's front drive! A large clubhouse was also built with locker rooms, equipment storage, and an upstairs broadcast booth. Afterward, Grenville became well-known for hosting huge tournaments and track meets.

During the mid-eighties, a large inground pool was installed next to the Farnsworths' house. It was big enough to hold pool parties for large groups of students. Lanes were painted on the bottom for students to train for their lifeguard courses or swimming levels. The pool was such a luxury compared to swimming in the river. It was even heated until winter set in. One time, I swam during a snowfall and was so cozy under the water as white flakes fell onto my wet hair. *This is the life!* I thought, amazed at our blessings.

If that wasn't enough, one more fitness facility was built in the late eighties. Where the barns and horses used to be, a large military-style obstacle course was constructed. It was donated by patron Sir Arthur Chetwynd, who was also the grandfather of one of our boarders. While this was an exciting addition to some, it sadly reminded me of better days. Whenever I looked at the obstacle course, I mourned the loss of our equestrian program. The school had sold all of its horses when I was around thirteen. The day they loaded the horses onto trailers, I watched in disbelief from the top floor of the school, my forehead pressed against the window, willing myself not to cry.

†

A year after the horses were sold, the school experienced a far more momentous loss. For reasons I never understood, Father and Mrs. Haig left Grenville in 1984 and Father Farnsworth became our headmaster. At first, the Haigs moved to the Community of Jesus. Then, we learned to our horror that they were getting divorced and that Father Haig had left the Community. Mrs. Haig stayed on the Cape and eventually married one of the Community's members. She's still living there, nearly forty years later.

The Haigs' departure shocked me. I thought about all the times when Mrs. Haig had made me feel so worthless and sinful, and how intimidating she was. If I so much as smelled her perfume down a hallway, I did everything in my power to avoid her. Her judgements about my body had cut especially deep. I'd spent years trying to win her acceptance, and by the time she left Grenville, my struggle with my size was only getting worse. The notion that her departure would give me a diet-free pass only lasted for a moment. Her message that I was a sinful glutton was well and truly imprinted.

Also, the Haigs' divorce confused me. Wasn't Mrs. Haig the model of perfection that we females were supposed to follow? She was always lecturing the girls on how to eat, dress, and act, as well as what God expected of women. She even hosted a talk show called *What Makes You Tick?* that was broadcast on CJOH-TV. We were often required to watch it in the dining room with the entire student body. In the show, guests would open up about their lives and Mrs. Haig would use her wisdom to help them discover what changes they should make, to live more fully and in tune with God. Think of her as a female Dr. Phil. Apart from the fact that she scared me, I was kind of in awe of Mrs. Haig, with all her apparent power and success. So, what went wrong?

Maybe it's Father Haig's fault, I wondered. *He's the one who left the Community altogether. How could he turn his back on his calling?* We were taught to shun anyone who did that. Breaking lifetime vows of obedience to the Mothers was unthinkable. Unforgivable. *He's going to Hell*, I thought. As always, the concept terrified me.

In truth, I didn't have much time to dwell on the facts, perplexing as they were. Grenville was as busy and demanding as ever. Even though I didn't understand the Haigs' departure, I figured that life would get easier without them in charge. To me, it was kind of a win.

For that moment, ignorance was bliss.

Chapter 11
Tightrope Walker

I couldn't wait for grade seven. For one thing, I'd get to wear the Grenville tartan kilt, a huge improvement over the loathsome navy tunic I'd outgrown. We'd also have different teachers for each subject and attend classes on the upper floors with all the older students. Best of all, I'd enter a much bigger cohort, with students from around the world.

My first orientation meeting, when all the boarding students gathered in the chapel, was ominous. The deans, principals, and headmasters stood at the front of the auditorium and lectured us sternly for two hours about all of the school's rules, restrictions, and expectations. They also hinted at the attitudes and unwritten rules that could land people in trouble. The collective dread was almost palpable as new students sat there, trying to process their new reality.

It was difficult being caught between two worlds. I wanted so badly for my new classmates to like Grenville and feel at home. More importantly, I wanted them to like me. I craved their acceptance. And yet, I knew that if I was the perfect staff kid, no outside students would like or trust me. I was expected to be a role model, with the best behaviour on campus.

Furthermore, as a staff kid, I was required to report on students—for anything and everything.

Of course, I did no such thing. Instead, I played an impossible role. For my teachers, I made every effort to be a model student. For the students, I did everything possible to appear cool. Especially when the teacher's back was turned.

But how does a thirteen-year-old who's been living in a closed Christian community her whole life go about looking cool? I'm not sure I ever quite managed it.

I spent as much time studying and observing the boarding students as I did my course content. I was intensely curious about their habits, clothing, beliefs, and interests; and it made me notice how different our worlds were. Still, I did my best to bridge the gap.

To gain friends, I'd let students copy my homework and turn a blind eye to peers who were fooling around. In the classroom, I downplayed my abilities. When tests were handed back and the inevitable buzz of "What did you get?" started up, I'd conceal my high marks and casually tell my peers that I did well. A friend once told me that I used to lie about my grades and tell her I got scores below what I actually achieved. She'd regularly sneak looks at my tests to see what I really got. All I remember was being afraid of looking haughty.

Despite my best efforts, I never felt comfortable around the other students. Sometimes, I felt like they were speaking another language. I had no idea what their inside jokes meant. Their innuendos left me bewildered. The last thing I wanted to do was look ignorant, so I never asked for explanations. I was learning that almost everything people said had a double meaning. A crude joke seemed to be hidden in every conceivable conversation.

What on earth are they laughing about now? I asked myself once. *All the teacher said was, "Where is Mark? Let's hope he comes quickly, so we can get started."*

All kinds of words seemed to set my peers off. For the life of me, I couldn't imagine what was so hilarious about words like *hard, head, blow,* or *hole.* Instead, I'd roll my eyes and snicker like I was in on it.

It didn't help that I had zero education about sex. The message at Grenville was clear: sex was dirty, a sin. The less we knew or thought about it, the better. Up until that time, all that I'd pieced together was that it was in our nature to be lustful, and that God wanted us to be pure. If you so much as imagined a sexual act, you were in league with Satan. Of course, I couldn't imagine sex because I didn't know anything about it.

When I got my first period, my mom mumbled something noncommittal about God's blessings. Then she explained, "God gives women a period once a month so that one day they can have babies. It's a gift from the Lord. Here's a box of pads. And here's an elastic belt. You attach it at the front and back. See?"

"OK," I muttered, equally horrified and perplexed.

Of course, I knew better than to ask my mom for more specifics. I didn't want to touch the subject with a ten-foot pole. A mortifying light session with Aunt Joan still haunted me at the time. Back in grade six, a few of us staff girls had been allowed to attend a birthday party—my first sleepover off campus!—at Susan Doner's house. Susan was a day student living in Brockville, in a big house on the river.

During the party, I overheard dirty jokes for the first time. I was lying in my sleeping bag, staring at the ceiling, listening to stories that Susan's friend was telling. I didn't understand the jokes or the context, but I felt rather creeped out by them—and more than guilty for eavesdropping.

A day or two later, I was told to report to Aunt Joan's trailer. I entered her home with a bowling ball of dread lodged in my stomach.

She called me into her bedroom so we could have privacy away from her three girls, who mysteriously seemed to live with her most of the time. She sat me down on her double bed and faced me. "Beth, did you go to a sleepover in Brockville last weekend?"

I nodded, already afraid of what was coming.

"Did something happen there that you need to confess?"

"I'm not sure what you mean," I managed, feeling like a trapped animal.

"Were you girls trading dirty jokes?"

"Not really." I stammered. Then, upon seeing her angry expression, I added, "Well, I didn't participate."

"So, you do know what I'm talking about."

Hoping to appease her, I offered, "Do you mean the jokes Magda was telling?"

Aunt Joan's face was scaring me now. "I think you know what I mean, and it seems to me that you are not willing to be honest about what took place. You would rather remain hidden, letting Satan take hold of your mind."

"Well, I …"

"Beth, if you're hiding some filthy stories, then you are choosing to be in league with the Devil. The only way to cleanse your mind is to be honest about what you overheard."

I was horrified. I couldn't imagine telling her what I'd heard. But I knew I had no choice.

I swallowed, gathering my courage. "Well, there was this one story that was really dirty. It was about a teacher keeping a boy for detention after school." As I continued, reluctantly recounting the details I remembered, my cheeks burned with mortification. There was something about the teacher stripping to her underwear, a ruler, and the teacher's panties being wet. I felt utterly humiliated as I repeated the shameful specifics.

When I finished, Aunt Joan pinned me with her penetrating glare. I silently begged her to let me go.

But she wasn't finished with me yet. "Beth, have you heard of the term masturbation?"

"No," I hedged, though I was sure I'd heard the word before. *In a sermon? Or an assembly?*

"Masturbation happens when someone is full of lustful thoughts, and they allow Satan to tempt them into acting on their desires. They stimulate themselves in their private parts. It might feel good, but it's a grievous, terrible sin. Now, you need to be completely honest with me. Have you ever masturbated, Beth?"

What? It felt like she was asking if I'd ever committed murder. *Do I tell her the truth? Will she even believe me?*

My hesitation seemed to incriminate me, because Aunt Joan dug further. "Do you go to bed with your hands under your covers?"

My confused expression didn't seem to register.

"Well, do you?" she asked again.

"I guess. Sometimes …" I trailed off, not sure of the correct answer.

"From now on, you are to keep your hands on top of your covers. You must defend yourself against Satan's temptation."

"OK," I managed, hoping that this was the end of it.

"And another thing," Aunt Joan went on. "Why weren't you open and honest about this sleepover as soon as you returned? How could you keep this kind of filth to yourself? Were you enjoying the memory of the stories you heard? Saving them up to fantasize in secret?"

My mind froze, as if it had been unplugged. So many disturbing accusations all at once. *How could I defend myself?*

Choosing my words carefully, I said, "I didn't know about masturbation. I still don't quite understand what it is. And I didn't want to even think about the dirty joke. It made me very uncomfortable. I was too embarrassed to tell anyone."

What I said was the truth, but I knew that it might not satisfy her. So I sat there, willing Aunt Joan to let me go.

"Well, I'm very concerned that you weren't honest from the start," she said. "I still wonder what you were trying to hide, and I'm not convinced you're telling me the full truth. You need to guard against your lustful nature, Beth. I'm afraid it's going to get you into deep trouble."

I was frozen, not sure what else to say.

"You need to plead with Jesus to cleanse your mind now that it's been contaminated," Aunt Joan continued. "Every time you even think about the story you heard, I want you to pray this inside your head: 'Lord Jesus Christ, have mercy on me, a sinner!' I want you to repeat that prayer over and over."

I complied by repeating the Jesus Prayer in front of her. She then led me in a longer prayer, asking God to cleanse my mind and help me to withstand the Devil's temptation in the future. And to forgive me for my hiddenness.

Over the next few weeks, I repeated that prayer frequently, trying to rid myself of my impurities. But what I truly wanted to forget was the shameful light session in Aunt Joan's bedroom.

†

In grade eight, I finally got some sex education. I was visiting my new friend Karine—a hilarious, smart, and gregarious girl from New York City—in her dorm room when she set me straight. In a single conversation, I learned all the basics, to my shock, horror, and embarrassment. On one hand, it was a relief to have an idea about the mysterious topic. But I also felt a great deal of guilt because of my curiosity. It was as if I had insider knowledge about a crime and my instinct was to confess it immediately. Carrying that knowledge around was a new weight I hadn't anticipated. I spent years wondering if I should admit that I'd received The Talk from a classmate in grade eight. In the end, I kept it to myself, like an explosive secret.

In middle school, I got another glimpse into the outside world when I received permission for two visits to boarding students' homes. During grade seven, I spent a weekend break at Marion's in Toronto and was amazed at the freedom in her life. We were allowed to leave her house, walk along the streets, get on a city bus, and travel to Square One, without any supervision! After hanging out in the mall, we snuck into an R-rated movie and watched *Flashdance*! I felt almost sick with guilt as I tried to take in all the sexual content. There was even a scene in a strip club! I barely followed the movie because I was terrified that we'd be caught, thrown out, and punished. *What if the leaders at Grenville find out?* I begged Marion not to share our adventure with a single soul. To her credit, she kept it quiet.

I was getting good at keeping some sins private, and I never confessed that offence to anyone. Not even to other staff kids at home. My caution allowed me to get permission to visit Karine in New York City for a week in the summer after grade eight.

That trip to NYC was an eye-opener. My favourite part was people-watching. I was mesmerized by the sheer number of humans packed in together like sardines. At every green light, we'd cross the street with hundreds of pedestrians. Everything was overwhelming: the skyscrapers, the endless yellow cabs all honking their horns simultaneously. Even though it scared me a little, I was exhilarated by the city. Everywhere we walked, I'd see bursts of colour from all the eighties outfits. Rock music would blare from boomboxes as street performers breakdanced inside the crowds encircling them. I wanted to dance to the music too! I could feel my body responding to the rhythm and wanting to break free. But I didn't dare.

One day we drove to a family gathering a few hours away. During the drive, I was huddled between two other teenagers in the back-seat, marvelling at the opportunity to listen to the radio. No one else seemed to notice the marvellous music the DJs kept serving up. Song after illicit song was broadcast to my wondering ears. I soaked it all in, losing myself in the sounds of The Police, Michael Jackson, Bonnie Tyler, Prince, and Phil Collins. For years, I'd heard students attempting to sing snippets of these tunes on campus without getting caught. I was determined to follow suit so that I wouldn't appear completely clueless. I wanted to identify popular songs and sing a few lyrics. But I never dared listen to the radio. The chance to take in all that music during the road trip without fear of reprisal was like no freedom I'd ever experienced. I didn't care if it was evil. I couldn't help but enjoy everything about it.

As the week went on, I became more daring. One day, Karine urged me to try on her jeans. Her suggestion alarmed me. I held the forbidden garment up, wondering if I should risk it. At Grenville, students were put on Discipline for having jeans in their possession, even if they were stored in their luggage in the basement. Wearing jeans signified that you were rebellious and wicked. Students had even been publicly humiliated for merely disliking this rule.

So when Karine offered me her jeans, I was conflicted. *Is Karine in league with the Devil? Should I reject her suggestion as a matter of principle? Or should I try to be a normal person for a moment? What harm will it do if no one finds out?*

Curiosity got the upper hand, and I squeezed myself into her jeans. Karine told me how to lie down on my back on the mattress and pry the zipper up with determined force. Once the jeans were on, and the button was successfully fastened, I stood at Karine's mirror, shocked at my appearance. The jeans hugged my curves and made me feel years older. *I could pass for a twenty-year-old*, I mused, feeling a delicious shiver of delight as if I'd bitten into forbidden fruit.

Karine asked me then if I wanted to wear her jeans for the rest of the day. "Are you sure you don't mind?" I asked, not quite believing my audacity.

"Of course not! It's about time you wore jeans!" Karine asserted.

The rest of the day passed in a blur of heady freedom laced with thoughts of guilt. *I can't believe I'm wearing jeans! I feel so normal! But does this mean I'm an agent of Satan? What if I get seen by someone I know?* Instinctively, I kept checking the faces of people we passed to ensure my safety, preparing to hide or run for it if necessary.

After I returned to Canada and settled back into life at Grenville, my encounters with the wicked world became distant memories. At first, I revelled in reminiscing about my secret forays into life on the outside. But as time went by, guilt took over. I was continually being targeted in light sessions and questioned relentlessly. "Beth, there is something off with you," they would say. "You seem like you're hiding something. What happened in New York that you need to confess?"

Eventually, the resolve to keep my rebellious secret crumbled. *Who am I kidding? I can't hide from God forever. I can't take this guilt anymore!*

I finally confessed almost everything, telling the adults about listening to banned music on the radio (though I left out the part about how much I enjoyed it); watching *Ghostbusters* (which I knew Grenville would deem inappropriate); and wearing jeans, assuring them that it had only been for one day and that I'd never felt comfortable in them. (As if that would help exonerate me.) In exchange for my honesty, I was told I could no longer be trusted to visit students off campus, and that I was too weak to withstand Satan's temptations. "Beth, you had better stop trying to make friends with boarding students. You're as idolatrous as your parents, putting others before God."

As grade nine approached, I felt like I was walking through a minefield. Though I was moved into the girls' dorm, I was reminded not to be too friendly with boarders. Rather, I was expected to be a spy. If girls had negative attitudes, were late, wore non-regulation underwear, or sang rock songs, I was to report on them. The list of infractions was endless.

But how could I share bedrooms, bathrooms, classrooms, tables, work duties, and extracurricular activities with the boarding students if they knew I was ratting them out? I wasn't prepared to do that. So I kept up the impossible façade. To the staff, I'd act like the model staff kid. To the students, I'd be friendly, relatable, and slightly defiant. It often felt like I was walking on a tightrope.

†

At the end of grades seven and eight, I won awards for the highest marks in most of my subjects. At graduation, I'd be called up to the front podium repeatedly to receive wooden plaques with my name engraved on them. Afterwards, carrying my armload of awards was almost embarrassing. Clearly, the teachers approved of my performance.

But with the students? I probably never achieved trusted status. Still, when they heard me singing along with their forbidden songs, their jaws would drop, and their comments were music to my ears: "How do you know that song? I didn't know staff kids could be cool!"

I'd shrug and smile with secret satisfaction.

Chapter 12
Under Threat

At Grenville we competed for every scrap of validation we could get. Living in shame will have that effect, I suppose.

I was desperate for positive attention. From anyone really, but especially my parents. I knew they weren't allowed to show me outward affection. But by God, I was going to make them proud of me, come hell or high water.

Naturally, my older brothers were my most obvious competitors. Even though we didn't live together, I was acutely aware of their successes. By the time I was in high school, I had my work cut out for me. Measuring up to them was a daunting task, to put it mildly.

Dan excelled at everything he did. He was a prefect, the yearbook editor, and the valedictorian of his graduating class in 1985. To top things off, he had played the lead tenor in *The Pirates of Penzance*, *The Gondoliers*, and *H.M.S. Pinafore*. "Our resident Pavarotti," the yearbook had dubbed him. Dan had tons of friends and fit right in with the boarding students. His yearbook caption ended with:

> Dan enjoys company and makes it a point to know every single student at Grenville. He will certainly do us all proud at Royal Military College in Kingston. (*Anno Domini* 1984/85, 33)

Garth was equally successful. He was the salutatorian of his graduating class in 1987, and his grade thirteen yearbook sang his praises:

> Garth's talents have spread over a wide range. This
> prefect excelled in the classroom, basketball, track and
> field, soccer, and cross-country skiing and running. In
> music, he played the violin and baritone and was in the
> choir, band, and orchestra. He was even invited this year
> to play with an Ontario Youth Orchestra at Massey Hall.
> His excellent leadership skills earned him the respect of
> many. Garth plans to attend university after working at
> GCC next year. (*Anno Domini* 1986/87, 32)

My older brothers' triumphs gave me hope for my future. After all, I
was a Gillis, and I suspected I had just as much talent as they did. If I
worked hard, I'd follow in their footsteps and reap similar rewards. I just
had to keep my head down, stay out of trouble, and do an outstanding
job at everything. Easy peasy.

Only, there were a few problems. For one thing, I seemed to be getting
in trouble much more often than Dan and Garth had. Also, I couldn't
seem to control my weight.

In addition, my efforts to be liked by my fellow students backfired
in grade nine. It started in geography class, which was taught by Uncle
Chuck, the headmaster's oldest son. From day one, I sensed that his
class would be an adventure, and not because we'd learn a lot. Rather,
the excitement was in seeing how many kids could get away with fooling
around and playing pranks on the teacher. I sat near the back and let it
all unfold before me.

Amazingly, Uncle Chuck seemed oblivious to the unrest in his classroom. At Grenville, students rarely acted up in class, even in grades
seven and eight, when you'd expect that kind of behaviour. Before grade
nine Geography, the worst I'd ever seen was muffled snickering and
occasional note-passing.

It didn't help that Uncle Chuck's demeanour invited ridicule. Whenever he was in a good mood, he'd get so excited about geographical

content that it was difficult to take him seriously. To preserve my dignity, I stopped answering questions in class. The last thing I wanted my peers to think was that I cared about landforms as much as our teacher did. I didn't misbehave, but I didn't do anything to stop the kids who did. In fact, I rather enjoyed watching their antics. Whenever Uncle Chuck turned his back on us, all kinds of tomfoolery would erupt. Several ringleaders would organize pranks that were harmless enough but completely rattled Uncle Chuck, like setting their watch alarms to go off during class, tying up the wall map's strings, or removing the lightbulb from the overhead projector.

The third time Uncle Chuck reported us to the administration the leaders arrived with targets in mind. They didn't single out the actual troublemakers. No, they went for three staff kids, including me. They soundly blasted us in front of the class, making it clear that if we'd been doing our jobs correctly, none of this misconduct would have happened. We were to be the teachers' allies, their reliable eyes and ears, reporting on every infraction. But clearly, we were rebellious and refusing to do our duty.

With that, the three of us were sentenced to Discipline—until further notice.

I was angry. Mostly at the leaders but also at myself. *Why can't I seem to get this right? Why can't I be more like my brothers? Maybe I should become that goodie-two-shoes that they expect of me.* It was a small comfort that I wasn't in trouble all by myself. And it made me feel cool to be taking one for the team. *Hopefully, the students will accept and trust me more now*, I thought, as I shoveled snow or scrubbed floors for hours on end.

While I worked, I was spoken to regularly by the usual scary staff. Miss James (a.k.a. Aunt Judy) became my most feared interrogator. She was the dean of women; my Phys Ed teacher; and my coach for basketball, cross-country skiing, and track. I already dreaded every interaction with her. However, when I was actually in trouble, she was doubly frightening. It seemed like she personally hated me, and she made me feel like I was a useless piece of pond scum, like I was ruining her life by existing.

During our light sessions, I'd stand with my head bowed, trying to survive the onslaught. Miss James's cross-examinations were so painful that I'd go blank inside my head. Focusing on her cruel accusations and pronouncements became too painful. You can endure being told how worthless, disappointing, rebellious, and evil you are for only so long.

On top of being on D for an entire week, I was kicked out of the girls' dorm and moved into the staff apartments until I could earn my way back. I was also assigned the task of writing a 1,000-word essay on respect.

Once that Discipline was over, I was more careful in class. I'd glare at students who were acting up, pleading with my eyes to get them to think twice. I never reported on them, but I made it clear I wasn't prepared to take the blame again.

After that incident, I felt like I had a target on my back. I kept my head down, focused on getting the highest grades possible and on doing well in extracurricular activities. But no matter what I did, I couldn't escape the constant feeling of being under surveillance. Around that time, I'd hear kids singing, "I always feel like somebody's watching me." It seemed like the perfect theme song for life at Grenville.

I never lost the feeling that my every move could be fodder for a light session. And those were happening more frequently than ever. Students were being chewed out left, right, and centre. Everywhere you went, you'd see a student being singled out by staff members, scolded for this or that infraction. Years later, I learned that the worst sessions were happening behind closed doors.

Occasionally, the whole school would gather for assemblies to clear the air or purge the student body of its evil spirit. These were essentially mass light sessions comprised of at least 300 staff and high school students. The headmasters, principal, and deans would preside at the front of the auditorium or dining room, and call on students one by one to stand up for public humiliation. Sometimes, students were required to walk to the front and face the crowd for their shaming. I'd watch with a mix of fear and morbid curiosity to see which sins each student would be accused of.

"Your problem is that you are in league with Satan!"

"We know what you've been writing to your friend back home. You're nothing but a rebellious, ungrateful liar!"

"The streets of Toronto are lined with whores like you!"

During those meetings, I'd silently beg, *Please, don't call my name!* I was so afraid of being called out that I barely registered what was being said to other students. It was like my brain couldn't take in more cruelty and suffering.

The meetings would last for hours. Sometimes we'd miss a morning of school to attend them, and other times, we'd miss more than a day.

Eventually, I detached from the proceedings and let my mind wander. After scouring my memory for possible infractions that might be exposed (I usually couldn't think of any), I'd start focusing on my upcoming tests, competitions, what was for dinner, what I'd wear next Saturday. As the years passed, I became even more adept at escaping in my mind. Somehow, I survived those meetings, but I don't have many clear memories of what words were hurled at students, or even at me. I've been told that they stood me up on several occasions. But try as I might, most of the details have been blocked out.

If this weren't bad enough, mandatory light sessions were scheduled at least once a week for staff kids. Every Tuesday at lunch about twenty of us gathered around the large rectangular table in a small conference room next to the dining room. The meetings were led by members of the A-team and occasionally, Father Farnsworth would preside. While lunch was supposed to last thirty minutes, our meetings often dragged on well past the scheduled time. If we missed class, so be it. On top of that, we'd attend Bible studies led by Father Farnsworth in his house once a week. Those often morphed into light sessions. You could never be sure.

The A-team was a group of staff members who met with the headmaster regularly to make decisions about every aspect of school life. It was comprised of the principal, the vice principal, the deans of men and women, the financial director, and the head of guidance. This group changed very little over the years, but its members were almost as feared as the headmaster. They held a lot of power and influence, and I felt compelled to stay on their good side.

Not a day went by in high school that I didn't dread the next staff kid meeting. I lived in a constant state of fear, wondering if I'd be next on the hot seat. By grade nine, I was already being treated like one of the most rebellious staff kids. Every meeting was a torment; I'd brace myself for each inevitable onslaught.

The meeting leaders made it clear that we were in training to become lifelong Community members. Not only were we expected to speak up and confess our sins, but they also required us to turn on one another. If we ever tried to remain silent during these meetings, we'd be targeted near the end for being passive, hidden, or in league with Satan.

I did my best to navigate the impossible terrain of each session. You never knew when you'd make a fatal step. All around me, my supposed friends were ready to pounce on me or anyone else.

"Beth, I've noticed you've been eating too much lately."

"Beth, I saw you speaking with a boy yesterday when you were walking down the hall. It seemed like you were flirting."

"Beth, why do you keep befriending students with bad attitudes?"

"Beth, I have a check on your new haircut. Did you pray about that?" (Sidenote: When someone had a check on something, it meant the Holy Spirit was guiding them to point out a sin about it.)

Once any accusations were raised, the meeting leaders joined the offensive. Other staff kids followed suit. One by one, they took aim and fired.

My mind would race, scrambling for an appropriate response. Still, no matter what I said, I'd be in danger of getting further into trouble. I'd try to keep my wits about me when all I wanted to do was dissociate, or better yet, disappear entirely.

I don't know how I survived those meetings. But week after week, year after year, I somehow did. I'd walk away from each one feeling battered, bruised, and completely spent. The energy it took to deflect blame or squash the instinct to defend myself left me shell-shocked.

Over time, I learned the easiest course of action was to agree with anyone who accused me of sin. But the more I cooperated, the more I internalized the projected shame. And I'd wear that shame like a favourite tattered sweatshirt.

You think I'm being haughty again? You're probably right.

You think I'm being flirty? I guess I probably am a stumbling block for the guys.

You think I'm eating too much? That's not news to me. I feel like a sinful glutton all the time.

Still, I couldn't let my guard down. There was a danger too in blithely agreeing to every accusation. I had to be on the defensive for fear of the endless disciplines that we staff kids could face.

The punishments for being in sin or rebellion were endless. On top of being on D, staff kids could face anything from silence disciplines to removal from the dorm to being under constant surveillance. We could be ordered not to speak to certain boarding students and reassigned to new tables, family groups, and classes to be kept away from them. We could also be pulled out of sports, band, choir, orchestra, and other extracurricular activities we actually enjoyed. The one consequence we feared most, though, was being exiled to the Community for rehabilitation. During our light sessions, we were never sure which consequences we'd face.

What I couldn't understand was the fact that my older brothers had avoided most of the scrutiny I was receiving. Especially Dan, who seemed to do everything right and never got into trouble. I knew he had a secret girlfriend. She and Dan had played the romantic leads in *The Pirates of Penzance* in grade eleven. But Dan was never punished for this. He even listened to the Devil's music on the sly. I once came across his stash of cassette tapes, and my jaw dropped to the floor. *How does he get away with owning these?* I wondered. His secret was safe with me, though.

In the spring of 1985, when Dan was about to graduate, he seemed on top of the world. He was popular, successful, and on his way to a bright future. Graduating as the valedictorian, Dan represented everything a good staff kid should aspire to become. He was also following in the footsteps of one of the Haigs' sons and heading to Royal Military College, which made me super proud.

But the following school year, the story about Dan changed dramatically. He was vilified in our staff kid meetings. From out of nowhere, we were told that Dan had defiantly left his calling; and now that he'd joined the wicked outside world, we were to shun him. During his first summer of boot camp in British Columbia, I sent him two care packages of homemade treats before I was told to stop. Instead, I was ordered to pray for his soul. If he came to his senses and returned to live at Grenville, we could let him back in our lives. Otherwise, we were to have nothing to do with him.

Other former staff kids who left were also defamed. We were told they were going straight to Hell. All we could do was pray for their salvation—and avoid ending up like them. I got the message loud and clear: Don't even *think* about leaving Grenville. Just behave, act like you're on board with everything, and stay under the radar!

Alas, staying under the radar was impossible.

As staff kids, we were forced to live in at the Community every March Break and one week every summer. I dreaded those visits. They never seemed to get easier. If anything, the older I got, the more threatened I felt when I spent time there.

Then in grade nine, I was informed that I'd be attending my first mother–daughter retreat at the Community. This, I was told, was a privilege. I feared everything about it, imagining three days of mass light sessions, led by the scariest people I knew.

I was not wrong.

The only good thing about the retreat was the food. The Community's sisters worked like an army of servants, preparing everything to perfection and serving us like highly trained wait staff. Meals were held in the Undercroft, a large meeting space in the chapel basement. To make things festive and welcoming, they had decorated with fancy table linens, hand-painted name tags, and fresh flower bouquets.

As good as the food was, I barely tasted any of it. The public humiliation lasted for hours and hours, day after day. During meals, when I thought we'd have a break, one of the Mothers would often speak into her microphone. And just like that, the food went from tasting delicious to inedible.

One by one, moms were ordered to stand up with their daughters, and Mother Cay or Judy would take turns interrogating them. Many of the women there were strangers to me, and the revelations kept coming. A daughter would learn some of her mother's worst secrets, and vice versa. It seemed like nothing was too personal. One mother sobbed as she revealed she'd once had an illegal abortion. Teenagers were coerced into publicly confessing their rebellious thoughts and actions, while moms were pressured to acknowledge their parental failings.

If participants didn't volunteer to stand up, the Mothers would call them out. I started to calculate the odds of making it through an entire retreat without being targeted. *Would we be one of the lucky ones?* The dread of awaiting our fate nearly did me in.

Early Saturday afternoon, I heard my name called along with my mother's. My stomach dropped to my knees. As I stood up, my whole body shook. I don't remember what they asked us. I was so terrified that my voice trembled whenever I attempted an answer. I felt like I was standing naked and exposed in front of 200 people.

They interrogated my mother and me for at least twenty minutes. Every question felt like an accusation. I cannot remember what was said, but I do remember wanting nothing more than to escape.

After what seemed like an eternity, the Mothers appeared deeply unsatisfied with my mother and me, as if they were detectives who weren't getting anywhere with their investigation. They made it clear that we were blocking the Holy Spirit and that they weren't finished with us. Then, as we both stood there, they turned off their mics and huddled with some of the other VIPs at the head table, whispering amongst themselves with serious expressions.

At last, they turned back to us. Mother Judy leaned into her mic. "Pat and Beth, it is clear to us that you are both steeped in sin. All you care about is being right. You are determined to say the correct things, but we sense it is all a sham. Your words ring hollow and seem phony to us. You are both refusing to allow the Holy Spirit to control your lives. I'm afraid your souls are in jeopardy. We need to take strong measures.

"Pat, one of your problems is that you care far too much about looking good. We want you to return to Grenville and gain twenty pounds immediately."

Wait, what? Hadn't I been under pressure to lose weight since I was five?

While I was still wrapping my head around my mom's discipline, Mother Judy addressed me. "Beth, we are very concerned about you. It's clear to us that you need to change from the inside out, and we don't think you can do that at Grenville. Not with your idolatrous parents nearby. Not with boarding students who are tempting you towards the Devil. We've decided that you need to live here at the Community. You will not be returning to Canada until you have changed."

Her words hit me like a sledgehammer.

Everything in the room went blurry. I gripped the top of the nearest chair with shaking hands, trying not to fall over. *I'm going to be held prisoner at the Community? Why?*

My mom looked stricken, but she didn't object to Mother Judy's pronouncement. She silently took it all in stride, as she had always done. As I was expected to do.

In a daze, I sat in my chair, tears streaming down my face. *How will I survive this? And what about school?*

The light session continued all Saturday afternoon and evening. But my mind had shut down, unable to attend to anyone else's business. No one offered me sympathy or concern while we ate or went to the dorms to prepare for bed. My mom just looked sad and stoic. That night, I cried myself to sleep, hoping I'd wake up and discover it had all been a bad dream.

After church on Sunday, when we reconvened in the retreat banquet room to resume the light session, I heard over the microphone, "Beth Gillis, please stand up."

I can't take any more of this. Standing up on quivering legs, I awaited more bad news from Mother Judy.

"Beth, we have been praying about your situation. Since you're only fourteen, God has decided that for now you will return to Canada.

"However, we are still very concerned about you. It seems that all you care about is achieving. You need to learn to become humble and give up your desire to be special. So, we are going to give you a new discipline. From now on, you will not be allowed to see your grades. Your teachers will not write your marks on your tests and assignments. You will not see your report cards, and your name will not be published on the honour roll, even if you've earned it."

My ears were ringing. Or maybe they were just being bombarded with my heartbeat. I could barely make out what Mother Judy said next.

"Beth, this is a gift to you. If you embrace it, you will feel closer to God. In time, you will be grateful."

I was filled with such intense relief that I could barely comprehend the magnitude of my new discipline. *I don't have to stay at the Community? I can return to Canada? I still get to be a student at Grenville?* Suddenly, my life at the school looked like it was glittering with stars and rainbows.

As we made the long trip home to Canada, the relief wore off. I kept worrying that the Mothers would change their minds again, and I couldn't shake the feeling that I was doomed. Even the fact that I was returning home didn't comfort me much. My mother and I had also been told to travel home in separate vans; and even though I was surrounded by staff girls (most of whom hadn't been singled out at the retreat), none of them could understand my fear. And none of them offered me the slightest ounce of compassion. I was on my own, again.

I never saw my marks again in high school. From grades nine through thirteen, I wasn't allowed to feel the pride of a project, test, or paper well done. My report cards were kept hidden from me and were never acknowledged. My name was never again engraved in gold paint on the carved wooden honour roll boards displayed near the chapel. I was no longer allowed to take pride in my academic achievements.

After that incident, my goals completely changed. I no longer counted on becoming a star student at Grenville. How would they let me become the valedictorian, or salutatorian, or a prefect, or even a leading actor on stage? So my new ambitions centred around survival. I tried to fly below the radar. I withdrew from life. And above all, I did everything possible to avoid being banished to the Community.

Chapter 13
To Eat, or Not to Eat?

With every passing year, I got even better at dissociation. My favourite escape involved fixating on eradicating my most shameful sin: gluttony.

Ever since Mrs. Haig had condemned me to a diet in kindergarten, I knew I'd never be safe until I conquered my appetite. By the time I was fourteen, I'd become frantic about fixing my weight. It was, after all, the only sin I could identify with any degree of accuracy.

Infuriatingly, the more I restricted myself, the more my cravings grew. Food was both my enemy and my greatest source of comfort. I never felt satisfied. If something tasted the least bit delicious, I wanted more.

I was also terrified of gaining weight. As the number on the scale grew, my fear intensified. My pledge to never weigh more than one hundred pounds became impossible to keep as puberty took hold. Not only did I gain weight, but I also watched helplessly as my body bloomed into the shape of a young woman.

My curves horrified me. Very few clothes fit. My growing boobs got in the way of everything. First, they looked terrible in my elementary school uniform, which was not designed for developing female bodies. My chest made the pleats of the tunic bulge out from the square neckline. Then, in grade seven, I found that the uniform kilt highlighted my rounding hips. When I played sports, my body mortified me. I was a fast runner, but I dreaded sprinting past the stands at the track and running down the basketball court. With cringing embarrassment, I pictured my boobs bouncing. I felt fat and sinful, my body a testament to my inherent wickedness.

Being embarrassed about my weight was bad enough. (For the record, I never weighed much higher than average.) But at Grenville, girls were taught to be ashamed of their bodies in general. The dire need for modesty was preached constantly. We were given the clear message that Satan used our womanly form to lure men into sin. It was our responsibility to ensure that no male was ever tempted by our demon flesh.

As a staff kid, I heard these messages so frequently that I was numb to them. It didn't faze me when girls were reprimanded for their wanton ways. I didn't even bat an eyelash when girls were called sluts or jezebels in front of the student body. I accepted that was what females were, and we had to guard against our nature, just like I had to guard against my appetite.

Everything the girls wore was subjected to strict scrutiny. We were inspected every time we passed eagle-eyed staff. Secret dorm searches were conducted while we attended classes, to make sure no contraband clothing was smuggled onto campus.

Here's an excerpt from a letter sent by the deans of women to parents in the summer of 1987 to reportedly clear up confusion regarding girls' clothing regulations:

> In general terms, the important thing to avoid is any clothing which is too tight or too short (above the knee), as well as skirts and dresses with slits where the opening extends above the knee, and form-fitting knitted suits, dresses or sweaters. Conversely, we do not approve oversized garments, shirts, tops, etc., or shirts worn outside skirts.
>
> Necklines on all garments cannot be too lowcut or too loose, which allows cleavage to be exposed when bending from the waist. Nor are lowcut back necklines allowed.

Dressier clothing for Sundays and special occasions must not be shorter than knee-length or longer than mid-calf, have no slits or open pleats above the knee, and be neither too tight nor too loose, with no lowcut necklines front or back.

Students are allowed to wear pants and Bermuda-length shorts for special events such as hikes, picnics, etc. No denim or corduroy jeans are permitted at any time, but dress corduroy and other dress pants in a neat, not-too-tight fit are acceptable. Sweaters may be worn over blouses, but T-shirts worn alone or layered with each other or with big sweaters are not permitted.

A full slip or camisole and half-slip must be worn with dresses and skirts, briefs must be regular waist style, with no hip-hugger or bikini types. Bras must be supportive; the thin tricot types are not acceptable since they are inadequate during sports. Nightwear may be knee, or full-length gowns or pyjamas. T-shirts or track suits are not acceptable sleepwear. (Grenville deans of women to parents, 1987)

On at least two occasions, my mom made clothes for me that I wasn't allowed to wear. The first—and only—time I wore the multicoloured sweater she knit for me, I was publicly shamed in the dining room. I was mid-bite when Miss James appeared out of nowhere, grabbed my upper arm and pulled me a few feet away from my table. "What do you think you are wearing?" she shouted loud enough for people at several nearby tables to overhear.

I cringed as I glanced up at her furious expression. "My mom made this for me for Christmas."

"Your mom made this?"

I nodded, feeling a familiar shame wash over me.

"Do you realize that your skin is showing?"

I looked down at my shoulder and saw the sliver of offensive skin. From my neck to my wrist were buttons that fastened the front to the back of the sweater. As a result, you could see glimpses of my skin near my bra straps and down my arms. "That's the style," I managed weakly, my body trembling.

"Well, you know very well that it's not even close to appropriate! What were you thinking wearing this in front of everyone? I can almost see your bra straps!"

Don't mention my bra! I begged silently, painfully aware that boys could hear her.

Knowing I wouldn't win this battle, I endured the rest of her tirade. I don't remember what else she said, but I felt terribly embarrassed and intensely disappointed. I didn't have many clothes, and I dearly wanted to wear this sweater.

The same thing happened a few years later. My mom sewed me a beautiful blouse that had delicate pintucks and inlaid lace across the bodice. To my horror, Aunt Susan took one look at it from across the dining room and came marching over. I won't repeat what happened next because it was almost identical to the first incident. This time, the offending article was deemed too see-through. Even though it was made of cotton, and I wore a full-coverage slip underneath. I wore that beautiful blouse for thirty minutes before it was confiscated.

Having noticeable curves was about as shameful as being fat. I fantasized about losing weight, to eradicate my curvaceous body. But the more I tried to control my eating, the more intrusive thoughts I had about food. I always wanted more than I was given, and I was constantly scheming for ways to get second helpings without anyone noticing. When I was in class, I'd daydream about upcoming meals.

If I got the chance to bake, for family nights or special occasions, I'd battle with my cravings the entire time, trying not to give in. But inevitably I'd eat more than I thought was OK, then feel the same old shame settle over me like an ominous black cloud.

Don't taste it, Beth! If you take even one bite, you won't be able to stop.

Ok, maybe I'll have a taste.
It's sooooo good! A little more won't hurt. Just one more spoonful.
Ugghh. I want to eat the entire bowl!
I'm such a loser! I'm such a glutton!
Lord Jesus Christ, Son of God, have mercy on me, a sinner!

This scenario played on for years. No amount of exercise or dieting seemed to eliminate my constant need to battle my cravings. My mind was continuously bombarded with ideas for weight loss, or a nonstop desire for food. And behind it all was the constant feeling of shame.

I'm not sure what the catalyst was for launching my most successful diet. In hindsight, I guess it was the fateful mother-daughter retreat at the Community. I was so traumatized by that event that I was desperate to get control over some part of my life. Why not conquer my most besetting sin?

Another question kept bothering me, too: *Why did the Mothers tell my mom to gain twenty pounds when I'm always being told to lose weight? I must look like a hideous, fat slob compared to her. I wonder what it would be like if I finally get thin. Will they approve of me at last?*

Thoughts like these catapulted me into the most rigorous diet of my life. During the summer between grades nine and ten, I became so sick of my constant cravings that I decided the only answer was near-starvation.

I stopped eating anything I considered fattening. Most dairy, carbs, and sugar were off the table. I'd drink lots of coffee and use artificial sweetener. If I ate a hamburger, I'd just eat the patty. If pizza was on the menu, I'd only eat the topping. Many foods I'd skip altogether, like casseroles, lasagna, or grilled cheese. I often opted for a salad with no dressing. For breakfast, I'd eat oatmeal without brown sugar, and it tasted disgusting. If I got extremely hungry, I'd allow myself a piece of white bread without butter.

My main goal was to eat only enough to survive. I let nothing past my lips that tempted me to binge. Hunger pains became my constant companion. But before long, the hunger felt like a badge of honour. I revelled in it, taking pride in my iron willpower. *Look at me, conquering these cravings! I've finally got this!*

Day after day, week after week, I grew more militant. I was constantly on the lookout, watching for danger. *I can control my food!* became my mantra, and I played all kinds of head games with myself.

Don't even try that!

If you taste it, you'll never stop eating.

Pretend it's poisoned.

The hardest part was working in the school's industrial kitchen. Girls were assigned the job of food put-away several times a week. This involved saving at least forty-five tables' worth of leftover food in huge buckets or trays. So I'd handle trays of pizza, stacks of pancakes, pans of coffee cake, and even extra desserts. My mouth would water as I steeled myself against the overwhelming temptation. We weren't allowed to eat on the job, but intrusive thoughts would bombard me mercilessly. *Just eat already! You're starving! You can binge in the walk-in cooler! No one will see.*

Somehow, with herculean effort, I'd withstand the overwhelming impulse to binge. And every time I conquered the desire to eat, I'd grow more confident.

The best part was, I could tell I was losing weight. Nothing was as motivating as feeling my clothes getting looser. I felt a thrill every time I could buckle my kilt tighter. When I could tuck my oxford shirt into my kilt and still have room left inside the waistband, I felt an exhilaration like I'd won the lottery. *So, this is what I've been missing!*

In addition to sports practises, I'd wake up at 5:45 a.m. every day to do Jane Fonda workouts. I'd sneak out of the dorm, run to the staff apartment video library, sign out the only VCR that was wired to all seven apartments, and press play. Then I'd sprint down the hall, sneak upstairs to my parents' living room, and start punishing my body. Jane would keep yelling, "Feel the burn!" and I'd revel in that exquisite pain. My arms, legs, butt, and stomach were on fire during those workouts. But I loved the feeling.

I was losing weight rapidly. This fact fuelled my desire to continue. I'd sit at the table at mealtime, sipping my coffee and pretending to eat the food on my plate. Urging those around me to eat became a powerful distraction.

"Are you sure you don't want seconds?"

"You can have my share of dessert if you want. Come on, you know you want it!"

After about a month, I started getting noticed. "Beth, you're getting thin! You look great! How are you doing it?"

That was all the fuel I needed to power my addiction. Finally, I was achieving the goals I'd been trying to meet since kindergarten! *Now, all I must do is keep this going! And never, ever slip up!*

Weight loss and restriction became my top preoccupations. I still participated in academics, sports, choir, orchestra, my assigned chores, and my weekend job as a house cleaner. I attended light sessions of all sizes. But no matter what was happening, my focus was on food and my weight. Even when I was publicly shamed, I tuned most of it out by focusing on how I looked. If I thought about looking thinner, I felt I could withstand anything. My new superpower was like a shield, protecting me from the shame that had hounded me for years.

After two months of extreme restriction, I started running into problems. First, I was struggling to find the energy I needed. Basketball was becoming difficult. I'd gasp for air and feel shaky. My ability to think straight was waning. This was made worse when dealing with my coach, Miss James. If I made mistakes on the court, she'd bench me and blast me later.

"Beth, there is something very off with you! Anyone can tell that you're out of the spirit on the court!"

"You seem very self-centred today, Beth! You need to stop your nerdling!" (*Nerdling* was Grenville sin-speak for being self-absorbed.)

I never knew how to respond. So, I endured her tirades and focused on weight loss.

When cross-country skiing season began in November, things got worse. Before the snow arrived, we did day after day of gruelling, boot camp-style land training that included running up and down the concrete stairs in the school's main building. We'd pound up those stairs as fast as possible, often bounding over two or three at a time. My legs would shake, my lungs would burn, and my head would pound. Three months into my starvation diet, I was getting increasingly faint. Once we got on the skis, I'd often feel like I was going to fall over, even when I was at a standstill.

I don't know how I got through the training on so little fuel. Somehow, I did it, and I managed to qualify for OFSAA, where the best skiers in Ontario gathered to compete. But I rarely enjoyed skiing. Miss James and Mr. Ortolani, our head coaches, both scared me. Probably because they specialized in terrorizing the athletes. Mr. O would hide in the woods and scream at us from behind trees as we passed him. "Faster! Push yourself, Beth! What's wrong with you?" We also had regular light sessions on the bus, in the ski shed, or after races.

I have no idea what they yelled at me during those light sessions. I only remember thinking about my weight.

Only the fastest skiers on our team got to wear competition uniforms, zip-up unitards with striking navy, red and white stripes. This was the year I finally qualified. But instead of feeling confident, I obsessed about how I looked. *I've never worn anything so revealing. I must look fat! What if people can see my curves?*

The truth was, the uniform was loose on me that season. I appeared to be a lean, mean skiing machine. But I felt fat. And I was weak and freezing most of the time. I became obsessed with my food intake, especially during competitions and strenuous practises in the Gatineau hills. *Beth, don't you dare eat the lunches they packed. Just eat half a sandwich. And maybe an apple. But only if you're starving.*

Paranoid about eating anything for fear that it would spark a binge, I made strict rules for myself and followed them to the letter. I feared that if I ever slipped up, I'd lose control and binge like there was no tomorrow. If I ever ate something that wasn't on my plan, I'd berate myself endlessly. *Why did you eat that raw carrot, Beth? You know you're not supposed to eat between meals! You'll just get hungrier the more you eat!*

The Farnsworths often invited groups of students to their house for Bible studies, occasionally combining these events with pool parties. On one such occasion, pizza was served between the meeting and the pool party. If that meeting actually morphed into a light session, I don't recall. All I was worried about was resisting the food. *Beth, the pizza is off-limits! No matter what people say, just refuse it!*

As I'd feared, people hounded me about not eating. Eventually, I was so worn down by the nagging, that I finally took one tiny slice. I ate it as slowly as possible, savouring every minuscule bite. Afterward I felt furious with myself. *How can you be such a pig? You weren't supposed to eat that! You're going to fast for the next twenty-four hours to make up for that show of gluttony.*

So I did. I was determined not to eat for the next day. I still remember the dizziness, the gnawing hunger pains, the smells of food wafting down the school hallways. It was hellish but empowering. I embraced the cravings as my punishment and made it through my twenty-four-hour penance. *These hunger pains are proof that I'm getting stronger. I'm conquering my sinful desires!*

As I got thinner, my clothing would hang off me. That worked well with the uniform because I could overlap my kilt further and further. I didn't have many casual clothes, but those I did own didn't fit anymore. Still, I kept thinking I was too fat.

Look at your stomach, you pig! Only half of your hipbones are protruding. You're a fat loser unless most of your bones are sticking out!

Despite the constant criticism from my inner voices, I was getting a lot of positive comments from other people.

"Beth, you're looking skinny!"

"You look amazing!"

"How much weight have you lost?"

All the comments fuelled my desire to keep shedding pounds. I was almost ashamed of the positive praise because it confirmed my fears. *If I'm getting so much praise now, that means I must have looked like a hideous fat slob before. I must* never *allow myself to gain weight again!*

In four months, I lost almost 30 percent of my body weight. After that, the scale became my nemesis. I was constantly frustrated because no matter how hard I tried, I couldn't seem to lose more weight. And my food cravings were increasing. I was afraid to eat anything in case I couldn't stop.

After several more months, I could barely function. I was freezing all the time. I was always breathless and dizzy, feeling like I might faint. Also, I'd lost my period for several months. That didn't bother me too much at the time. *One less hassle!* I told myself. Still, I wasn't sure how much longer I could maintain my self-imposed starvation. And my terror of gaining weight only grew.

The worst problem was, my new body was attracting attention for the wrong reasons. If guys thought I looked good, they kept it to themselves. At Grenville, boys knew better than to openly flirt, especially with staff girls. But the staff and other staff kids were noticing, and instead of being rewarded for finally conquering my sin of gluttony, I was accused of a host of new transgressions.

"Beth, we are very worried about you. You seem to have lost a lot of weight. It's obvious you're trying to attract attention from the boys. Are you in a secret relationship with someone?"

I'd defend myself against the constant accusations, assuring everyone that I was just trying not to overeat. That I was eating enough. That of course I wasn't interested in boys! (I was, though.)

"It's clear that you are far too concerned with your looks," the adults would respond. "You are so self-centred and preoccupied with your body! Something is very off with you and needs to change. For starters, you need to eat more!"

Staff kids would chime in, too. What annoyed me most was that only a year prior, they'd publicly humiliate me for eating too much food. Now here I was getting vilified for eating too little. I could never win.

For the second half of that school year, I was under constant scrutiny. During light sessions, I was accused of trying to attract the attention of boys and ensnare them with my lustful flesh.

To my horror, I was put on a force-feeding regime. My new table heads would load up my plate with obscene amounts of food. I'd sit there with dread, looking at the plate piled high with food I considered off-limits. I was afraid to eat any of it, much less the massive quantities they were giving me. And when I refused to eat it, reinforcements would be called in. After most meals, staff members would gang up on me, yelling at me about my sins of vanity and wilfulness.

Meanwhile, my mind would be racing. *Haven't I been in trouble for my gluttony all my life? Why are they trying to sabotage my success? Do they know how* desperately *I want to eat the food they're forcing on me?*

It felt like it was me against the world. Even my parents didn't seem to notice what I was going through. I was hoping they'd finally be proud of me, now that I was skinny. But secretly, I was desperate for them to show concern. My greatest wish was that they would swoop in, take charge, and rush me to get professional help. But they just kept their heads down, working like beasts of burden, oblivious to my problems.

Meanwhile, I kept up my private battle to maintain control over my body. By sheer force of will, I kept this up for several more months. Finally, when I'd lost my period for an entire year, I was taken to Dr. Best, a local doctor who treated the Grenville staff. She didn't seem concerned. And it didn't help that she was so skinny that she made Twiggy look fat. I felt like a whale compared to her. She ordered an ultrasound and ran blood tests which revealed I was dangerously anemic. With some iron pills, she sent me on my way.

But no pills could help me get over my intense fear of eating or gaining weight. And about fourteen months into my most successful diet, my body began fighting back.

It started harmlessly enough. I was eating plain rice cakes. They tasted like Styrofoam, but I couldn't stop. Alarmed, I redoubled my efforts. But the more I restricted myself, the more my body screamed, *Feed me!* I'd eat more and more, no matter how hard I tried to stop. I was terrified of my appetite and did everything in my power not to assuage it.

Still, mother nature overruled my desire to restrict. Time and time again, I'd binge on foods I was desperate to avoid.

And with that, I began to be targeted for my old sin of gluttony once again. Only this time, the voices in my head were the loudest and cruelest critics.

You can't be trusted around food! You're going to gain back all the weight you lost! You're a hopeless failure! You're an embarrassment! You're a fat pig!

I was desperate to regain control. I couldn't bear the fact that I'd tasted success only to feel it slipping from my grasp. But the more I tried, the more I seemed to fail.

My weight started fluctuating wildly. It was a never-ending cycle of restriction and bingeing. With every bite I ate, and with every pound re-gained, I felt myself sinking into an abyss of despair.

Little did I know that the shame was about to get far worse.

Chapter 14
Scarlet Letter

In grade eleven we studied *The Scarlet Letter* by Nathaniel Hawthorne. Set in Puritan New England, the novel explores themes of sin, guilt, and public shaming after Hester Prynne conceives a child out of wedlock. When I read the book as a teenager, I had no idea that I was about to be branded with my own scarlet letter.

It all started back in grade ten when I had developed a crush on a boarding student named Matt. He was tall and athletic, with dark eyes that seemed to seek me out in a crowd. His quiet sense of confidence also drew me in. Whenever our gazes met, I got butterflies. We shared several classes, and I was secretly thrilled whenever I got seated near him. He was smart and enjoyed a good debate. I'd banter with him, never quite flirting but trying to engage him in conversation. And hopefully, get him to notice me a little.

I knew better than to openly flirt. Spies were lurking everywhere. At least eighty-five staff members were living on campus, not to mention all the prefects who were expected to report infractions. If a co-ed couple was seen talking in the hallways or walking down the front drive, the deans would call the culprits in for separate, intense interrogations and order them to never speak to each other. Or worse.

Despite the risk, I really wanted Matt to like me. Yet, I was deeply insecure. It was the year of my Big Diet, and I was consumed with self-doubt. I thought he might never find me thin or pretty enough.

So we forged a hesitant friendship throughout grade ten. We never dared to engage in one-on-one conversation. Instead, we met in groups of friends in the rare opportunities we had to socialize. The closest I ever got to Matt was on a chairlift at Big Tupper Ski Resort in New York. Three of us were on the lift, so Matt and I weren't alone. I was delighted to be sitting so near him, but terrified that we'd be seen by a staff supervisor. Luckily, we got away with it.

As the school year passed, I became more and more aware of Matt. Still, even though I felt tiny sparks fly whenever we were near each other, I often wondered if it was all in my imagination.

That summer, Matt mailed me a letter from his home in the States. But I didn't get to experience the delight of opening it—or receiving it. Instead, I was called into the living room in the Steinbachs' apartment and confronted by six sombre staff members.

"Beth, we are here to uncover what you've been hiding from us," someone began.

Gulp.

"For months now, we've been guessing that you were dieting to attract a boy's attention. We have given you multiple opportunities to confess your sinful motives. But it looks like you have repeatedly lied to us. How long have you been hiding a special relationship?"

I stood there, dumbfounded, before stammering, "I don't know what you're talking about."

Several pairs of eyes glared at me in disapproval. "Beth, sit down."

I did, almost out of necessity. My limbs were shaking.

Mrs. Steinbach held up an envelope. "This arrived, addressed to you. Would you like to explain why a male boarding student is writing you letters?"

At first, I shivered with excitement. *Did Matt write to me?* But the thrill fizzled out as I realized my dire situation. *What can I say that will exonerate me?*

"I don't know why a boy is writing to me," I said carefully. "I don't even know who sent me the letter."

I waited then, hoping to be given more information. After a silent standoff with the adults, I was told the letter was written by Matt.

My initial excitement turned to terror. *What did Matt say? Did he write anything that might hint at affection?* If so, I needed to know.

"Matt is one of the friends in a big group that we've formed in our grade," I struggled to explain. "I'm just as surprised as you that he wrote to me."

I desperately hoped the staff would believe me. But I didn't get that lucky.

"Beth, I don't believe that for a second."

"A teenage boy doesn't write letters to a girl unless she's led him on."

"Were you losing weight to attract this boy? Make him desire your body?"

"Do you fantasize about him?"

Mortified, I dodged and deflected the attacks as best I could. But there's only so long a brain can operate while in a state of terror. After a while, all I could think about was survival.

Somehow, I endured that light session. I did my best to protect myself, admitting nothing about my secret crush on Matt. But I never got to see his letter. I left that meeting feeling more paranoid than ever. The staff put a new fear of God into me that day. If I so much as *thought* about a boy romantically, as far as they were concerned, I'd be heading straight to Hell.

It was also made clear to me that I wouldn't be permitted to write letters back to Matt. And that we'd be watched very closely when he returned for grade eleven. For weeks after the light session, I lived in a heightened state of fear. I was used to the feeling of being watched and accused of all kinds of sin. But I was torn. On one hand, I wanted to follow the rules. On the other, I craved the illicit thrill of being liked, noticed, special.

Despite the risk, I wrote back to Matt. It's hard to respond to a crush's letter that you haven't even read. But I did make it clear that he could *not* mail a reply to me directly. I told him that if he wanted to write back, to address my letter to Joe, a staff kid my age whom I thought was trustworthy. The plan worked like a charm. Joe became my go-between for the rest of that summer. Our letters were not the least bit romantic. Still, I took great delight in knowing there was a boy somewhere who thought I mattered enough to write to me.

†

Summers weren't much fun for teenage staff kids. Apart from one week off, and a mandatory week at the Community, we worked full-time to prepare the school for each new year. The older I got, the more arduous our work became. On top of regular cleaning, we'd paint dorm rooms, hallways, stairwells, and classrooms, often perched high on ladders or scaffolds. We'd help sand, stain, and assemble bunk beds. We'd even spend hours, sometimes late at night, bent over the floors, armed with razor-sharp scrapers, our knees soaked in harsh chemicals designed to strip waxed floors, the fumes irritating our eyes and airways.

We were also expected to attend morning prayers and Holy Communion every day. Our communal meals regularly morphed into light sessions.

That summer, I was briefly staying with my family while the dorms were being cleaned and renovated. At 3:00 a.m. my dad woke me up. "Beth, get up and get dressed as fast as you can! We must report to the chapel immediately."

Disoriented, I tried to follow his orders, though my limbs didn't want to cooperate. *What's going on? Has there been a disaster?*

As soon as I was dressed, I left the apartment with my parents and sleepy seven-year-old Robby. We joined the bleary-eyed throng of a hundred-plus staff members and their kids trudging silently through the long hallways towards the chapel on the other side of campus.

As we entered the dimly lit chapel, we were ushered to specific seating areas. "Staff kids, sit up front. Men, sit on this side, women, on that side." The atmosphere felt ominous. I was used to mass meetings, but not in the middle of the night. My stomach churned as I stole glances at Father Farnsworth and his wife, seated in plush armchairs at the front of the chapel.

Eventually, Father Farnsworth stood up and declared that God had revealed our community was contaminated with an evil spirit. We needed to be purified immediately, or Satan would take over our school. There wasn't a moment to lose.

I was so filled with fear that I still cannot recall much that was said that night. But I felt a cold sense of dread, as I watched people being stood up and verbally attacked, one after another. It felt particularly harsh, given that all the youngest staff kids were there, witnessing the vicious public humiliation of their elders. I was too afraid to turn around and look at adults who were being yelled at. And as usual, I was terrified that my parents would be targeted.

Several hours in, all the elementary school children were told to stand, including Robby. One by one, these kids were shamed in front of the entire chapel. Father Farnsworth went from one child to the next, pointing out their sins loudly so everyone could hear. When he got to my precious little brother, he declared, "Robby, your problem is that your parents didn't raise you right."

Oh boy. Here we go again.

My heart broke for Robby, feeling every bit of his pain. He hung his blond head, and a tear slid down his face. He was so small, bewildered, and alone. Instinct told me to brace for more.

Sure enough, my parents were ordered to stand up. Father Farnsworth kept digging into his steaming pile of shame manure and dumping it onto their heads. I was frozen in fear, wondering when he'd call my name.

My time came soon enough. When I was ordered to stand up along with all the teenage staff kids, I was so terrified that my brain refused to store the memory. To this day, I cannot remember what sins were heaped upon me that night. I only recall the trembling.

The meeting lasted for hours. We didn't leave until the sun was streaming through the windows that lined the upper walls of the chapel. But we didn't get off easy. Father Farnsworth ordered each of us to compose letters of confession and bring them to his house, where he'd meet with us one on one. If he felt we'd been honest in our letters, he'd pray with us for absolution. But, if our letter rang false or hollow, we were promised further consequences.

I left that meeting on shaky legs. Sleepless and starving, I made my way back down the hallways, feeling the weight of the daunting task ahead. This wasn't my first letter of confession, and it certainly wouldn't be my last. My parents had already been required to write notes to the Mothers and the Farnsworths frequently, and I'd witnessed them be publicly shamed for not being honest enough in those letters, time and time again.

With great fear, I began writing. *What sins should I include? If I omit my crush, will I be in even worse trouble?*

I don't recall what I confessed that day; I was either too scared, or too tired, or my brain was too overwhelmed. Regardless, Father Farnsworth wasn't one to speed through a confession. Typically, he asked a lot of probing questions, digging for more details. Nothing was to be held back, and it was his habit to prod and pry until our sin was cleaned from every dark nook and cranny. We had a lengthy exchange, with me searching for the right words, being careful not to incriminate myself too badly.

Somehow, I emerged from that one-on-one relatively unscathed. Father Farnsworth might have been running out of steam since he'd been up all night. Whatever the reason, he wasn't as ruthless as usual. He accepted my offering of sins, and I was released after a lecture and a prayer of absolution.

Still, that 3:00 a.m. light session freaked me out. It also served to usher in an era of heightened vigilance and paranoia at the school.

†

One part of life at Grenville that always caught me off guard was the all-too-regular visits from the Angel of Moves, as we jokingly called them. At least twice a year, staff were ordered to move from one residence to another. It was like a dreadful game of musical chairs, without any winners. The moves were always framed as God's will. Being in control was a sin.

After that fateful 3:00 a.m. meeting, more moves were announced. The teenage staff girls were told that we'd be living all together in a staff apartment. The leaders revealed that they were very worried about us. So we were being ordered to live together in the light. (Red flag much?)

At first, I thought it sounded like fun. But that fun never materialized. We lived across the hall from two staff women—our appointed dorm mothers—who conducted surprise light sessions about our sins almost daily. They also encouraged us to turn on one another with an intensity like never before.

Things got really tricky for me when Matt returned in the fall for grade eleven. I had to keep everything hidden, especially my feelings for him. Not that there was much to hide. Our so-called relationship consisted of lingering looks, brief smiles across crowded spaces, and occasional conversations with friends. We showed up at each other's basketball games, cheering from the sidelines. We were both good cross-country skiers, too, training and competing together. We never dared to flirt on the ski team. Still, I got a thrill when every night, during study hall, our eyes would meet across the dining room.

The idea that Matt might like me was the most precious gift I'd ever received. I was desperate to feel like I mattered to someone. But I kept it all inside. I didn't let Matt know how much he meant to me. And I didn't dare tell a single soul. No one could be trusted, especially the other staff kids. Apart from them, I didn't really have any friends. Sure, the boarding students were friendly, but it was hard to get to know them well, for obvious reasons.

Living on a tightrope was exhausting. I knew one wrong step would be fatal. So I pretended to be the perfect staff kid, a shining example to the students. The other staff girls were constantly on the lookout for my sins, even after we all moved back to the dorm. I was forced to contribute during light sessions and accept the corrections I regularly received. Meanwhile, I was trying frantically to diet, lose weight, and avoid bingeing. Even worse, I was thinking about Matt all the time. I was trying to get close to a forbidden boy who couldn't possibly understand the life I was living.

In December of that year, I bought a bottle of Ralph Lauren cologne for Matt. It took me months to save up and I agonized over what to get for him for Christmas, since I wasn't sure we were an actual couple. But I knew he liked me, so I took the risk. Then, just before the Christmas banquet, I asked him to meet me so I could give him something. He agreed, and shyly said he also had something for me.

I dressed with extra care, donning a new gown my mom and I had made. It had a red velvet bodice and a full skirt made of red, green, and blue plaid taffeta. For once, I felt pretty.

Breathlessly I made my way to our meeting spot. When I saw Matt, I suggested we'd get more privacy if we ducked into the staff link: a glassed walled corridor connecting the dining room to the staff apartments. I don't know what I was thinking then because the staff links were anything but private. We had just enough time to exchange gifts without interruption. Matt appeared to like my cologne. Then he stunned me by pulling out a green velvet box. Inside was a delicate gold ring, with a tiny diamond sparkling inside the shape of a heart. I was speechless. I'd never been so surprised and delighted by a gift. Without thinking, I reached up and hugged Matt.

It was the first time we'd ever touched. For a few seconds, our bodies were pressed against each other. It was exhilarating, to say the least. But the reality of our situation quickly ended our magical moment as we heard a door swing open.

"Merry Christmas!" I declared awkwardly as I pulled away. "I hope you have a good holiday!" *And thank you for this awesome ring,* I mouthed. *I love it!* I beamed at Matt and quickly took the ring to my room, where I hid it under my mattress.

I spent the next few weeks on cloud nine. Nothing bothered me. *Do I have a boyfriend?* Neither Matt nor I had said as much, but I couldn't help leaping to that glorious conclusion.

Around that time, auditions were taking place for the annual G&S production. I was finally old enough to join. That year, we were putting on *The Yeomen of the Guard* and I wanted the female lead. Every instinct told me not to bother trying out. *There's no way they'll award you the main part, Beth! Have you forgotten Father Farnworth's warning?*

But a small, resilient flame flickered inside me. I couldn't drop the notion that I might be worthy of the role. After all, my brother Dan had been the tenor lead for three years in a row. Didn't I have just as much talent? Plus, boarding students who had heard my voice urged me to try out. So I did.

The audition process forced me completely out of my comfort zone. My inner voice was constantly yelling, *You're too fat!* I couldn't shake the terrifying knowledge that, if I did get the lead role, every eye in the audience would be on me. Just the thought of that was almost enough to stop me from trying out. But somehow, I drummed up the courage and let my inner diva emerge for the occasion.

And then I waited. For weeks.

I told myself that if I didn't get the lead, at least I had Matt. His gold ring was safely hidden under my mattress. I often wore it to bed. The secret knowledge that he cared for me gave me the courage to face any outcome.

Shortly after Christmas break, the cast list was posted—and I almost fainted. I'd been cast as Elsie Maynard, the romantic lead of *Yeomen*!

I could hardly believe it. But even so, I kept my joy firmly in check. All too often, I'd seen students train for months only to be kicked out of the productions just weeks or even days before opening night. So I curbed my enthusiasm and kept my happiness—and my fears—to myself.

Truthfully, I was feeling like a mess inside. I hated hiding and tiptoeing through life. I wanted to be free to talk about how wonderful it was to get a ring from a great guy. Or how scared I was that he'd lose interest. Or how afraid I was that I wouldn't be talented enough to pull off the demanding role I'd been given. Or how paranoid I was to play the lead at my size.

†

In early January, I made a big mistake: I confided in my friend Julie when we had a rare moment to ourselves.

Julie was the only other staff girl hiding a relationship, so I felt there was little risk in my revelation. I told her about how much I liked Matt, how I'd wondered for months if he liked me too, and finally his gift. Julie was all ears. "He gave you a ring?" She gasped.

"Yes! Can you believe it? Here, I'll show you." I retrieved it from my mattress. "Look at this!" I said, still not believing it myself.

Julie seemed almost afraid for me. "You'd better keep that hidden. You're not wearing it, are you?"

I assured her that I wasn't. But then I wondered out loud, "Who would notice though? Should I wear it? Like on Sundays?"

Julie gave me a look that seemed to say, *I wouldn't if I were you.*

It felt good to share my precious secret, even though I experienced all kinds of unsettling emotions. Sharing it made the situation seem more real, like I hadn't dreamt it. Still, I couldn't shake the worry that I'd taken a risk, and I couldn't control the outcome.

A few weeks passed and my life felt like a whirlwind. Daily rehearsals for the operetta were underway and I began training for the role of a lifetime. When I received my script, I could hardly contain my excitement. *This is really happening!* I felt like pinching myself repeatedly.

Then one day in mid-January, I heard my name being paged. "Beth Gillis, please report to the Phys Ed office." The woman paging me was Miss James, the person who, next to our headmaster, scared me the most at Grenville.

With mounting dread, I quickly made my way to see her. *Beth, just get this over with, whatever it is.*

Miss James was talking to Mr. Poth, her coworker, when I arrived. I tentatively knocked on the open door. As she turned around and saw it was me, her face clouded over, like I was the last person she wanted to deal with. There were no other chairs, so while she sat and glared at me, I stood there awkwardly, wondering what I'd done this time.

"Beth, what have you been hiding?"

"Um … I don't know."

"Don't lie to us. You know very well there is something you've been keeping secret. Something that could get you into a great deal of trouble."

My heart started hammering. I pressed my sweaty palms down my kilt as I frantically searched for words that would save me. But nothing came.

With an exasperated sigh, Miss James leaned sideways and pulled her desk drawer open. I watched in horror as she reached inside and pulled out my velvet ring box.

Intense fear gripped me. *My life is over.*

"Would you care to explain this to me?" she asked, her voice drenched with accusation.

As usual, I trod carefully. "That is a gift I received from a friend."

"Really? And who might this friend be?"

Beth, there's no way out of this. Tell the truth. You've done nothing wrong. Well, nothing too terrible. It's not like you've kissed him or anything.

"Matt gave me that ring just before the Christmas break," I admitted. "I was afraid to wear it because I know we aren't allowed to date, or even have an exclusive relationship. So, I kept it hidden."

"Keeping things hidden seems to be your specialty," Miss James countered.

"Well, I …"

"What exactly are you trying to hide from everyone?"

"The ring—"

"Why on earth did Matt give a ring to you? What have you two been up to?"

I cringed at the accusation in her voice. "We haven't done anything!"

"That's a lie!" she yelled.

I quickly looked away. *She's never going to believe me*, I thought hopelessly. Still, I tried to plead my case. "I've had a crush on Matt since last year. I wasn't sure if he liked me back until he gave me this ring."

"You expect me to believe that he gave you a gold ring with a heart on it out of the blue?"

"When he gave it to me, I was stunned. Honestly." Even to my ears, my words sounded unconvincing.

"Beth, there is nothing honest about you. We can't believe a word that comes out of your mouth. Satan has you wrapped around his finger.

Clearly, you've been sneaking around behind our backs, leading Matt into grievous sin. You've pulled him into your web of lies, just like a black widow. I am so ashamed of you, Beth. And I'm sure you're hiding a whole lot more."

"I'm not hiding more. We didn't do anything together."

"Stop lying! You above anyone should know the rules! Furthermore, you know very well that it's your responsibility to keep the boys around here safe from temptation! But clearly you don't care about anyone but yourself! Now tell us once and for all, what else have you done with Matt that you need to confess?"

An awkward silence filled the room. *Beth, just stick to the truth*, I reminded myself, then said, "In the summer we wrote letters to each other, even though it was forbidden. I had him address the letters to Joe."

"Joe knew all about you two? So, he's in league with you as well. Interesting."

My heart sank. I'd just betrayed a friend. "He only knew about the letters," I offered, knowing it wouldn't make any difference.

"Did you ever get physical with Matt?" Miss James asked then. "Did you ever let him touch you?"

"Well ... we hugged once. In the staff link. Right after he gave me the ring."

"You expect me to believe that's all you did? I wasn't born yesterday." Her voice was dripping with scorn. "Did you two ever sneak away to be alone together? Did you ever kiss? Did he ever touch your body?"

On and on she peppered me with increasingly alarming and personal questions.

"Did you let him see your breasts?

"Did he put his hands into your underwear?

"Did you touch him below his belt?

"Do you masturbate thinking about him?"

I was so shocked that I couldn't think straight. "No!" I cried, again and again. But my protests seemed to fall on deaf ears. *What must she think of me? Obviously, she assumes I'm a slut. And what about Matt? He's being painted as a pervert, or worse.*

I was so mortified and disgusted by Miss James's interrogation that I forgot Mr. Poth was still in the office, listening to every word. That is, until Miss James turned to him and asked him to explain how I'd ruined Matt's life.

In embarrassing detail, Mr. Poth described how destructive girls can be for teenage boys. How they can so easily be led away from God, and how they can't focus on their obligations. How lusting after a girl can ruin a guy's life if he follows his base desires. Clearly, Mr. Poth didn't believe my version of things.

Then Miss James added, "You know, Beth, we had high hopes for Matt. He seemed to be taking responsibility and was on track to become a prefect. Now, we find out that he's been led astray by your cunning and deceit. You encouraged him to lie and sneak around. You made him break the school's most important rules. You turned him away from God, and there is no sin worse than that."

With every word they said, I sank lower into my cesspool of shame. At the start of the interrogation, I'd viewed our relationship as it was: fledgling and innocent. But by the end, I felt more like a wanton harlot, snaring innocent boys for my wicked pleasure. *How could I have led Matt so far astray?* I was a staff kid who knew better. Instead of doing what was expected of me, I was a terrible influence and deserved nothing but contempt and disdain.

Panic took over as I considered my hopeless future. *I'm going to be punished severely. I'll be put on Discipline. And what about my role in the musical?* My mind raced through worst-case scenarios.

"Beth," said Miss James, "you are going on Discipline until further notice. We cannot allow you to infect the spirit of the school with your sin and your lies. While you are working, I want you to consider how much you have to be ashamed about. You must cry out to God for forgiveness. We will be checking in on you as you work over the next few days. I expect you to have more confessions to make. I have no doubt you're hiding much more than you've admitted. You have a lot of repenting and changing to do.

"Now, go with Miss Mayberry to get changed out of your uniform. We will let you know where you'll be sleeping later tonight."

Dazed, I turned around to see Miss Mayberry waiting outside the office. She looked severe as she instructed me to walk in front of her down the hallway. From behind, she could monitor if I attempted to make eye contact with anyone.

We made our way to my room, where I took off my uniform. As I hung it up, I wondered how long it might be before I could wear it again. A week? Maybe even two? I'd never been on Discipline for longer than a week. But this time things felt deadly serious. I had the feeling that I'd be lucky to be back in school anytime soon.

Once I was escorted to the kitchen, my life dissolved into endless drudgery. I was assigned every demeaning job the staff could invent. Days turned into a blur of scrubbing industrial coolers, freezers, ovens, kettles, deep fryers, and grills. After every meal, I'd be assigned to the pot sink, where I'd scrub unending pots and pans, caked with every kind of nauseating mess. Every evening, the floors had to be swept, scrubbed, and mopped. I wouldn't stop working until around 9:30 p.m., and be up the next morning at 6:00 a.m. to help with breakfast prep.

I was drowning in an ocean of shame. Students and staff weren't allowed to talk to me. Almost no one dared to make eye contact. Around mealtimes, I'd be surrounded by students bustling in and out of the kitchen, carrying on with their busy lives. I'd be escorted to the bathroom, to my bed, to my meals. I'd eat with prefects who never spoke to me. It made me feel more despised than a prisoner.

Yet I was constantly on the lookout for Matt. *What is he going through? Is he OK?* Amazingly, he wasn't put on D. Every few days, I'd spot him in the dining room or entering the kitchen for his assigned duties. Even when he was on dish crew, which lasted at least forty-five minutes, he never made eye contact with me. It was like I was invisible. Or too shameful to even look at.

The longer I worked, the more paranoid I became. *Will I ever be forgiven? Will Matt still like me? Will I get to go back to classes soon? What about my exams?*

More than anything, I was plagued with the fear that I'd lost my role in the play. I attempted to bravely hope for the best while preparing for the worst-case scenario. *Maybe I'll get to keep the part. I'll do my time, learn my lesson, and maybe everything will go back to normal. Or maybe I'll never be forgiven, and I'll lose everything that matters. Matt, my role on stage, my last shreds of dignity.*

It didn't help that I was subjected to light sessions at any time without notice. Father Farnsworth, Miss James, or Mrs. Childs would confront me in the kitchen, right in front of anyone, urging me to confess more sins. "We know there is more going on, Beth. You need to be pleading with Jesus to reveal the deeper sins that are binding you to Satan. You're not being completely honest yet. You will never change unless you allow God to break you open and cleanse every part of you."

The more they said this, the longer my discipline lasted. One week turned into two weeks. I'd never been punished for that long before. I missed all my classes and wasn't given time to work on schoolwork in the evenings. I missed all the rehearsals. I was moved into a staff apartment to live under surveillance. My despair grew like a malignancy.

I was urged for confessions so often that I never had a moment's peace. My mind constantly searched for sins that I might reveal during my next light session. At every encounter, I'd pour out my latest revelation, hoping it would appease my interrogators. But they never seemed satisfied. "Beth, keep praying. We know there is something missing."

†

As the weeks passed, more and more students joined me on D. Eventually, there were at least two dozen of us. I didn't dare talk to the other students. But somehow, I pieced together what was going on.

The deans were conducting a massive crackdown on supposed relationships. We all knew boys and girls weren't allowed to date. But the deans were searching out couples who secretly liked each other, just like Matt and I had dared to do.

Soon, they were running out of jobs for us. Students were scrubbing baseboards, washing every leaf on the dining-room plants, dusting the rungs of 500 chairs, or cleaning rust off the dish carts. The kitchen staff got cruelly creative with my assignments. One day, I was taken to get changed into track pants to work outside and clean out the school dumpsters. I had to use a ladder to scale up and over the dumpster wall, then crawl into the stinking bags of garbage, and throw them out onto the snow until I could access the dumpster's internal walls. Then I was forced to scrub those walls with a strong chemical to remove the worst grease, grime, and caked-on filth.

The memory of that task still makes me shudder. It was such a vile job that I was laughing through hysterical tears while doing it. At one point, I moved a bag of rotten garbage and screamed when I found a dead crow lying underneath it. Refusing to touch the dead bird, I went inside the kitchen to ask Mr. Barnes for help. After he removed it, I was told to resume scrubbing that horrifying dumpster until it was clean before starting the next one. And so I did.

Two weeks of Discipline turned into three. With every passing day, my hopes faded. I began thinking I'd never be forgiven. I felt like the worst sinner in the school and was riddled with guilt. Because I knew there was more to confess. I was hiding something I didn't want anyone to know. And the more I was pressured for honesty by my interrogators, the more afraid I became of the consequences should I share it. *What if God has told them my deepest sin? I might be on D forever until I confess it all.*

It took me days to work up the courage. By then, it was clear I didn't have anything left to lose. It hadn't been confirmed, but I was pretty sure I'd lost my role in the musical, Matt, and even my schooling.

So finally, through bitter tears and excruciating embarrassment, I confessed my greatest shame to Mrs. Childs. "I'm a thief!" I sobbed.

I went on to explain how last year, when I'd been plagued with intense cravings after months of dieting, I'd stolen a chocolate bar at Woolco. And even though I'd been filled with deep shame and regret, it hadn't stopped there. Another time, I stole a sports bra from Dave Jones. I'd needed one for years but had been too ashamed to ask my parents. After I'd tried on the bra, I'd impulsively put my shirt back on over it, and left the store. I'd also stolen a Harlequin romance from the lady who had hired me to clean her house. Mrs. Passmore had shelves of them, and I was so curious about sex that I couldn't resist taking one.

There's often a sense of relief that comes with exposing shameful secrets. But I didn't get to experience that comfort. Instead, my confession landed like an exploding bombshell. Mrs. Childs was shocked at the depths of my depravity. And she didn't mince words telling me as much.

I was immediately escorted to Father Farnsworth, who expressed his disgust in the strongest of terms. To make his point agonizingly clear, he took me to the boiler building and led me down the concrete staircase to the bowels of its basement. The room was huge, with blackened cinderblock walls at least twenty feet high. A massive boiler that burned woodchips to heat the entire campus dominated the space. Father Farnsworth ordered me to step much closer to the boiler than I thought was safe, then peer into the side door as he opened it. The heat emanating from the boiler was extreme; I felt the sting of it on my face. Dread and terror engulfed me as I stared at the raging inferno, its flames leaping and swirling, devouring everything within. All the while, Father Farnsworth warned, "Beth, this is nothing compared to the agony and suffering that awaits you, if you don't change."

Eventually, he prayed with me and asked God to save me from eternal damnation. Despite the prayer, I was beginning to think there was no hope for my soul. That experience compounded my fear of Hellfire and the sense that it could very well be my destiny.

†

Everything got worse over the next few days. It was confirmed that I'd lost my role in *The Yeomen of the Guard*. Furthermore, I wouldn't be allowed on stage in any capacity. I'd let Satan into our school and was a terrible influence on the students. I was also told that if I were a boarding student, I'd surely have been expelled.

From there, I was ordered to visit the managers at Woolco and Dave Jones as well as Mrs. Passmore. To my immense shame, my father was ordered to accompany me. The person I wanted to impress more than anyone in the world had to witness my disgrace. I sat in the offices of those store managers, my head hung low, tears streaming as I confessed my offences, feeling like the lowest worm that ever slithered. Both managers were very kind and accepted my apology and offer of restitution. Mrs. Passmore was just as gracious, smiling as she reminded me that everyone makes mistakes.

Decades later, I live by the belief that honesty is the best policy. But looking back at my sixteen-year-old self, I'm not so sure. The confession of those actions landed me in such hot water that my life was forever impacted.

I was on Discipline for twenty-nine days of abject misery. And I lost everything that mattered to me. I was treated like a criminal and made to believe I deserved nothing better.

When, at last, I was pulled out of the kitchen to attend my last meeting, the leaders said, "Beth, we are very worried for your soul. We cannot risk having you stay here, infecting the spirit of the school with your lust, lies, and deceit. You're being sent to the Community of Jesus. You will live and work down there until you have completely changed. You will not attend school. If you plead with Jesus to change you, remain humble, needy, and repentant, we hope you'll be able to return to Grenville and finish high school someday."

With that, I went dead inside. *My life might as well be over.*

I followed the leaders' orders like a zombie, tears streaming down as I went through the motions of packing. My body felt like it weighed a thousand pounds.

Before I left, I was allowed to say goodbye to my mom. When she hugged me, she cried fervently in my ear, "Beth, I don't want you to go to Hell."

Under the threat of everlasting Hellfire, I was banished from my home and country. Ironically, I was headed to a place that resembled Puritan New England three centuries earlier. It was there that I'd continue down my path of public shaming, just like Hester Prynne.

Chapter 15
Banished

My banishment to the Community did change me. Though not for the better.

Right before my departure, I learned that another staff girl was being shipped away with me. Amy and I had been off-and-on roommates since kindergarten. This didn't mean we were close. The way staff kids were taught to report on each other left little trust between us.

Neither Amy nor I spoke during that ten-hour drive to Cape Cod. I thought it was weird that I had no idea why she was in trouble. *What terrible sins has she committed?* I didn't dare ask. I wasn't about to tell her mine.

I'd made the ominous trip to the Cape many times. But never in a car, driven by two taciturn dads, to be dropped off and abandoned indefinitely. When we got to the US border, we were detained while our fathers tried to explain our reason for entry into the States. The customs officers were suspicious and pulled us all in for questioning.

"You're taking the girls where?" they asked. "For how long? Who exactly will be their guardians? You don't have names? Will they be enrolled in school? No? What are they going to be doing down there?"

Our dads became visibly flustered and had difficulty reassuring the officers that we were going to be fine.

We're not going to be fine at all, I thought numbly.

Once we arrived at the Community, two sisters met Amy and me outside the Bethany house and told us where we'd be living. We were assigned to different houses and went our separate ways.

I was placed in a house called Hebron. Aunt Jane's serious face intimidated me right off the bat. She ushered me into the kitchen and tasked me to help with dinner prep. Then, during dinner, I met two other aunts, three new uncles, three children, and a baby.

Can I trust any of my new wardens? I thought, terrified to be surrounded by so many new people. *Do I have a choice?*

My first light session began after dinner. I had to disclose my entire story, with all its painful, embarrassing details. The grave expressions of each adult acknowledged my worst sins and deeds. "Beth, you have been gifted a golden opportunity to change," I was told. "If you're willing to listen for God's voice to convict you of your sins and honestly confess them, you'll truly learn to live the life of the cross."

Desperate to please my new captors, I resolved to live up to their expectations. How else was I going to earn my way back to Grenville? So all day long, I'd dutifully clean bathrooms, fold laundry, cook, clean dishes, vacuum, and iron while contemplating my wickedness.

Whenever I was tasked with ironing—honestly, it seemed endless—I had to listen to cassette tapes of the Mothers preaching. There were so many in the collection, you could say I was spoiled for choice. Until you saw the titles, which were anything but appealing.

What should I pick today? I've almost memorized "Battle for Your Mind". What about "I Repent of Me" or "Idolatry, Anger and Lust"? Or maybe "The Way Out of Jealousy"?

I'd make my selection and glumly press play, willing myself to learn from their wisdom. On and on their voices would drone, and my despair was so intense that I considered their words very carefully. I sensed that my only hope was to become a willing disciple.

Wait, what? They just said that you know you're cherished by God if He's punishing or chastising you. Hmm. I guess God must really love me.

Somehow, that didn't make me feel much better. But I tried to imagine God up in Heaven, pleased with my efforts at repentance. The Mothers kept on preaching about how we need to thank God whenever He loves us enough to sanctify, redeem and cleanse our sin. Then, I followed them in prayer.

Thank you, God, for taking such strong measures. Help me to be grateful for the purging and the scourging.

I had so much time to think as I worked. Time to ruminate on my sins, my faults, my worries, and mostly my grief. Before long, I was praying continually or preaching the Mothers' words to myself.

Beth, there is something wrong if the Holy Spirit isn't daily convicting you of your sin. Whatever you do, don't let any sin remain hidden.

Dear God, I kept pleading, *Show me my sin! I don't want my mind to be a breeding ground for Satan!*

†

During every meal, I was asked to answer the question, "What sins has God revealed to you today, Beth?" I had to be ready to spill on cue. I hated doing this, but I was determined to do everything I could to please my household. If they wanted honesty, they were going to get it. So, I carefully analyzed every emotion I felt, considering which sin to confess. If I was sad, I'd admit to self-pity. If I was angry, I'd expose my rebellion. If I felt scared, I'd admit my desire to be in control. If I felt isolation and despair, I figured I was jealous.

In my head I kept repeating the phrase I heard on the Mothers' recordings. *Beth, your problem is* you! *The only way out of you is to confess, repent, and plead with God to change your heart.*

Before long, I was searching out my adult supervisors between meals, to confess my feelings or sinful thoughts as soon as I noticed them. One time, I told Aunt Lilian, "I keep thinking about stealing food in the pantry. Especially that granola we made last week."

In response, Aunt Lilian sternly warned me to stand against my gluttony, then reminded me to pray the Jesus Prayer whenever I was tempted. "Lord Jesus Christ, have mercy upon me, a sinner," I'd mutter repeatedly, hoping Jesus could stop me from bingeing. Because I knew I couldn't stop myself.

Another time, I admitted, "I keep thinking about my friends back at Grenville. I'm dying to be back in class. And to be back on stage. I'm so jealous that they're moving on with their lives and I'm here, being a nobody."

"Beth, you need to give up that jealousy," was the reply. "Refuse Satan entry into your mind. It is clearly God's will that you are here, where you can starve your over-inflated ego. I can also tell you are wallowing in self-pity. You must pray and ask God to help you let go of your need to have your way, and to be admired."

And so, I prayed. All. The. Time.

Lord, show me my sin.

Lord, please stop me from craving food.

Lord, help me be honest.

Lord, please forgive me for my pride, jealousy, anger, self-pity, greed, deceit and …

For hours and hours, I'd toil away at household chores in isolation. Crying, praying, confessing, and attempting to change myself.

†

Not long after I arrived at the Community, we were given direction from the Mothers about Lenten disciplines. Instead of a grape fast (thank God!) we were commanded to attend every single chant service. That meant bundling up all the children and trudging across the compound in the biting winter weather up to six times a day. The Community had adopted the practise of singing the Gregorian chant services that originated in the early Roman Catholic church. Lauds (6 a.m.), Terce (9 a.m.), Sext (noon), None (3 p.m.), Vespers (6 p.m.), and Compline (9 p.m.) were mandatory. Only the brothers were required to attend the 3:00 a.m. Matins service.

It's hard to describe those chant services. It felt like we had time-travelled. Dozens and dozens of sisters and brothers would process into the church wearing off-white hooded robes, heads bowed in reverence. Then they'd sit in the nave, eyes cast downward as they chanted. The music sounded otherworldly and gave the church a perpetually sombre atmosphere, which seemed appropriate for Lent, and my mood. In no time, I was singing along in Latin, following the complex melodies written with black square notes on a four-line staff. We'd bow together while singing, and kneel whenever we made a mistake. It was strange, challenging, and off-putting.

After several weeks, I could sing long sections of the services by rote. My mind would often wander and worry. *What if I never get to go home to Canada? How do I prove that I've changed? What if the Mothers force me to become a sister?* The latter was by far my biggest fear. It propelled me to keep following every order and fully cooperate with my program of penance. *If I keep praying, confessing, and working hard, maybe they'll think I'm worthy of going home.*

But no matter how hard I tried to repent and change, some of my demons wouldn't go away.

For one thing, I couldn't stop craving food. I was still frightened of gaining weight. But the only pleasurable thing left in my life was food.

I was continuously on the lookout for opportunities to sneak food when no one was around. I'd creep into the pantry and dip my finger into a jar of honey. It was so sweet and mouthwatering. Then I'd open the jars of homemade granola and take out a few chunks. A few turned into many, then handfuls.

Horrified and full of regret, I'd hurry away, relieved that I hadn't been caught. But a few hours later, I'd find myself back there, scrounging for morsels of comfort all over again.

Every night, I wanted snacks before bed. But I hated asking for permission. So, if I got the chance, I'd sneak something. Still, I never felt satisfied.

With every episode of stolen food, I'd be wracked with guilt. *Beth, you were sent down here for stealing, and now look at you! When are you ever going to learn?*

Tormented by shame, I finally confessed my struggles to the adults. "I can't stop sneaking food! I keep trying to stop and keep praying to God for help, but it isn't working. I can't be trusted near a kitchen. I want to eat anything and everything. I've been sneaking things like peanut butter, crackers and granola. I even ate some of the ginger ice cream from Sunday School!" (That was especially shameful because it was reserved for the uncles.)

I was met with grave-faced admonitions to rebuke Satan and his temptations. And not long afterward, private counselling was arranged. I'd never been to a therapist before, and I didn't know anyone who had. But I was desperate for help, so I felt grateful for the offer.

It turned out that the counsellor was one of the Community's priests. Dr. Showalter asked me all kinds of questions about my childhood, and I cried a lot in his office. Unfortunately, the solutions he offered were not at all helpful, in hindsight. At the time, though, I hung on to his every word.

For one thing, Dr. Showalter reinforced the notion that my parents weren't good for me. "Beth, you need time to grow in God, all on your own. You don't need the distraction of idolatrous family members who won't stand against your sin."

I also agonized about my inability to manage my food cravings, as well as my insecurities about my body. I told Dr. Showalter about my lifelong struggle to lose and keep off weight. How I'd starved myself and became dangerously thin. How I'd been force-fed and started bingeing. How I couldn't bear to inhabit my—God forbid!—size twelve body.

Looking back, I wonder why I didn't question why a fat middle-aged man would give me the following advice: to go on a diet. Not just any diet, either. I was put on the 3D Diet that Dr. Showalter's wife Carol had created in 1975.

Marketed as America's first faith-based diet program, *3D: Diet, Discipline and Discipleship* was a spiritual guide, a Bible study, and a daily devotional marketed to Christians who wanted to lose weight in fellowship. The 3D Diet's materials were published by Paraclete Press, owned and operated by the Community.

Not only was I required to meet with other 3D dieters, but I also had to help assemble the 3D kits purchased by Christians living all over the country. I'd make the ten-minute walk to Galilee, a huge mansion overlooking Cape Cod Bay that was owned by members of the Community.

Its basement was like a huge warehouse and housed countless boxes of 3D materials.

Going back to a strict diet was demoralizing. *I can't believe I have to go through this again! When will I ever learn?*

The fact that this diet directly equated overeating with sin didn't help my self-esteem. I was already deeply ashamed of my gluttony. But this diet rubbed my nose in it. I didn't enjoy sharing my struggles with even more strangers at the meetings. I'd look around at the middle-aged women and feel so hopeless. *What's wrong with me? Why aren't any other teenage girls going through this?*

Still, I was determined to succeed. I was going to change! I'd done it before, and I could do it again. So I battled my impulses like I was battling the Devil himself. I restricted, counted calories, and carefully chewed each bite. To slow myself down during meals, I'd use chopsticks. (Eating cornflakes with chopsticks takes forever!) I'd also steel myself against my cravings and tap into the iron control that had once helped me shed so many pounds.

After lunch each day, I was given thirty minutes of rest time. But instead of resting, I got permission to walk around the Community. I never enjoyed the scenery on those walks because I was so laser-focused on speed. In my makeshift room—which, by my third move, was an office that converted into sleeping quarters each night—I'd do squats, leg lifts, crunches and push-ups before bed.

Gradually, I noticed my efforts were working. This spurred me on to more weight loss. My self-esteem climbed, and I felt tiny bursts of pride as the weigh-ins confirmed my progress.

Dr. Showalter would praise me for my success. That felt so good and motivated me to keep going. Clothes became looser. I revelled in my newfound control over my sinful desires. God was blessing me. My body was proving my devotion to discipline and discipleship.

As a result, I was told that I'd be allowed to join the Community's orchestra. I was thrilled to use one of my talents again.

Music was a huge deal at the Community, just as it was at Grenville. But here, the performing arts were taken to a whole other level. Their choir was coached by world-renowned directors from King's College and St John's College. In fact, the choir flew to Cambridge, England that winter for three months of rigorous training. (The following year, the group was named Gloriæ Dei Cantores and embarked upon decades of successful recording and performances all around the world.)

The Community also had the Spirit of America, an impressive marching band that toured extensively. There was also an orchestra and smaller ensembles that entertained the public regularly, as well as a drama program that presented musicals and plays, receiving wonderful acclaim.

Once I joined the orchestra rehearsals, the conductor, Dr. Pugsley, intimidated me from the start. He struck me as someone who was equally fastidious about his appearance as he was about his directing. Every musician was so eager to please, and so attentive to his leadership. I followed their lead, and hung on his every word. It seemed imperative to make a good impression.

The expectations were impossibly high. All the musicians were amateurs, with day jobs and countless responsibilities. Still, I got the feeling that perfection was expected. Our rehearsals were punctuated with many frustrated critiques from the conductor. "Do it again!" he'd say. "Something's missing! Clearly, you aren't trusting in God!"

Once, just days before the July 4th concert, Dr. Pugsley slammed down his baton and yelled, "You people are completely wrapped up in yourselves! You're so concerned about playing everything right that you're blocking the Holy Spirit."

He looked down in exasperation. You could hear a pin drop as he contemplated his next words. I dreaded what might come next.

"I want all of you to memorize the music for the concert by tomorrow's 2:00 p.m. rehearsal," he eventually said. "If that means you must stay up all night, then so be it. God is calling you to sacrifice for His glory. If you can't make this deadline, then you will not perform."

I was stunned. The music we were playing was not easy. (Any amateur musician who's played Aaron Copland's *Rodeo* would agree.) I could barely play some parts of it, even with the score. *How am I going to memorize it? Will I get kicked out of this too?*

I looked at the adults around me. Their stricken faces said it all. I knew how busy they all were. No one at the Community had free time. I hadn't once seen a TV turned on in the months I'd been living there.

I left that rehearsal afraid and confused. *Why does God demand the impossible? Why must we always feel like we're doing everything wrong?*

At dinner that evening I asked for extra time to practise. The adults didn't seem the least bit surprised by the draconian task ahead of me.

Down in the basement, I worked for hours to learn my music by heart. It was nearly hopeless, attempting to memorize the notes, the rhythm, the bowing, the rests, the entrances and cut-offs. Still, I wanted to prove myself. I wasn't about to squander this chance to be part of something so exciting.

The next day, when we reconvened for rehearsal, not a single person was absent from the orchestra. *Did all fifty of us memorize this in one night?* I was full of nervous anticipation, wondering if we could pull this off.

Dr. Pugsley arrived and the room hushed instantly. Without scores, we all sat on the edges of our seats, instruments ready, poised to prove ourselves. He opened his score and raised his baton. The entire room took a deep communal breath. With his first downbeat, we were off. Every eye glued to the conductor's, we played the entire piece without a hitch. I could hardly believe it. When the music ended, we all exhaled collectively. I tried to read our leader's expression. *Is he finally satisfied?*

For the moment, Dr. Pugsley was pleased. He declared that we played much better, since we were depending upon the Holy Spirit instead of our scores. We went on to perform on the 4th of July to a sold-out audience, completely by memory.

†

As the summer progressed, the uncertainty of my future became a constant torment. *Will I ever get to go back home? Will I ever finish high school?*

My old life was a distant memory. Even though I wasn't allowed to write letters or receive phone calls, I'd heard through the grapevine that my brother Garth had been appointed the salutatorian of his graduating class. *Great.* I was constantly being reminded of how low I'd sunk. I also heard that Julie, the girl who had betrayed me over Matt, had been named the MC of the graduation banquet. This huge honour was annually bestowed upon the most deserving grade eleven student. Intense jealousy dragged me further into the pit of despair.

Meanwhile, I focused on my journey of repentance. Daily light sessions became commonplace, and I willed myself to keep cooperating and confessing. I tackled my diet, discipline, and discipleship like it was my job. My weight kept creeping down, which made me feel triumphant yet paranoid. *How long can I keep up with this restriction?*

Most people probably envision summers on Cape Cod with images of beaches and sparkling ocean waves. While I did go to the beach occasionally that summer, the Mothers also declared that our skirt bathing suits were too immodest. All my life, we'd been required to swim in suits that were almost impossible to find in stores. Shopping for a full-coverage swimdress was like hunting for a unicorn. But somehow, all the women and girls wore them. If we couldn't find them, we'd sew them.

Evidently, some of the men had confessed they were struggling with lustful thoughts when seeing us women on the beach—even in our skirted suits. So, the Mothers proclaimed that far too much of our demon flesh was on display. That was how I found myself shopping with Aunt Jane for modest sundresses at a local clothing store. Eventually, I found a pink-striped one made of heavy cotton. And so my memories of Cape Cod beaches consist of me trying not to die of embarrassment or drown in a dress that covered my body from neck to knees.

That summer was filled with chores, worship, chant services, light sessions, and dieting. But on special occasions, I'd watch the Spirit of America band march in parades with the rest of the Community. I'd feel such excitement and pride whenever the band approached, decked out in impressive uniforms that commanded attention, moving with skilled precision and playing even better than they marched. *Look how special we are!* I'd think.

That thought was continually hammered home. Everything we did at the Community was to the highest standard. The houses, gardens, and grounds looked immaculate. Each home was large and expensive looking, built in the quintessential Cape Cod architecture. Everyone dressed as well as they could afford, in a conservative New England style. Delicious meals were prepared with care, and households were run like a business. When they weren't at work, every member helped with countless communal endeavours. And when it came to the performing arts, the Community members would exude passion, skill, expertise, and humility. Every presentation seemed to portray the message, "Look what God can do with true believers!"

I internalized all of this. It was almost intoxicating, the prospect of being a member of Christ's elite. It seemed that as God's chosen ones, our lives put outsiders to shame. I vowed to spend my life serving Jesus and offering my gifts for Him to use. All I had to do was stand against my ego and selfish desires.

†

Over time, I was allowed to sew new clothes for myself, since I'd dropped a few sizes. One day, I went to see Dr. Showalter in a new dress I'd made. He gushed about how nice I looked—so much so that, despite my triumph, I felt awkward and self-conscious. He asked me how much weight I'd lost, and I proudly told him thirty-three pounds. He then praised me for all the hard work I'd done since arriving back in February. It was the first time in a while that anyone had made me feel worthy. I went away from that session determined to never gain weight again.

Then in August, the first Master Schola retreat, where church musicians from around the world would gather, was held at the Community. I'd heard rumours that my father would be attending. I had always been so proud of his talent and dedication to the music program at Grenville. Of course, the fact that I was living in disgrace, prohibited from contacting him, made me nervous about our relationship. Still, I was hoping to see him in passing.

During large retreats, it was all hands on deck behind the scenes. Community members were determined to impress their visitors. I helped in the industrial kitchen, cleaned the dorms, and weeded the gardens. But during the event, I never set eyes on my dad. Not even during church on Sunday. I wondered where he was, and I tried not to dwell on my feelings of hurt and abandonment. *Why doesn't he make an effort to see me? Do I even matter to him?*

At my next appointment with Dr. Showalter, he dropped a bombshell: after my father had arrived for the retreat, there had been an incident. Apparently, he'd done something the Mothers had deemed shameful, and they'd spoken very strongly against his sin. As a result, my dad left the retreat in rebellion and anger. He'd disappeared without a car, and no one knew where he was. It appeared that my dad had turned his back on the Community, his calling, and his family.

The shock of this news made my head spin.

My dad left? Where would he go? I thought, panicking. Nobody left our communities without being shunned, with the clear message that they were choosing a path that led straight to Hell. Adults had taken vows of obedience for life. So when they left, they did so knowing that they were leaving God's call. Those who stayed rarely spoke their names; they were lost to us.

What's going to happen to my dad? And to our family? My dad had always been so stoic and steadfast. He was one of the most loyal staff members I knew. He was committed to the cause, passionate about music, dedicated to education and helping students reach their highest potential.

Then Dr. Showalter dropped another bombshell: it had been decided that I could go back to Grenville after Labour Day! I'd return on probation, and if I kept living the life of the Cross, and didn't let myself get corrupted by other students, they were confident that I could be trusted to resume my education. I'd be under supervision in the Farnsworths' and Childs' house, so that I wouldn't be tempted to go astray.

I get to go home? Are you serious? I was so relieved that I could hardly contain my excitement. My hard work and dedication to my repentance had paid off. *I did it! I did it!*

No, Beth, I reminded myself soberly, *God did it!*

The last few weeks in Cape Cod were a mix of excitement and fear. I learned that the other staff kid I'd been banished with wasn't allowed to return to Grenville yet. Apparently, Amy had been biding her time and hadn't done the work to change as I had. This made me feel proud yet paranoid. *Will I be able to keep the weight off? How will I handle the pressure of catching up? Or fitting in?*

Truthfully, I was scared to resume my life at Grenville. I'd worked extremely hard to repent and change, but I knew that one wrong step could land me back into trouble. Was I up to the challenge? I had a new sense of God's call on my life, and I didn't want to get derailed by sinful desires that had brought my life to ruin already. At the Community, I'd learned how to properly live the Cross life; and I was determined to take that knowledge back home with me. *Just deny all your desires! You've got this!*

Armed with this determination, I boarded a school caravan for the long drive back to Canada. On top of everything else, I was worried about my dad. I'd earned my way back to Grenville, but now my dad's disgrace would surely become my new shame. *What if he doesn't come back?* I couldn't let myself consider that possibility. All I knew was that if he did return, it wouldn't be easy. The leaders would break his spirit as they had broken mine.

Chapter 16
Probation

By the time I returned home to Canada, I was used to feeling paranoid. Being on probation didn't help matters. I was housed in an apartment with two A-team administrators who were effectively running Grenville alongside Father Farnsworth. Living with them scared me.

My memories of those last two years of high school are hazy at best. Almost every recollection is permeated with a sense of dread. I was on high alert, trying to be the model staff kid.

Project 88 was launched that September. To raise money and publicity for the school, select students trained all year long to cycle 8,200 km across Canada. All of the senior students were encouraged to put their names forward to be considered for the team. Part of me was keenly interested. I was athletic, and I wanted to be part of something exciting. But I was scared to express my interest.

Tentatively, I brought up my indecision with the adults at home. They made it clear that I wouldn't qualify. "Beth, being on the cycling team is an honour. You have a long way to go before being trusted with such a privilege. That cycling team will be representing God and Grenville Christian College across Canada. Face it, you're not ready for such a responsibility."

As much as those words stung, I agreed with them and put the idea on the shelf where so many of my previous hopes had gone to die. It didn't make it easier that Julie, my former friend, was chosen to be on the bike

team along with Jeff—her longtime crush and secret boyfriend—and
Matt. So all year long, I watched from the sidelines as they trained as an
elite group of students that, once again, I wasn't worthy enough to join.

Every time I saw Matt, I felt the proverbial knife in my chest twist
further. He never once made eye contact with me. I didn't dare speak
to him either. I often stole glances, but he never reciprocated them. The
burden of his rejection was almost unbearable. Matt had been the only
person on the planet to show me affection, and now he was acting like
I no longer mattered.

Feeling like a nobody never got easier. My grades were kept secret,
so no one knew I was smart. I wasn't truly friends with any boarding
students because I was too afraid to be seen fraternizing with outsiders.
Amongst the staff kids, I felt like a failure. I was the only senior staff
kid who wasn't a prefect or student leader. Ten days after his dramatic
escape, my dad had returned to Grenville with his tail between his legs.
Since then, both of my parents had been demoted, and I felt their
humiliation like a physical ache. Not only had my dad been banished
from music, but my mom, the school's most fluent French teacher,
had recently been prohibited from teaching. Her new janitorial roles
seemed demoralizing, especially since I knew how intelligent she was.

To make matters even worse, I was gaining weight again.

If you've been on a strict diet before, you know that weight loss
doesn't last. Your body rebels, and long-term restriction always leads to
bingeing. Of course, I didn't realize my experience was normal. I just
thought I was a sinful glutton and a food addict.

Despite my vow to never gain weight again, I was hungry all the time.
My fear of food was at an all-time high, and I tried not to eat anything
that might trigger a binge. But you can only hold back the floodwaters
of appetite for so long. The dam kept breaking, and I'd binge whenever
I had access to food. I'd sneak into the coolers in the school's industrial kitchen and wolf down leftover pancakes, or hide in the storeroom
behind the cereal shelves and inhale handfuls of Cheerios. In the apartment, I'd silently creep into the kitchen whenever I could and slather
bread with butter and sugar. If someone walked in, I'd pretend to be

doing the dishes, frantically trying to swallow. All the while, a crushing sense of shame engulfed me.

Eventually, the binges became so intense that I took extreme measures. I'd heard that some girls were vomiting their food. The idea intrigued me. What if I could erase my worst sin? It would be like a confession without shame. Or a feast without guilt. I had to try.

My first attempts at purging didn't go well. *Why can't I vomit this hateful food?* I'd sputter and choke as my fingers tried to work their magic. *If I can just throw up this food, I'll be able to maintain control!*

Persistence paid off. After several attempts, I got the hang of it. Soon, purging became my secret weapon. Though I was hyper-vigilant and tried to avoid foods that triggered me, it was such a relief to know my binges could be erased.

The only problem was, the binges got more frequent, more intense, and more debilitating. I was craving much more food than ever before. Once a binge began, I felt like there wasn't enough food in the world. Since I'd spent so much time working in the school kitchen, I knew where all the stashes were. I'd climb the ladder to a loft in the store-room, hide behind stacks of boxes, and open a bulk container of Oreos. Then I'd eat and eat and eat and eat, petrified that someone might discover me. Finally, when I couldn't breathe or take another bite, I'd drag my aching, bulging body down the ladder and search for a private toilet.

These episodes left me physically incapacitated and paralyzed with guilt. My throat burned, my eyes stung as they watered, and my body felt shaky and utterly drained. *What if I get caught? What if they find out that I'm still a glutton after all? What if I gain weight* again? I vowed to keep my shameful secret to myself, hoping it was a temporary problem I could conquer.

While I was stuck in my private hell, I hardly noticed the suffering of students all around me. A few of my peers were always on Discipline, and while part of me sympathized, I didn't think much of it. *Anyone can survive D for a week or two. Take it from me.*

However, students seemed to be getting into trouble much more often now. In the late fall, Father Farnsworth concocted a new form of Discipline called Cold Grits.

We were introduced to it during a girls-only assembly in the chapel. (The boys got their own version soon afterward.) We'd been sitting silently in the pews, waiting for the axe to drop, when a large group of girls filed to the front of the chapel, facing the audience like victims in a firing line.

Well, this is new. What's going on? I listened, perplexed, as Father Farnsworth introduced Cold Grits and what these girls had to do with it.

The headmaster, who was from the American South, said that hot grits were delicious, but once they cooled off, they tasted like shit. *Did he say that out loud?* I thought, stealing a shocked glance with my neighbour. He then explained that these girls had the potential to be as good as hot grits if they stopped being negative and sinning in their minds. Since their attitudes were so bad, they were good for nothing, just like cold grits. They were breaking the rules not with their actions but in their thoughts—and until they completely changed, they were going to be on a special kind of discipline.

Then, to prove his point, the headmaster and the deans publicly humiliated each girl, one by one. A host of accusations, threats, and cruelties were hurled at the girls, who stood there defenceless and exposed.

We also learned that those girls had been awakened before dawn and forced to run laps in the gym while singing hymns like "Onward, Christian Soldiers." One girl—I'll call her Alia—got yelled at because she refused to sing while running. When she explained that she was Muslim, the leaders countered. "You could still have sung the chant that Miss James composed for the occasion! In fact, let's have you sing it here, with the rest of the girls." When Alia adamantly refused, Miss James threatened that if she didn't join in, they'd expose her most shameful secret to the audience. (Decades later I learned that Alia's parents had sent her to Grenville because they blamed her for having been raped.)

Alia glared at Miss James as tears escaped from her defiant gaze. We watched her move her lips unwillingly while they performed the army chant for us:

"Mom and Dad, I'm on Cold Grits
"For being bad and throwing fits
"Not for long, you've got my word
"'Cause up at 5 is for the birds."

Once the administration finished publicly shaming each girl, they asked prefects to chime in. For once, I was relieved that I didn't have a prefect pin.

"I want to be your friend, Alia, but you are always so negative. I wish you would trust that I care about you. That God cares about you."

"Debbie, I keep telling you not to sing rock music, but you never listen. You've got to stop! For your own good!"

After the prefects were finished, the rest of us were encouraged to stand up and take a turn. Several keeners jumped on the bandwagon. I felt immense pressure to join in. If I stood up and spoke truth to any of those girls, I'd impress the leaders. They might even consider me ready to move back to the dorm or give me a leader pin, meaning that I'd be a prefect in training. But I couldn't do it.

The meeting lasted all morning. As usual, I tuned much of it out by thinking about my other worries. Like what was for lunch, and whether I'd be able to control my appetite. But I tuned back in when the leaders announced the discipline that these girls would receive.

First, each girl was assigned a prefect who would be her big sister and escort her everywhere. They wouldn't even be allowed to go to the bathroom without supervision. Next, they were put on silence. We were told not to speak to them, even in the dorms. Also, every day at 5:00 a.m., they'd have to run laps in the gym. They could go to classes and wear uniforms, but they wouldn't be allowed to eat with the rest of the student body. On top of that, they were to report for work duties whenever they weren't in class.

The last nail in the coffin was what I hated most about Discipline: it was to last indefinitely until each girl had changed.

Finally, near the end of the session, Miss James called out, "Jacqueline and Kim, I see you sitting back there, slumped in your pews. You'd better watch out. Your names were almost on the list." And so we all left that meeting knowing that our names could just as easily be on the next list.

✝

After five months of living under intense scrutiny in the staff apartments, I was finally allowed to move into the dorm. I was assigned to a room with another staff girl who was on the illustrious bike team and could keep an eye on me. We lived with two boarding students, one of whom was Alia. It must have been torture for her to be placed with two staff kids, because everyone knew we were tasked with spying on students.

Little did she know that I felt as much under the microscope as she did. Still, the move was one step closer to feeling like a normal student again.

With that move, I gained enough confidence to audition for the annual G&S operetta. Knowing how much it had hurt to lose my lead role the year before, I was afraid to put myself through the process again. But I knew I had the talent, and if I could conquer all my other demons, then maybe I could finally pull it off.

The play was *The Mikado*, and I tried out for the two main female roles. I don't remember much from the audition, but it must have gone well enough because I was awarded the role of Katisha. The delight I felt was immediately eclipsed by crippling self-doubt. Could I do the part justice? Katisha was a hilarious, obnoxious, deliciously dramatic villain. Her character required immense stage presence and outrageous mannerisms. How could I manage all that while I was so intensely insecure and concealing an eating disorder? I felt unequal to the challenge in almost every way.

Still, my love of G&S and the hope of being a somebody propelled me forward. As rehearsals began, I waded into uncharted waters with all the courage I could muster. Little by little, my confidence grew, and I felt like I was tapping into long-dormant strengths. But I couldn't shake the feeling of dread. *What if I gain more weight? What if I can't handle the spotlight?*

All the while, I still couldn't control my eating. Fighting the cravings was like being caught in a tsunami. Despite my attempts to avoid the foods I craved, time and time again I'd lose all control. After that, I'd find a toilet and dispose of the evidence of my colossal mistakes.

My bulimia soon became unbearable. What had once seemed like a solution became a dirty secret that haunted me 24/7. And since I was a staff kid, I was obliged to attend light sessions every week. At those meetings, we were expected to share our struggles in a group of at least twenty, including staff members from the A-team. If we didn't, they'd be pointed out by someone else. I struggled for months, trying to decide whether to share what was going on.

One day, I finally blurted out my shameful secret. The room fell silent. And when a response came, it wasn't one of concern for my well-being. Rather, Mr. Ortolani shook his head, saying something about being disgusted. He added that he was glad I wasn't on the bike team, since those students were capable of self-discipline.

Miss James looked at me like I was the spawn of the devil. "Not only are you giving in to your gluttony, but you are lying to everyone by vomiting to hide the evidence!" she said. "Your deceit is shocking! I am absolutely appalled by you, Beth. Especially after all the help you've been given. You have received more care and intervention than any staff kid in Grenville's history. And here you are again, refusing to live the Cross life. Choosing to follow your evil desires, every single time you face temptation. You should be utterly ashamed of yourself!"

Tears streamed down my face. *You can't imagine how ashamed I am!* I wanted to say. *I know that I'm the worst staff kid ever. I can't be trusted. I can't resist Satan, no matter how hard I try.*

Numbly I listened to other staff kids who took turns rebuking me. I was so demoralized that I couldn't even let their words sink in. I was already drowning in shame, so what did more accusations matter?

Eventually, the leaders leaned together to whisper about my fate. Dread gripped my stomach in its familiar vice. *What are they going to do to me this time?*

"Beth," they began, "we are extremely worried about you. There will need to be some serious measures taken. To begin with, we are assigning Karen to be your big sister. You will need to be under constant supervision. Do not go anywhere without her. That includes the bathroom, eating meals, and walking anywhere in the school or dorm."

I gulped, feeling a painful lump in my throat. *This is going to be the worst!*

"But that is not all. You are dealing with a battle over good and evil, and Satan has been winning. To turn your life around, drastic actions are necessary. We have decided that the role of Katisha will go to your understudy. You cannot be on stage while you're so steeped in sin."

Those words almost knocked me to the ground. But the leaders weren't finished with me yet.

"You can still be part of the production, in background roles. You will play viola in the orchestra, and on weekdays after class, you will help sew the costumes."

So not only am I losing my role on stage, but I must sew the costumes in my free time? And sit in the orchestra watching my peers perform?

The wretchedness I felt then is impossible to describe today. I knew I'd failed again, and I was beginning to think there was no hope for my future.

As the weeks and months dragged on, I subjected myself to the humiliation of being escorted everywhere by a staff girl only one year my senior. She was a prefect and seemed to do everything right, which drove me up the wall. Still, her presence was the deterrent I needed as I battled the desire to binge. I never *ever* wanted my eating habits to be the subject of another light session.

Making the costumes was a torment. Every day, I'd report to the sewing room after classes and work, usually alone, on some of the most exquisite costumes I'd ever seen. Bright silks and satins were used to create the kimonos for the production. With every stitch, I was reminded of my failure and shame. How could I have sunk so low?

As much as it hurt, I kept reminding myself that I had no one but myself to blame. *You did this to yourself, Beth! If you weren't such a sinful glutton, you'd be on stage with the rest of your peers. You should be ashamed of yourself!*

Playing in the orchestra only made me feel worse. As the opening night drew near, every rehearsal served as a reminder of my disgrace. I'd play my viola, fighting back tears while the actors brought down the house. At least I wasn't alone in my humiliation. That year, at least three other students lost their lead roles, due to their supposed sins. So when the play debuted, three main parts were filled by adults: two male staff members, and Robert, a former student who returned from university to play the tenor lead, and who eventually starred on Broadway.

†

At the time, students planning to attend Canadian universities had to complete grade thirteen. But you could graduate after grade twelve if you were heading to college. Matt was one of my classmates planning to graduate early, since he had been accepted by a military college in the States. That school year, I'd watched him from afar, never daring to speak to him. Matt trained for ten months to cycle across Canada with the bike team and belonged to the inner circle of those representing Grenville. Even though we were in the same grade, I felt invisible around him.

On the day before graduation, I finally summoned the nerve to ask Matt to sign my yearbook. He awkwardly agreed and asked to take it with him for a minute. My heart hammered as I passed it to him. *Is anyone watching?* I didn't care. This was my last chance to communicate with him. I tried not to get my hopes up as he settled under a tree to write.

What Matt wrote brought tears to my eyes. It wasn't exactly closure, and it didn't bring me relief. But it wasn't nothing:

Dear Beth,

Well, we have had some good times and some bad times. I really wanted to say something to you about what happened last year. I suppose the only thing worth saying is that I am sorry. After the whole incident, I was pretty messed up. I don't think I ever really realized what we were doing. The beginning of this year I was messed up too. But I think everything turned out the way God wanted it to. I hope to write when I'm at VMI next year, but I'm not making any promises. We really should keep in touch. I do care.

Matt

Matt's bittersweet acknowledgement that he cared meant more to me than I wanted to admit. Letting him go was so painful, even though he'd moved on months before. I knew in my gut that I'd never hear from him again, though his words hinted otherwise.

Chapter 17
Boiling the Frog

My final year of high school felt like intensive training to become a Grenville staff member. I was still a student, living in the dorm, but I was expected to act as though I were already on staff.

During that year, my twenty-year-old brother Garth was told by the leaders that they felt he was called to become a brother at the Community. Like several other staff kids from Grenville, he obeyed. Garth travelled to Cape Cod, moved in with the brothers, and became a novice, like a monk in training. About a year later, he changed his name to Brother Matthew, and publicly took lifetime vows of chastity, poverty, and obedience to the Mothers. Three decades later, my brother still lives there.

Such was the level of control over our lives and minds that I never considered a different path. By the time I was eighteen, I believed the warnings about my oldest brother Dan, who had chosen to leave after high school. He was going to Hell and I had no desire to follow in his footsteps. His freedom didn't tempt me.

Knowing that I was called by God to be a staff member didn't make the preparation easier. That school year tested my resolve as I faced challenge after challenge. In effect, we staff kids were being taught to deny our desires, hopes, and dreams, and to willingly submit to God, without questioning.

Expectations were becoming increasingly rigorous, too. The leaders called us to reject worldliness and sins of the flesh more than ever before. I was used to modesty mandates, but a series of light sessions about bathing suits still caught me off guard.

While I was in exile at the Community, Grenville's dress codes for swimming had also changed. Apparently, females needed to wear shorts and a loose tank top with wide straps overtop a modest one-piece swimsuit. (Males were required to wear T-shirts or tank tops and long swim trunks.) Since I'd never owned a regular one-piece in my life, I borrowed one from a boarding student for our senior trip. Days later, I was called into a light session, where it was declared that my bathing suit hadn't been supportive enough—and that people had noticed! I was accused of wearing an inappropriate suit to attract attention and tempt the boys.

Embarrassment washed over me. How could I explain that during that trip, I'd felt so uncomfortable, ashamed of my status, my body, and my lack of friends, I'd spent most of that time helping with food prep and clean-up, hoping to impress the staff with my subservient behaviour? Only once had I ventured into the lake for a volleyball game.

It was easier to keep my mouth shut and endure the reprimand. The meeting concluded with the proclamation that I go shopping with a staff lady to find a proper swimsuit.

The excursion was agony. I had to model every single suit in the changing room. I could barely look at myself, much less have another woman critique me so intimately. I couldn't stop my inner critic from screaming at me. *Your boobs are way too big! Nothing hides them! You're so fat! You need to lose weight immediately!*

Finally, I found a suit that was well-constructed, modest, and supportive. It was a Jantzen and far too expensive, but I was so desperate that I bought it with my meagre savings. (Even though it would never actually be seen.) My chaperone agreed that it ticked all the boxes, and that shopping torment ended.

A couple of days later I was told to report to one of the staff apartments. When I walked into the living room, I was met by five staff women, three of whom were on the A-team. Their severe expressions told me I was in deep trouble.

Aunt Judy held up my new bathing suit—which I'd last seen hanging in my locked closet—and asked, "Is this what you bought on your trip? How dare you buy a suit that is so high-cut?"

Her accusation stung. Immediately I saw the suit from her perspective. *The bottom does look high-cut! What was I thinking?*

Lamely, I explained how it had been difficult to find a suit that supported my chest. "This was the only one I found that seemed to work," I added.

"Beth, it's clear that you're trying to get away with the sexiest suit possible," Aunt Susan piped up. "Who are you trying to impress?"

"No one!" I protested, feeling utterly defeated.

It didn't matter what I said. After a barrage of accusations, Aunt Judy proposed that I model the suit for them.

Knowing I had no choice, I closed myself in the bathroom. My limbs shook as I changed into the offending suit. The idea of leaving the privacy of that bathroom, wearing far less material than I'd ever worn in public, filled me with horror. I glanced at my reflection. At least the bottom didn't look very high-cut once I had it on. I took a deep breath. *Just get this over with.*

Peering down the apartment hallway to ensure no man was in sight, I worked up the courage to emerge from the bathroom to stand before the panel. Ten critical eyes scanned my body. I couldn't bear to watch their gazes scrutinizing my chest, my stomach, my hips. So I turned my head to stare out the living-room window to the river beyond.

"All right, Beth," one of the staff women said eventually. "Face the back of the room." As I slowly turned she continued, "Now bend down, and touch your toes!"

What? I looked over my shoulder at them, confused.

"Go on, touch your toes so we can see if it rides up when you bend over."

Drowning in shame, I tentatively reached down, trying not to picture my embarrassing backside. After a few moments, I stood up.

"Now turn around and reach down to touch your toes, facing us. Do it slowly, so we have a proper view."

As if in a trance, I did what I was told, shuddering as I imagined my evil cleavage that was most certainly on full display. When I stood up again, dizziness took hold. The room reeled as I noticed my judges conferring, forming a verdict.

"The suit is OK after all," Aunt Joan eventually said. "It isn't as high-cut as it appeared on the hanger. You can go change now."

I left on shaky legs. *The suit might be OK, but I'm not.*

†

In mid-August, the staff kids got to spend a glorious day at Canada's Wonderland, a theme park near Toronto. We worked most of the time during the summers, but when we got time off, we knew how to have fun. The day was packed with nonstop excitement, from the SkyRider and the 3D Action Theatre, to the delicious funnel cakes. We were sent off in fours, all of us wearing Grenville golf shirts with long pants, and at one point, my group and another did something daring: we visited the park's karaoke studio to consider making a music video together.

"Wouldn't it be fun?" A great deal of arguing ensued as we counted the pros and cons. I thought it was risky, but I couldn't help wanting to push the envelope for some reason. We got caught up in the thrill of being filmed and eventually went for it.

The first problem was, we didn't recognize any of the hit songs that were listed. When you're not allowed to listen to pop music, it's nearly impossible to choose a karaoke song. Eventually, we found "You've Lost That Lovin' Feelin'," which we recognized from *Top Gun*, a movie Father Farnsworth loved. (Minus the fast-forwarded sex scenes.)

The next problem? We really didn't know the song—and we all had stage fright. I hid behind the synthesizer stand and pretended to play the keyboard while awkwardly singing a song I barely knew. *I should probably not be standing still*, I thought at one point. *Maybe I should sway a little or something?* I couldn't wait for the filming to be over. *I probably look so fat! I hope no one is watching this!*

When the video was finished, we pooled our money and purchased a VHS copy. I was already regretting the cost since I had no intention of watching our performance. *I won't be doing that again,* I thought, sighing.

I didn't think much more about the music video until a couple of days later, when all the teenage staff kids had to report for a meeting. A few dozen of us piled into one apartment and waited nervously. It didn't take long before the adults informed us that many of us had ruined the trip to Canada's Wonderland with our rebellion, deceit, and worldly behaviour. I don't recall what kinds of incidents other kids were called out for. I only remember worrying that somehow, they knew about the music video.

Sure enough, we were next in line. One of the meeting's leaders produced our VHS and announced our evildoing to the group. We girls were interrogated and accused of all manner of sins. Fear gripped me. *Please don't show it,* I silently begged. *You can say what you like about me, but please don't show it.*

My prayers went unanswered. I watched in horror as a dean turned on the TV and inserted the evidence of our sin into the VHS player.

Mortified, I couldn't bear to watch the video. It was even cringier than I feared. *I look so fat! What was I thinking, wearing those pants?*

When it was over, the critiques intensified. One girl was criticized for the way she swooped her voice like a seductive pop singer. Another one was targeted for the way she played the drums. "That beat is straight from the Devil, and you were loving it!" When they got to me, someone yelled, "You know better than to take part in a stunt like this! You were the oldest one in the group! You're supposed to be the example for the rest of the girls."

I nodded in shame. *I do know better! I regret everything!*

But the meeting's leaders weren't finished with me yet. "Beth, your behaviour in that video is by far the most shameful. The way you were swinging your hips to the beat! Do you know how lustful you appear? You look like a wanton woman, begging for men to notice you!"

Stop! I implored inside my head. *If you only knew how ashamed I am of my body, you'd know I was trying to hide my hateful hips!*

As the meeting closed, the leaders declared that we were all ungrateful wretches and didn't deserve to be Grenville students. Our punishments were doled out, including extra manual labour, and loss of various privileges. I left that meeting knowing I'd failed again. I was about to start grade thirteen and I hadn't even earned a student leader pin. On top of that, I felt even worse about the accusations of being lustful and wanton. The experience of having my body critiqued in front of my peers was worse than any punishment. Decades later, I still shudder at that memory.

†

By the fall of grade thirteen, I was keeping very much to myself, even though I rubbed shoulders with boarding students around the clock. Light sessions for staff kids were getting increasingly intense, too. To be prepared for my future, I was required to meet with young staff members who had already graduated. Our group was called Corpus Christi (CC) and I dreaded those meetings more than anything. The group had no sense of empathy. Everyone in it was there to attack or be attacked. Often, I got in trouble with them for being passive, which wasn't acceptable. We were expected to be aggressively rooting out each other's sins.

Like with the bathing suit and Wonderland incidents, I was often caught off guard. One time, I'd gone to a three-day public speaking competition in Westmount, Montreal. Like other competitions I'd attended, it was an exercise in sheer terror. I excelled in dramatic recitations, but impromptu speaking petrified me. I only attempted these competitions because I was chosen to represent the school. Plus, the part of me that craved validation was never satisfied.

I was sent with my English teacher and two other Grenville students: Amy, who had finally returned from her Community exile, and Kevin, a boarding student and prefect. We enjoyed one another's company whenever we weren't competing. On the last day, our coach had to help with the final tallying, so we were left without supervision for over two hours. We opted to walk the streets, gazing at the Westmount mansions in the drizzling rain. As we walked, we sang in three-part harmony, practising choir pieces. It was more entertaining than anything I'd done in a long time. We couldn't have been nerdier if we tried. After an hour, when the drizzle turned into a downpour, we waited for our teacher in the school minivan. More singing and chatting ensued; and for once, I felt comfortable. I truly enjoyed that day.

Which meant that I was completely unprepared when Miss James pulled me into her office two days later. She'd caught wind of the hours Amy, Kevin, and I had spent without supervision in Montreal and was gravely concerned. So she launched into her trademark interrogation tactics: What did I do with Kevin and Amy while our teacher was busy? Was I ever alone with Kevin? How on earth did I think it was OK to spend time in a car with a boy without a supervisor? What else was I hiding? Had I let Kevin touch me? Was I fantasizing about him?

Her pointed questioning was so absurd that after the initial shame, I felt an unfamiliar surge of anger. I knew for certain that I wasn't guilty. *How dare she accuse me of attempting to seduce Kevin? Can't she see how hard I've been working to prove myself as a model staff kid?*

I explained that I felt no attraction to Kevin (which was true). We were simply friends and classmates. I described our actions in detail and stood by my decisions. Defending myself to Miss James was always an exercise in futility, though. Her penetrating glare confirmed her belief that I was guilty.

That encounter left me feeling dirty and demoralized. I felt like I'd never be trusted. My anger over the accusations didn't erase the shame, either. Being painted as a wanton seducer was taking its toll. I never wanted to be seen speaking to boys.

The next CC light session after that was open season against me. After I endured another round of accusations, the meeting leaders announced, "Beth, we think it's time that you got your hair cut short, like all the staff women here."

What?

"You don't seem to be taking God's call seriously. This is an action that you need to take to prove that you are ready to commit your future to God."

Don't touch my hair! I wanted to scream. I'd hoped to grow my hair ever since I was little, but I hadn't been allowed to do so until my exile at the Community, where haircuts weren't provided for me. After returning to Grenville, I kept growing it out, and now it was past my shoulders. Visions of staff women and their short, tight perms flooded my brain. *I'm still a teenager! I don't want to look like an old woman! I'm not ready!*

I wept in silent misery. Nothing about me was acceptable. I'd been taught to be ashamed of every aspect of my body. And now, my one redeeming feature was going to be chopped off. I knew there was no way I could argue my way out of it. I'd seen too many other girls get their hair cut short against their will. Even boarding students, with long hair down to their waist, had been whisked away to the Majestic Styling Lounge in Brockville, where most staff women got their hair done.

I showed up to my hairdresser, accompanied by an assistant dean who was calling the shots. When Diane was told to cut my hair short, she frowned, searching my face for confirmation. I tried to look like I was OK with the plan, but Diane knew me better than that. She'd been doing my hair since grade four and seemed to sense that something was off. I sat in her chair, wishing I could protest. But I knew that if I didn't cooperate, things would be even worse for me back at Grenville. So, I reassured her that I wanted a change.

Reluctantly, Diane got to work. Even though she cared about my welfare, it felt like she was removing the last shreds of my self-worth with every snip.

When I got home, all eyes were on me. Embarrassment engulfed me as I fended off reactions and criticism left and right. A few perceptive students pointed out that I looked like a staff member. Others said that I looked twenty years older.

Great, I thought sarcastically. *Just what an eighteen-year-old wants to hear.*

†

The rest of grade thirteen passed by in a painful blur. When I think back on that school year, all I remember is feeling defeated. The recollections I have of it are like a bad dream that you can't quite recall. It's like my capacity to make memories shut down during that time.

I do recall that for some absurd reason, I auditioned for the lead role in *The Pirates of Penzance*, that year's G&S play. How I kept that spark of hope alive is still a mystery. I guess I knew I was one of a tiny handful who had the talent. Also, it was my last chance to prove I was equal to my brothers. Amazingly, I landed the role I wanted: Mabel, who sings one of the most difficult soprano arias Sullivan ever composed.

However, Kevin—the boy I'd supposedly tried to seduce in Montreal—got cast as Frederick, the lead tenor. So right from the beginning, my chances of keeping the part seemed precarious. *Are the leaders really going to let me play opposite Kevin? How am I going to pull this off?*

As I said, the details are a blur, but for the third year in a row, I lost the lead role. Once again, my sins got the better of me. I don't recall which ones, but I was still struggling with my eating at the time. Which meant that I was confessing those struggles regularly. I'd be hounded during the CC meetings about my inability to control my cravings. At one point, Mr. Ortolani leaned back on his chair and scoffed, "Beth, if you're worried about weight, stop eating so much. It's that simple."

At that moment, I hated Mr. Ortolani almost as much as I hated myself.

I suppose it says a lot about my mental state that I can't remember how or why I lost the part of Mabel, but I do remember the diet I started then. Life was so unbearable that in February of grade thirteen, I tried Weight Watchers for the first time. I borrowed the materials from a staff member who had recently shrunk her body, and it felt like a lifeline.

I didn't go to any meetings. Instead, I powered through the program on my own and harnessed my willpower for those last few months of high school. I was determined not to graduate feeling fat. As the pounds melted away, I basked in my renewed confidence. By the time June arrived, I'd lost at least three dress sizes. As graduation approached, I focused on my food and my body and ignored all the other disappointments.

When it came time for *The Pirates of Penzance* to be performed, the actors who played Mabel and Frederick shone on stage. I sat directly below them, playing my viola, and revelled in my hunger pains.

Later, when a classmate I tutored in math was chosen to be valedictorian, I concentrated on my daily calorie intake.

During the final month of school, when I was called up in front of the student body to be awarded an embarrassingly late prefect pin, I focused on my triumphantly loose kilt instead.

And whenever I endured the sight of the gold-embossed names on the honour roll, without mine included, I took comfort in my reflection.

Still, there was one memorable blow that even weight loss couldn't erase.

Father Farnsworth often made guest appearances at our CC light sessions. Whenever he did, my fear would spike off the charts. At one point, the topic of our future roles came up and I revealed that I was hoping to be a teacher at Grenville someday. Father Farnsworth's response brooked no argument: "Beth, you will never be a teacher at Grenville. With your ego, you have been called to fill a menial role. Like working in housekeeping or the kitchen. If you want to stay close to God, you'll have to stay low."

His words sounded the death knell on my dreams. I graduated from a high school where performance was everything, feeling like a nobody with no hope for my future. But at least I was thin.

Chapter 18
Getting Fired and Other News

As I look back at my years at Grenville, I keep asking myself, *What made me stay and become a staff member there?*

The answer is simple. I felt I had no choice. I had been taught that I was called by God to serve as a lifelong member of our community. By the time I was nineteen, that belief was absolute, and I didn't dare question it. I knew it would require sacrifice, and I was better prepared than most.

If I left, I'd be turning my back on God and be shunned in the process. Why would I choose to sacrifice my family, my friends, and my eternal salvation? The leaders had preached endlessly of our certain downfall if we dared to leave. Sometimes I'd picture myself alone on a street corner, selling my body to survive. I couldn't bear to imagine how low I'd sink if I turned my back on God's will.

I took great pride in my calling. All my life, the notion that we were members of God's elite had been drilled into me. Grenville had been growing for years; new buildings were being built, enrolment was increasing, and its reputation was soaring. Our music and drama programs were second to none, our sports teams excelled, and 99 percent of our graduates got accepted into their desired colleges or universities. As a result, an intoxicating sense of superiority was instilled into us. We believed our staff formed one of the most dedicated, dynamic, and effective teams of Christian education in the world. We were carrying out the Lord's most essential work, which was moulding the lives and hearts of children. What could have been more important than that?

It was with this sense of conviction that I began my adult life in the summer of 1989. During those first few years, I performed all kinds of menial jobs. I started in laundry, cleaning the clothes, sheets, and towels of 200 students. Every day was a race against the clock. The machines were taller than me and rumbled louder than a freight train. I'd blast the *Les Misérables* soundtrack and sing at the top of my lungs while folding thousands of items, sorting them into individual tubs, and delivering them to each student.

There was a lot of pressure on Grenville's staff. We were kept busy from dawn until midnight (even later if you were assigned nightwatch). When we weren't working or at chant services, or our mandatory daily prayer vigil, we were in light sessions. Our staff meetings almost always caught us off guard. Nearly a hundred of us would pile into the cramped community room, faces worn and full of anxiety. Then the leaders would enter and make traumatic decrees such as, "We feel some of you are getting too comfortable in your jobs." Or, "God has told us that many of you are living in idolatry with your housemates."

Disciplines would be issued, moves would be announced, or jobs would change. At first, I didn't mind the job switches, since I didn't like mine to begin with. But I felt for the teachers who were told at a moment's notice that they were to change subjects or even worse, leave the classroom to work on housekeeping. I also hated moving my living quarters all the time. One year I was moved eight times!

I often had to live with people who frightened me. In my first year on staff, for example, I lived with Father and Mrs. Farnsworth.

During that time, Father Farnsworth decided that I needed to break the so-called idolatrous bond between my mother and me. He also wanted me to hone my skills at confronting the sins of others. So, he gave me the discipline of correcting my mother. Every day I was required to point out her sins in the presence of a witness. Then I'd report back to the Farnsworths about each confrontation. I can't believe I went along with this. The discipline made me feel like a monster and it further damaged my relationship with my mother, which by now was practically non-existent. I can still picture her stricken expression, every time I pointed out her sins. I can feel my revulsion—both at myself and her—as she meekly accepted every hateful word I said as though it were a message from God.

No matter where I lived, random light sessions would happen. Sometimes they were a direct result of confessions we were required to write to our leaders every two weeks. I always hoped the contents of my letters would remain confidential. But for some reason, my superiors always seemed to have the inside scoop on my latest sins.

When I was twenty-three, I was assigned to be a dorm mother on the second floor of Murray Hall. My roommate was my age, and for once I felt comfortable. I bought a large boombox to celebrate my new freedom. That year, I'd also been given a job as a front-office receptionist, answering the school's only phone, using a bulky switchboard that had six incoming lines. My job was to connect every call or take a message. That meant locating someone, out of approximately 450 people, at a moment's notice. It was a huge responsibility, and I loved the challenge.

Soon, that all came crashing to a halt, too. First, I was called out in a staff meeting after I purchased the soundtracks from *Robin Hood* and *Sister Act*. During the meeting, it was decreed that the music had a Devil's beat and that I was a terrible influence on the girls in the dorm. Much to my dismay, those CDs were confiscated.

Things got worse after that. As Christmas approached, the school was preparing for a visit from the Mothers for the annual staff retreat. My fear and dread became so unbearable as their arrival drew near that, during a stop at the Brockville drugstore, I caught sight of the shelves lined with treats on sale for Christmas, and the voices that had plagued me my entire life shouted, *Just eat a bunch of chocolate! You'll feel so much better!* Praying the cashier couldn't read my mind, I paid for a Pot of Gold and hid it inside a bag before being driven back to Grenville by another staff member. (I wasn't allowed to drive yet, even though I'd had my licence for four years.)

As soon as I got to a bathroom, I opened the box and shovelled the chocolates into my mouth. The taste was pure bliss at first. But soon I was eating in a frenzy. *I can't even taste this anymore. I've got to slow down!* I couldn't stop, though. I kept gobbling the chocolates, one by one, two by two, until all I could think about was vomiting. The habit had been getting worse again for over a year, and I'd tried to keep it hidden, thinking I could stop whenever I wanted to.

But at that moment, I had no choice. Up came the chocolate, like a foul explosion, stinging my throat, splattering my clothes, the toilet, and the floor. I was left shaking, emptied of calories, but full of self-loathing.

During the Mothers' Christmas retreat, the Grenville staff were bombarded by the full arsenal of firepower our leaders could shell out. Everyone was a potential target, and we spent days in fear, wondering who was next. At one point, each of us was urged to make a full confession on paper. I was used to this, but the intensity of this retreat forced me to hold nothing back.

My letter contained my greatest shame: I was bingeing and purging again. I revealed that I'd eaten an entire box of chocolates just before the retreat and thrown it all up. I wrote of my guilt, my remorse, and my desperate determination to stop.

Days later, I was called to Father Farnsworth's office. My heart hammered as he spelled out my fate. I was told that my bulimia was such a grievous sin that he could no longer keep me on staff. My gluttony and deceit were so out of control that he didn't want me anywhere near the students. I was being fired, effective immediately.

My life is over. Again.

Being fired at Grenville didn't mean I would leave. I'd taken lifetime vows of obedience to the Mothers two years earlier, during a public ceremony in the Community's chapel on Cape Cod. But it did mean that I'd be forced to work in a demeaning capacity without pay. I lost my salary and my job at the front office. I was also moved from the dorm to a room in one of the staff apartments, where I'd live and work as a maid with two couples who worked in administration. I wasn't allowed to be a coach, sing in the choir, play in the orchestra, or supervise the students in any way. Instead, I'd work in the staff kid daycare, clean the apartment, do the dishes and household laundry, and care for the household babies. In my free time, I'd sew costumes for G&S productions.

So noticeable was my debasement that rumours flew around the school. Decades later I would learn that students had started a rumour about me. The story they'd concocted was that I was being punished for having had an affair with a man from Brockville. If only they had known the truth.

For eight months, I lived in abject humiliation, paying for my sin of bulimia. I was so afraid of relapsing that I was afraid to eat. I also suffered through continual light sessions, where my every move was picked apart. At one point, the dean of men scolded me after he saw me checking my reflection. "You need to stop being so self-centred, Beth! Your size doesn't matter!" That seemed like mixed messaging if I'd ever heard it.

As this punishment wore on, I continued to endure intense scrutiny about my eating, my body, and my weight. I'd be subjected to draconian exercise disciplines, all in the pursuit of taming my sinful body and appetite. Every day that summer, I was forced to swim seventy-two laps in the school's large pool in twenty-five minutes. I wasn't trusted to complete the challenge without an overseer counting my laps and timing me. By lap thirty-six, I'd feel like I was sinking. It was the feeling I'd battled for decades: the feeling of drowning in literal shame.

During that time, my maternal grandpa wrote to me, just after my grandma had died. I'd never received a letter from him before. My family had rarely visited their home in Springfield, Ohio. My grandpa was fastidious, cuttingly cynical, and hilarious. I was in awe of his big Tudor-style house, his habit of blasting classical music, and his delightful use of the most erudite vocabulary.

Grandpa Eutsler's letter stopped me in my tracks. *Beth*, he wrote, *I am concerned that you are only dabbling in higher education.* He then offered to pay my entire tuition for a four-year degree at Wittenberg University and extended me free room and board in his beautiful home.

I was afraid to consider Grandpa Eutsler's offer, even for a moment. The prospect of leaving Grenville seemed tantalizing, especially when I was living in such despair. *Is God testing me?*

Letters from outsiders were always fuel for light sessions. This time was no exception. I was told that my grandpa's words were the voice of Satan. "Beth, it's clear that the Devil knows your resolve is weak. Why else would he be tempting you this way? You need to treat this as your opportunity to defeat Satan's power over your life!"

Determined to prove my loyalty, I did as I was told. I wrote a *Thanks, but no thanks* letter to my grandpa, explaining that I felt God's call to work full-time on staff at Grenville. I assured him that I'd been taking two or three courses per year at Queen's University in Kingston and that I'd graduate sooner or later. Of course, I didn't tell him I was often berated for my ambition to get a degree, chastised for my haughtiness whenever I got high grades at Queen's, and repeatedly told I had no need for further education since I wasn't called to become a teacher. (Some of my peers were already teaching at Grenville, without having earned a degree—a fact that drove me crazy.)

Despite the pushback, I was determined to get my degree. And it nearly killed me. My assignments had to be finished late into the night, after I'd completed all my other duties. During those six long years, I was never once allowed to drive one of Grenville's cars by myself. Every time I made the sixty-minute trip to Kingston, for class or research, I had to find someone to drive me or accompany me. (And it couldn't be a man, because … *sex?*)

I finally earned my degree from Queen's when I was twenty-six. It was a day I'll never forget because after never knowing my grades in high school, I was awarded the Kathleen L. Healey Prize from Queen's University, graduating with the highest grade point average of all the part-time students. Grandpa Eutsler never got to see this, though. He died only six months after writing me that letter.

†

After getting fired for being bulimic, it took me over eight months to earn my way back onto Grenville's payroll. I was given a job in the business office and was allowed to supervise students again. But that didn't mean the pressure was off.

I was moved into an apartment with Miss James—my former Aunt Judy who had been tormenting me since I had lived with her in elementary school. As always, she made me intensely uncomfortable. By this point, she had been the dean of women for quite some time, and had morphed into a kind of Aunt Lydia from *The Handmaid's Tale*. She expected dorm supervisors to spy on students and report to her about everything. If we didn't get dirt on them, or if we missed any of their infractions, we'd be in deep trouble.

One thing I hated was conducting dorm searches. Miss James initiated these frequently; and whenever she did, students weren't allowed to enter the dormitories for any reason. We'd have to breach their school-issued padlocks, rifle through their belongings, and search for anything suspicious: bikini underwear, jeans, medication, lighters, music, and even personal correspondence.

The searches were often conducted right before school breaks. Sometimes students who were found with contraband weren't allowed to go home. One March break, I was looking forward to being a supervisor on a school trip to Europe. (I could only afford the trip because my grandpa had left me money in his will.) The day before we were to leave, we conducted a massive dorm search. Cigarettes were found, and a full-scale interrogation ensued. It turned out that three girls had been smoking that week, and none of us supervisors had discovered them.

Once the dorm-wide light session concluded and the perpetrators were put on Discipline, Miss James met with us dorm supervisors. She was outraged that we hadn't caught the smokers sooner. "Clearly, none of you are living in the Spirit!" She then announced that I wasn't fit to be a supervisor on the Europe trip. For the next twenty-four hours, I thought I wouldn't get to go, all because I hadn't known girls were sneaking some smokes.

After that incident, I looked for every opportunity to impress Miss James. During a dorm search months later, I was ordered to examine the luggage in the locked storage room. Inside a suitcase, I found a small plastic package that appeared to be a medical item. Not knowing what it was, yet anxious to win Miss James's approval, I turned it in to her. The girl who had been secretly storing contraception was expelled as a result.

Whenever I think of the unjust cruelty that student suffered, I feel a sharp stab of guilt. I can't remember her name. But I hope she'll read this one day and know how terribly sorry I am for taking part in her abuse.

Chapter 19
Boot Camp

I don't know how I survived 1995.

Ironically, it seemed like everything was finally going my way before that dreadful year began.

Mid-1994, a young staff member named Mark had drummed up the courage to ask me out. Of course, he didn't ask me first. I imagined his request going up through the chain, from his household elders to Father Farnsworth, all the way to headquarters in Cape Cod. These things had to go through proper channels.

He braved that for me?

I was genuinely surprised and delighted by Mark's interest in me. His deadpan sarcasm and sharp wit drew me in. Mark was tall and athletic, with unruly black hair and gorgeous brown skin from what I assumed was his Indigenous heritage. We'd banter and joke about the chaos of our busy lives since he had joined the staff. My only hint that he liked me was the way I'd occasionally catch his dark eyes looking my way. That thrill never got old.

Mark, a former boarding student from Ottawa, had been persuaded by Father Farnsworth to join the Grenville staff. The hope was that once he was properly indoctrinated, he'd take lifetime vows of obedience to the leaders, like the rest of us had. Several other boarding students had done the same. In fact, Kevin—yes, the one I'd supposedly tried to seduce—had joined the staff, and then went on to become a brother at the Community. Like my brother Garth, he is there to this day.

I was twenty-four by this time, and starting to worry I'd never marry. We were only allowed to wed vowed members of the community, and there were precious few choices. The young staff ladies far outnumbered the single men, and the feeling that I was terminally undesirable plagued me constantly. So Mark's interest offered a glimmer of hope. For a few blissful weeks, I revelled in the fact that someone thought I was special. Maybe even attractive?

Unfortunately, Mark and I never got to enjoy dating. As I learned quickly, couples who were going out required constant supervision. Whenever Mark and I spent the occasional meal and evening together, we'd share the experience with ten other people from our assigned households. The closest we got to an outing was a one-day salmon fishing trip in upstate New York. I joked that the only reason I'd ever go fishing was to spend time with a man I liked. (Fish still gross me out.) But even that trip was jammed with a vanload of others. Mark and I didn't even sit next to each other.

I never really got to know Mark well. Our relationship provided endless fodder for light sessions, and our every move was scrutinized and picked apart in excruciating detail. Within a couple of months, I was afraid to be seen speaking to Mark. Unsurprisingly, we drifted apart.

†

As Christmas approached, another staff retreat loomed. Mother Betty would be visiting from Cape Cod, and I was dreading her arrival. On her first day, she met with the young single staff ladies. The session lasted for several hours, and though I felt afraid throughout it, I was relieved that we all seemed to survive unscathed.

I couldn't have been more wrong.

The following evening, twelve of us were called to another meeting. We piled onto the floor of the dean's apartment, oblivious to the fact that our lives as we knew them were over. Then Mrs. Farnsworth arrived to deliver the news: Mother Betty had serious concerns about our spiritual growth after her meeting with us. She sensed that as a group we were too entitled, too self-centred, too ungrateful. Worst of all, we seemed to possess a desire for attention from men. We were called bitches in heat—a term that stung—even though I'd heard it hurled at other women so often.

I can still feel the ominous dread that settled over us as we sat, in shock, on the shaggy brown carpet of that third-floor apartment. We were being charged, condemned, and sentenced without a trial: "You ladies are being put on Boot Camp. Listen carefully as I explain."

The rules of life were as follows: All twelve of us would live together, under the supervision of Dale and Jan, two older single staff, who would sleep in the apartment bedrooms. We'd eat all our meals together, for the express purposes of light sessions. Our lives would be scheduled down to the minute. When we weren't at chant services or our jobs, we'd be working full-time on cleaning projects around campus. We wouldn't celebrate Christmas or exchange gifts with anyone, not even family. No TV, music, or reading was allowed. Shopping or spending money was forbidden, unless specifically sanctioned. No showers or baths were allowed, either. Instead, we'd be taking sponge baths in assigned areas within the girls' dorm.

I could hardly believe my ears. *What fresh hell is this?* (Is what I would have thought if I'd been cool enough.)

In addition, we'd be moving into the apartment where we were sitting. Each night, we'd move aside the living-room furniture and set up army cots and our green North Face survival sleeping bags—the ones we'd been forced to purchase in preparation for the End Times. Each of us was also given one cardboard box for our belongings. We were told to bring only two outfits, plus pyjamas and underwear. No makeup, hair products, styling tools, or jewellery were permitted.

Right after the meeting, twelve old army cots made of wood and canvas were delivered to the dorm. They smelled of mildew and were a mystery to assemble. *How will I sleep on this?* I needn't have worried. I was about to begin living in a state of such chronic exhaustion that I'd be able to sleep standing up.

At 5:00 a.m. every morning, we were woken for exercise. We'd run laps in the gym, then take hasty, embarrassing sponge baths in our allotted locations. Along with two others, I was assigned the girls' laundry room dump sink. The act of standing there, in our underwear, awkwardly squeezing water onto our sweaty armpits, was beyond humiliating. "At least the boarding students aren't here to walk in on us," someone offered lamely.

I cringed at the idea. *Surely this will be over in a week or two. The students can't be allowed to see us like this!*

Dale and Jan lined up the most difficult cleaning jobs on campus. We scoured the boiler room's cinderblock walls, which were at least twenty feet tall and caked with decades of black soot and grime. Perched precariously on rickety ladders, we scrubbed the filthiest surfaces I'd ever tackled (apart from those dumpsters). The fact that we were cleaning next to the very boiler that had so often terrified us with visions of the fires of Hell wasn't lost on me.

There was no shortage of work for us. One day, we must have scrubbed at least thirty-five ovens, all over campus. On other days we could be found painting around the school: the dining room, the office-floor hallways, and even the stairwells. Staff members who were enjoying their break kept asking us why we were working so hard. But what could we say?

On Christmas morning, we each received a new red bucket and a sponge. "Merry Christmas, ladies!" our wardens trilled, laughing as if our gifts were an inside joke.

Yay, Merry Christmas, I thought gloomily, as I considered the dreadful possibility of the sponge bath rule lasting longer than one more week.

Every night I set up my army cot, stretching the canvas to form its rock-hard surface, and hoped for the oblivion of sleep. Despite the discomfort, I fell asleep quickly during those first few weeks. I'd never been so tired. Or so demoralized.

I was used to hard work, relentless light sessions, and deprivation. But the shame of looking my absolute worst every day was a cruel blow. Before, it would take me no longer than five minutes to curl my hair and apply enough makeup to make myself look decent. But never in my life had I been forbidden to groom myself. My hair was still short, and it looked terrible without a blow dryer, curling iron, and some hairspray. I'd show up at church, feeling like the ugliest woman on the planet. It didn't help that I was only allowed to wear the same two outfits. Growing up so self-conscious, I'd always dressed my absolute best. So it was beyond mortifying to show up in the same clothes day after day. I avoided Mark's gaze like the plague.

When will this discipline be over? I'd think. Most of the other women agreed that there was no way it would continue once the students returned from break. But as the end of our holiday approached, my hopes about the end of our boot camp dwindled. Our light sessions were getting increasingly intense, and I had an ominous feeling that things were only going to get worse.

Unfortunately, I was right.

Just before the students returned, we were informed that every aspect of Boot Camp would continue, including rules for clothing and grooming. "How are we supposed to take sponge baths in the students' laundry room?" I asked, horrified. We received only a vague exhortation to pray about it, and God would provide us moments of privacy.

Weeks turned into months. Every aspect of our lives was drudgery and degradation. I was acutely aware of students watching us, taking note of our fall from grace. At Grenville, students noticed everything. We were used to looking professional. Several women in our group were teachers; the rest of us worked in offices, dealing with students all day long. We couldn't escape their scrutiny. I got sick and tired of deflecting their questions, like, "Why are all of you living together in the same apartment now?" and, "Why are you always wearing the same thing?" and, "Did you change your hair?"

The only way to survive was to submit. If we ever asserted ourselves, we were punished. Permission had to be granted for the tiniest privileges. Like going to town for necessities. And it was never a simple yes or no answer.

One time, in my frantic rush, I knocked my toothbrush into the toilet by accident. Shuddering, I fished it out and cleaned it thoroughly with dish soap. Even though the toilet had been full of clean water, I couldn't stand the idea of putting it in my mouth.

Filled with dread, I approached my Boot Camp leaders to ask permission to accompany the students on their Saturday trip into town, explaining why I needed a new toothbrush. Their response was predictably frustrating: "Have you prayed about this yet? Are you certain that God wants to expose you to all the temptation that awaits you in town? You need to spend more time asking God to reveal His will, and then get back to us."

Their words left me consumed with self-doubt. *Am I being too entitled, asking to buy a new toothbrush? Is it even worth it to go through all this fuss?* Unsure, I followed orders and prayed. But as usual, I got no reply from Heaven. What bugged me most wasn't the fact that I was being told to pray about something so inconsequential, but that God didn't think I was worthy enough to make Himself heard.

Finally, I decided to tell Dale and Jan that God had made it clear to me: it was His will for me to get a new toothbrush. Reluctantly, they allowed me to go into town on Saturday. Only then, I was wracked with guilt about lying. *Who am I kidding? God never spoke to me!*

†

There was no reprieve that year. I felt my spirit break a little more each day. One night, while lying on my rock-hard cot, I couldn't sleep, despite my bone-deep exhaustion. Tears blurred my vision as I looked hopelessly out the window at the large stone cross shining like a bright beacon from the top of the school's main building. Despair engulfed me. *Is this all there is? Does God love me at all? Do I even matter?* I couldn't bear to consider the answers. By that point, I hadn't seen much of Mark over the past few months. I was too embarrassed for him to see me.

And then one day, Mark was gone for good. After he escaped (without a word to me), I learned he'd been enduring his own private Boot Camp since Mother Betty's visit. I never found out what it entailed, but I was certain it must have been brutal. What else would cause my thoughtful, earnest, hilarious not-quite boyfriend to disappear without a trace? I was left despondent and heartbroken.

Of course, I wasn't allowed to wallow. Dale and Jan made it clear to me that Satan was using Mark to tempt me away from God's call. "Put him out of your mind, Beth!" they said. "Don't even let yourself think about him!" So, I suffered silently, never telling anyone how much I missed him. How much I worried about him and wondered where he was. How much I despaired that I'd be single forever, living like a beast of burden who didn't matter to anyone.

Winter changed to spring and then summer. All the while, we kept sleeping on those terrible cots, wearing the same two outfits, and looking like death warmed over.

As June approached, we all took part in a fundraiser for our new multimillion dollar church. It would be christened the Chapel of the Good Shepherd and it was a real showstopper. A quasi-cathedral that was our collective pride and joy. To help raise funds, we Boot Campers cycled for a three-day marathon after cold calling alumni and Grenville supporters. I hated begging for money. But I loved the cycling. We even got to stay in a motel where we slept in actual beds. When our leaders announced that we could use the showers, we all shrieked with excitement and disbelief. Never mind that the facility was shabbier than the Rosebud Motel. Under that dodgy shower head, I thought I'd died and gone to Heaven.

Even as summer unfolded, it seemed like Boot Camp would never end. All throughout July and August, we'd rise at 5:00 a.m. to exercise before a long workday commenced. Finally, as September drew near, it was announced that we'd be moving out of the crowded living room where we'd been sleeping for eight months. Boot Camp wasn't over; only our living situations were changing. We were allowed to sleep in real beds again! But my enthusiasm died when I learned I'd be sharing a bedroom with Dale, one of my Boot Camp wardens. *Great. Just great.*

Boot Camp lasted for an entire year. The leaders finally declared it over as the next Christmas approached. We joked that we should make t-shirts reading, *I survived 1995*.

Decades later, I look back on that year and wonder how I endured it. On one hand, it was so demoralizing that my spirit felt completely broken by the end. On the other, it strengthened our indoctrination. Not once during that year did I seriously consider leaving Grenville. I knew I was deeply unhappy, but I figured that was the sacrifice God required to truly live the Cross life.

What's even stranger is that I didn't realize I'd been given a way out. When my Grandpa Eustler died the year before Boot Camp started, I received part of his inheritance, which he had split equally between his children and grandchildren. The $40,000 fortune dazzled me. Still, I invested most of it, setting some aside for donations to our communities. Not once during that year from Hell did it occur to me that Grandpa Eustler had gifted me the funds I needed to leave Grenville.

When Boot Camp ended, I was proud of myself. I'd been tried by God, and I'd passed the test. Nothing would shake my resolve to honour my lifetime vows. But what I didn't realize was how deeply Boot Camp had hurt me. It had hijacked my capability to question others, to follow my intuition, to desire, to trust. It would take decades for me to undo this damage.

Unfortunately, Mark didn't get that luxury. I don't know what turns his life took after he left Grenville, since we completely lost touch. But I know now that just over a decade after his escape, he died by suicide.

Chapter 20
The Last Straw

In the aftermath of 1995, life seemed grand to me. I didn't mind the hectic pace or the never-ending demands. I'd survived a year of Boot Camp! *Time for another light session? Bring it on!*

I was also resigned to the idea that I'd probably be single forever. Still, I wasn't ready to take single vows, as many of our staff had done at the Community. The very notion depressed me.

By the time I was twenty-six, I'd taken part in far too many weddings as either a bridesmaid, a chorister, or a violist in our professional string quartet. The thrill of watching the bride appear in all her glory was being replaced by deep fear and longing. *What if I'm never a bride? I want a man to love me! I want to prove to the world that I'm worthy!*

Life became all about pushing those thoughts down. Instead, I focused on finishing my university degree and becoming indispensable in my jobs. No sense dwelling on what I couldn't have. Like a man. Or love. Or sex. Or babies. Or permission to drive.

Then one day, I was called to a meeting that left me discombobulated. Craig, a staff member eleven years my senior, was there with two senior staff members. Awkwardly, he declared that he felt God was calling us to start a relationship.

I was stunned—and not at all pleased. Craig worked in the finance department, and I'd been working closely with him for years. In no way did I desire his attention. He'd struck me as uptight, awkward, and legalistic.

Craig was, in many ways, the exact opposite of Mark. He'd never been a student at Grenville, and I cringed at the way he acted around teenagers. He seemed completely out of touch, and I understood why he was sometimes ridiculed. Also, the gruelling light sessions I'd endured about Mark were still fresh in my memory. Who in their right mind would submit to all that aggravation, for the sake of a person they didn't even like?

When I turned Craig's offer down, the other staff members intervened. "Beth, why don't you give this relationship a chance? It could be God's will. What have you got to lose?"

My dignity, I thought sardonically.

After offering several excuses as to why I didn't feel we should try dating, each of which was refuted by the other staff members, I reluctantly agreed to the idea.

What followed caught me truly by surprise. Over the next several months, my perspective on Craig transformed.

Craig's attention was like ice water in the desert. After enduring such intense deprivation during Boot Camp, I revelled in his thoughtfulness and affection. I'd find treats or love notes on my desk at work. He always wanted to spend time with me. He made it clear that I was important to him, and wasn't afraid to say it. "I just can't get enough of her!" he publicly declared one day. I couldn't decide if I was delighted or embarrassed.

As our relationship progressed, Craig became less uptight and more carefree. He'd openly flirt with me in the office, and we'd often laugh and enjoy each other's company during our workdays. I felt myself falling for him, even though he regularly exasperated me.

Half a year into our relationship, I wrote Craig this poem:

> When I complain, you're positive
> And when I'm cold, you're hot
> When I like noise, you turn it off
> Where I'm dramatic, you are not.

I gobble food, you take all day
Raw cookie dough's my downfall—
You take one look and say, "No way!"
When I'm upset, I rant and rave
But you're inclined to go and pray.

Seven months ago
I didn't think we'd stand each other
At least not for very long
I only gave your offer a try
If by some tiny chance I was wrong.

Well, I was wrong!
To think that now I miss you
After just one hour!
It's something I just can't explain—
To deny it—I have tried in vain.
You're very special to me Craig!
Despite our differences which are vast
I'm sure our friendship is meant to last.

Despite our progress, the process of dating at Grenville was still painful
and frustrating. We were chaperoned all the time, which seemed ridiculous, since Craig and I had worked in the same office for years. Even
worse, we were expected to confess any time we had dirty thoughts.
If I even let my mind drift to the mysteries of the marriage bed, I'd
feel compelled to admit it, and then suffer the humiliation of intrusive
interrogations. As a result, I tried hard to remain detached and keep my
thoughts pure.

After the first time Craig and I held hands, I wrote this in my journal:

He's been trying to hold my hand several times over the
last few months, and I never cooperated till this week.
Figured it wasn't worth having to confess it later. But

in the bus on the way to Toronto when he grabbed my hand, I gave in, and it was so worth it. He was so affectionate. We felt so close. It was hard to stop and has been difficult to lay off since. Sometimes it makes my insides curl up—a pretty nice feeling.

Just before I graduated from Queen's University in the fall of 1996, Craig proposed. By that time, I was quite sure I wanted to marry him. The alternative seemed far too bleak. So, I said yes. That night we went out to dinner alone for the first time. It was also the first time I'd ever been kissed, albeit awkwardly. I felt like I'd finally arrived.

Soon after our engagement, we travelled with Craig's brother, who was also on Grenville's staff, to Nova Scotia to spend Thanksgiving with his parents. I felt so free! We were trusted to spend time alone together. I can still feel my pulse race as I recall our first make-out session in his parents' house. Everyone else had gone to bed, and we were finding it difficult to head to our separate rooms. I'd never felt so desired.

Of course, we were expected to confess any time we dipped our toes into the forbidden waters of intimacy. Frustratingly, Craig would always beat me to it. Then I'd endure mortifying light sessions about suppressing my lustful impulses.

Tiptoeing through a minefield would have been easier than planning a wedding at Grenville. Especially since I constantly got in trouble for trying to be in control or desiring to be the centre of attention. Then there was the fact that I was obsessing about my weight more than ever.

Cracks began appearing in our relationship. Craig was having doubts. I was accused of living in unreality and was ordered to stop all wedding plans and let God dictate the timing. I begged God to help me let go of my desire for a beautiful wedding. But as I did that, I felt my fear rising. How many times had I yearned for things, only to have them taken away? My journal was filled with anguish as I grappled with my wedding-related sins:

> I've been forcing myself not to think about wedding plans, not to get upset or jealous of others' plans; not to

even want to make my own plans. I expect to be pretty much annihilated if people really knew how badly I want to jump into the whole process.

Around that time, my left knee mysteriously began hurting. It worsened quickly, and walking became excruciating. I'd often had knee pain during my teenage years, but this was disabling. Eventually, an orthopaedic surgeon confirmed that I needed surgery. And he warned me that I'd never again be able to do impact sports that involved running and jumping. *Great.*

I'd always relied on exercise to manage my weight or punish myself for bingeing. Being physically unable to participate in athletics spiked my fears about my body to an all-time high. I was so afraid that my skinny fiancé would be repulsed by me. Craig had been the source of so much comfort, telling me that my size was fine with him. But even his reassurance didn't seem up to the task now that I was sidelined and on crutches.

A month after the surgery, when it felt like our wedding was doomed, Craig and I were given the order to go ahead and make our wedding plans. I got excited again as we discussed dates. I even made plans to shop for a wedding dress. It all seemed too good to be true.

Then, a week after Valentine's Day, while my desk was still covered with his cards, flowers, and gifts, Craig announced that he wanted to break up with me.

He proceeded to close himself off, refusing to speak to me or make eye contact. I was completely shocked and heartbroken. It felt like I'd lost everything. My best friend, my hope for our future, my ability to breathe. Every moment was agony, especially since we worked in the same office. You could have cut the tension between us with a butter knife.

I had no idea why Craig broke off our engagement. He never offered an explanation. All I knew was I could hardly bear the rejection, the loneliness, the hurt. Sometimes I felt so angry at him that I lost my senses. One day, as I passed him in an empty hallway during March break, his refusal to look at me made me snap. I flung the contents of my hot cup of coffee at him. Immediately, I regretted my rashness. He acted like I was insane—I probably was—and continued to ignore me as we cleaned up the mess.

Over the next few months, I poured my grief onto paper. At one point, I wrote this:

> I feel like killing myself. I really do. I have never felt so utterly depressed in my entire life.

It took an entire year for the pain to subside. The whole time, I worked alongside Craig in the finance department, stoically enduring his indifference. I'd often cry silently at my desk, and he'd act like we'd never even been a couple. Eventually, I became so miserable that I lost my tolerance for nonsense. It was like Craig's rejection was the last straw. I'd always been held back by rules, decrees, and attacks about my sin, and I couldn't take it anymore.

One day, I was hauled into a light session with two women who worked in administration. One of them launched into a familiar diatribe about me being out of the spirit when driving with her the previous day. I was twenty-six years old, and I still hadn't been cleared to drive the school cars by myself. Meanwhile, all the staff men my age had been approved when they turned twenty.

Years of simmering fury now boiled inside me. The woman who was expounding about my so-called sin had complimented me while I deftly drove her family to appointments in Ottawa. Her duplicity enraged me. Unable to tolerate another second, I pushed my chair back, stood up, and glared at my accusers. "You are lying!" I heard myself scream. "Just yesterday, you were praising me for my excellent driving! I can't stand this anymore. I am so angry at the two of you! If I had a gun, I'd shoot you both!"

The two women stared at me, shocked. I glared back at them, shaking and feeling strangely triumphant. The ferocity of my rage amazed me. But I held my ground and refused to apologize.

That was a breakthrough moment. Within a few months, I was allowed to drive alone. I also began to question everything.

Ironically, the other thing that freed me was exercise. After months of rehabilitation from my knee surgery, I was advised to try aquafit. Since it was doctor's orders, I got special permission to attend classes at the local YMCA. My knee gradually got stronger, and so did the rest of my body.

Soon, I was attending all kinds of fitness classes. I delighted in the loud pulsating music, so forbidden in my life. The sweat, the endorphins, and the feeling of my muscles strengthening was so empowering. Six months after my surgery, I was several sizes smaller, and fitter than I'd ever been.

Despite this, I worried that the leaders at Grenville wouldn't let me continue my workouts in town. *What if I become a certified fitness instructor? Would they allow me to keep my membership?*

It didn't take me long to work up the courage. Promising to offer fitness classes at Grenville, I requested permission to get my certification. Amazingly, it was granted!

Soon enough, I earned my certification and started teaching step, Tae Bo, and aquafit classes at the YMCA, the Royal Brock Hotel, and Grenville. I delighted in my independence. Sure, my life was busy. But little by little, I was spending more time off campus, and I felt an intoxicating new sense of confidence.

Around that time, Father Farnsworth retired from his role as headmaster. I had the feeling it wasn't his choice. Either way, it was a relief for me. There was a sudden palpable sense of change at the school. Some rules were updated to boost declining enrolment. For instance, we were allowed to wear jeans! I got my first pair at the age of twenty-seven. (Of course, I endured a light session concerning the fit of mine.) Girls were also allowed to wear bathing suits without t-shirts and shorts! Staff were even allowed to buy their own cars! Not long after that last decree, I leased a brand-new black Toyota Corolla. With each new freedom, I found myself transforming. And as I spread my wings, I grew increasingly uncomfortable with life at Grenville.

The sense of suffocation was constant. I felt attractive and confident, and I wanted a man. I couldn't stand living in a three-bedroom apartment with eight other women. Nor could I tolerate the absurd criticisms launched at me during light sessions any longer. "Beth, are you letting your hair grow? Have you gotten permission? Do you really think it's God's will?"

For the first time ever, words like these made me angry instead of paralyzing me with dread. But I'd keep my disdainful reactions to myself. *Do you know how idiotic you sound? If it's not God's will for my hair to grow, then I really don't care.*

Incomprehensibly, fourteen months after Craig broke off our engagement, he met with me in the presence of two A-team members and begged me for another chance, saying he'd been wrong to break things off. I was flabbergasted. By then, my feelings for him had dissipated. What bugged me even more was that he wanted me back after my recent weight loss. His previous behaviour had been so hurtful and inexplicable that I had no desire to give him another chance.

After that conversation, I vented to my journal:

> I can't believe that he actually asked me to marry him after fourteen months of being virtual enemies! Don't ask me what he was thinking. Anyway, he's been pestering me with gifts, cards and treats. I must be strong in resisting him. I will not marry an idiot!

Craig wouldn't take no for an answer. For months, he tried to win me back. He was so relentless that I nearly conceded. But his awful treatment of me during our breakup was so fresh in my memory that I could never forgive or trust him.

Still, I knew that by rejecting Craig, I'd remain a spinster staff member, most likely forever. I wrestled with this knowledge, and my discontent reared its ugly head constantly. Eventually, I came to a frightening conclusion: *If I can't get married here, I don't think I want to stay.*

Even as I repeatedly turned Craig down, I ached with loneliness and a growing need to break free. Here's what I wrote in my journal:

I am a caged animal inside. I feel like tearing down the bars of my cell constantly. I want to run wild and free. I am full of desires. There's a terrible war inside me. Things I used to enjoy hold no excitement anymore. What am I going to do?

I began following my intuition, and little by little I broke free in my own ways. I'd listen to popular music in my car. I made friends with my fellow fitness instructors. I'd buy worldly clothes that made me feel attractive. I even visited with my wayward brother Dan, whom I'd been taught to shun.

During one such visit, Dan persuaded me to go out clubbing. Initially, I was fearful. But soon after I entered the den of iniquity, the fear evaporated. I'll never forget the illicit pleasure of the music thumping, the strobe lights, the bodies moving so freely in the dark. I let myself go, allowing the music to take over my body. It seemed as natural as breathing. I felt sexy, strong, and daring. At one point, a stranger moved in behind me and I let him press his body close. I'd been aching for a man's arms, so I dropped all inhibitions and revelled in our mysterious intimacy.

That experience changed me. Every chance I got, I'd sneak off campus, after all of my apartment mates were asleep. I'd change into my sexy clothes—jeans and a black tank top—and head to Bud's on the Bay in Brockville. Without a drop of alcohol, I'd dance with abandon by myself, tapping into a secret magnetism that seemed to attract strangers from the sidelines. Men who couldn't keep their hands to themselves told me that I was a fantastic dancer, that they couldn't take their eyes off me, that I was beautiful. Whenever the music slowed, they'd hold me tight, rocking back and forth. Sometimes tears would slide down my cheeks as I experienced the forbidden pleasure of being desired.

I was extremely lucky that I didn't get assaulted. At age twenty-eight, I was ignorantly putting myself in harm's way time and time again. More than once, I drove men home if they were too drunk to drive, then I'd have to extricate myself as they tried to undress me or themselves. I had no clue what I was doing. I'd never had any sexual education, and I didn't know anyone I could confide in. There was no internet, no way to learn what I needed to know.

Also, each time I snuck out from Grenville, I'd creep back in during the early morning hours reeking of cigarettes (gasp!) and hide my clothes where no one would smell them. A few hours later, I'd be dressed in my Sunday best, attending choir practise before church. One time, Mrs. Ortolani exclaimed, "Why does it smell like smoke in here?" I shrugged, pretending to be disgusted—and hoping she wouldn't get too close to my hair.

Thrilling as my secret escapades were, I couldn't stand living a double life. I was plagued by guilt and shame over my shocking behaviour. It also didn't take a genius to realize the bonds I'd make on the dance floor were fleeting and offered no real connection.

For the first time in my life, I was living against God's will, but I didn't care to change. It wasn't worth it to confess my terrible secrets. I knew the punishment that awaited me, and I wasn't prepared to subject myself to that treatment. I now saw myself as a black sheep in a white flock.

I can't keep up this charade forever.

But what choice do I have? I'd think. *If I leave, I'll be without a salary, a home, any friends, and most of my family. I'll be turning my back on God and breaking my lifetime vows. Also, I'll go to Hell.*

I was so inexperienced that I still hadn't realized my inheritance from my grandfather—which had grown, thanks to the investments I'd made—was waiting to rescue me. *Homes and cars cost far more than the money I have. What good is $45,000?* I would think.

For months I agonized over my future. Finally, I wrote a letter to Grenville's administration, revealing that I was deeply unhappy and didn't feel I could keep living in accordance with our vows. Knowing that I possessed specialized training in the financial office, I made a daring proposal. I asked that the school allow me to move off campus, let me keep my office job, and triple my salary.

For three agonizing weeks, I waited for a response, hoping that my audacity wouldn't result in a direct lightning strike. Eventually, two members of the A-team met with me to convey the news: they had agreed to my terms! I could hardly believe my good fortune.

The only reason my request was granted was, unbeknownst to me back then, several other staff members were considering leaving. My proposal had come at a time when the administration was worried about keeping the school running with its remaining residential staff.

For the next two years, I lived with one foot in, and one foot out. By day, I worked at Grenville; and by night, I delighted in my partial freedom. What I craved, though, was connection. With friends, a man—anyone, really. I'd walk the streets of Brockville, looking longingly at homes. *I wonder if I'll ever live in a house. Or have a family. Or friends who care.*

Dancing by myself—and with men I didn't know—lost its appeal. So I kept searching. Surprisingly, I found belonging in the unlikeliest of places.

My love of horses propelled me to call a local ranch I found in the Yellow Pages. The man who answered sounded like a cowboy from the Wild West. "We ain't in the trail-riding business since the Ice Storm, but you get your white ass on out here and we'll get you on a horse!"

Laughing, I took him up on his offer.

Bob Perkins and his friends welcomed me with open arms. In no time, I was surrounded by his beer-drinking neighbours and trail-riding with him on weekends and even by moonlight.

Bob was unlike anyone I'd met before. He looked like he'd walked right off the set of a Western, moving with the swagger of a man who wasn't afraid of anything. His swearing would make my toes curl. I often told him that his appalling grammar hurt my ears. Whenever I used fancy vocabulary and he followed suit, we'd exclaim, "Bobby said a big word!" and nearly fall off our horses in laughter.

I started spending all my free time at Bob's place. Whenever I wasn't there, he'd call me, and his first words were, "Comin' out?" We'd talk into the wee hours, drinking endless cups of Maxwell House. Despite our fourteen-year age difference and our backgrounds that were worlds apart, we developed a deep connection. Bob had four children from two previous marriages and wasn't interested in tying the knot again. Still, a few months into our friendship, he told me, "Lady, I'd marry you in a heartbeat."

Eventually, I moved into Bob's farmhouse. Explaining that to my parents and colleagues was terrifying. In my imagination, I'd sunk from being a black sheep to a harlot who was contaminating the school's holy halls.

Little did anyone know that Bob was waiting patiently to consummate our relationship until I was ready. It was like he instinctively knew how to handle a twenty-nine-year-old virgin with care. For six months, we slept side by side, lovingly spooning together, before I felt prepared. All the while, he challenged me to confront my beliefs, my shame, my fear of Hellfire. Gently, he helped me to question and cut chains that bound me to my past. Whenever I fretted over my future, my career, and my worries about breaking all ties, he'd exclaim, "Lady, you don't owe that place one fucking thing!"

It was difficult to believe that. Up until then, I felt nothing but obligation to Grenville. I was so indoctrinated that I could hardly forgive myself for moving away. I craved the security of my job there. I worried about going to Hell, since I knew I'd strayed too far to ever go back.

As this was happening, Father Farnsworth was still actively involved in members' lives, even though he was retired. He cornered me one day and delivered the lecture I'd been dreading: "You know you're sacrificing your eternal salvation. But it's not too late to move back and make amends. God can forgive anything if you're willing to repent."

Surprising myself, I found the strength to tell Father Farnsworth my truth: "I can't move back now. Too much has changed for me. If God loves me, then He will help me find my way. If not, I'll do it without Him."

After that conversation, I knew there was no going back. Little by little, Bob helped me imagine a future apart from my past. His friends, who called me The Flying Nun, were always popping in unannounced. One day, one of them asked, "Why don't you become a teacher? You'd be perfect! Just go back to university for your Bachelor of Education. It's only a one-year program."

This was news to me. It didn't take me long to decide to become a teacher, as I'd always dreamed. Within a year, the trajectory of my life was completely altered.

I gave my six months' notice to Grenville, renounced my vows to the Community, and threw my gold cross ring into the St. Lawrence River. I also got accepted into the faculty of education at Queen's University and moved away from Bob. With my Grandpa's inheritance, I bought my own house and paid my way through a year of university, graduating debt-free.

In the end, Bob and I weren't meant to stay together. Our breakup was as agonizing as it was necessary. For two years, he'd been my best friend, my love, and a voice of reason. He welcomed me into the scary outside world and helped me close the door on my former one. I'll always cherish him for this.

Weirdly, I also have Craig to thank. If I hadn't sampled the sweetness of being loved, I never would have been so miserable without it. He gave me that first taste, however fleeting. And the fact that he withdrew it was a blessing in disguise. Without that heartbreak, I might never have become aware of the deep misery that permeated my life and doomed my future.

Paradoxically, our breakup had the opposite effect on Craig. He eventually moved to the Community and became a monk. He is still there today.

PART TWO

"My tongue will tell the anger of my heart,
or else my heart, concealing it,
will break."
William Shakespeare

Chapter 21
Freedom?

The next few years were a whirlwind. With my exit from Grenville complete, I was determined to succeed in the outside world, despite the dire warnings I'd heard all my life. At age thirty-one, I had a lot of catching up to do. So I hit the ground running.

At university, I was laser-focused on becoming the best teacher I could be. When I began to practise teaching in public schools, I found I was a natural. I was terrified, of course. But it was almost a relief to realize that in a classroom, there are so many needs to be met that one doesn't have time to dwell on anything else. Fortunately, I sensed that the kids loved me, and I instinctively loved them right back.

Teaching required all my talents. It was like I got to unpack each one from a long-lost storage locker. *Welcome back, artistic, dramatic, musical, academic, fun-loving Beth! Where have you been all this time?* Little by little, I got reacquainted with all the parts of myself I'd buried during my years at Grenville.

One month after earning my Bachelor of Education, I received a call that I'll never forget. The principal explained that out of seventy-five applicants, I was one of five selected to be interviewed. Heart hammering, I tackled my first-ever interview with all the enthusiasm and hope I held for my future. Despite my nerves, a strange peace descended over me as I answered every question posed by the panel of principals.

Two days later, I received another call. "Beth, we want to offer you a full-time contract …"

Yes! Yes! Yes! When I hung up the phone, my hands were shaking and tears were streaming. *OMG! I'm going to be a teacher!*

My social life didn't unfold as easily as my teaching career, however. After I left Bob, it felt like I was entering the outside world on my own all over again. Weekends stretched out in an eternity of loneliness. Sure, I had mountains of schoolwork to do. But the isolation of living by myself tormented me. Much as I enjoyed my independence, part of me kept wondering what my former friends were doing. I'd picture them so busy at Grenville, surrounded by like-minded people. Free as I was, I missed being part of their elite group.

Christmas is especially brutal when you're alone. I felt like I didn't belong anywhere. One year, my younger brother Rob made a rare trip back to Brockville to join me. Our parents, who lived ten minutes away, didn't invite us to join them, as their lives didn't seem to include outsiders. With no family but each other, we resorted to a strange evening of church hopping, attending three consecutive services in an aimless search for comfort or connection. We found neither. I went to bed that Christmas Eve feeling so lonely that my chest ached.

Late one night, while lying on my secondhand couch watching mindless TV, I saw a commercial for Quest Personals. It seemed like it was aimed directly at me. Curious, I fired up my high-pitched screaming modem.

People today complain about the hardships of online dating. Imagine doing it with dial-up internet! I'd wait for photos to appear on my monitor, one agonizing centimetre per minute. For a year, I bravely sifted through inquiries (deleting any with poor grammar), chatted with strangers, and met men I barely knew. The main problems I encountered, aside from a lack of chemistry or shared interests, were that the guys I met were afraid of long-term commitment. I was hoping to get married and have children, not just dating for the hell of it. (Yes, swear words had entered my vocabulary by then. I blame Bob.)

When I was just about to give up entirely, I received a message from a man whose profile mentioned his desire for long-term commitment. Even better, he could form complete sentences. There were no pics, but I replied anyway. We got chatting, and despite my intention to quit online dating, I became intrigued by him. When we first talked on the phone, I was relieved that his voice wasn't weird (as so many seemed to be) and we talked effortlessly. Soon, I was dating Garry, a six-foot redhead with kind eyes. Strangely, he felt like home to me.

Over the next two years, Garry and I visited Grenville for occasions like Christmas and Easter. It was my hope to keep things friendly between the people in my new life and those from my past. More importantly, I was determined to prove to Garry that Grenville wasn't a cult. (He'd mentioned my background to a few of his detective colleagues in the Ottawa Police Force, and one of them had casually replied, "Grenville? That place is a cult.") When Garry asked me about this, I scoffed and said, "Lots of former students say that because they're bitter. It's just a nasty rumour."

After Garry's first church service at Grenville, Father Farnsworth spoke to him briefly, but enough to leave an impression. "Beth," Garry said, "there's something sinister about that man."

I couldn't argue with that, though I thought Garry might have been exaggerating. Still, I hoped he'd see that my former home wasn't some weird religious sect. Outsiders couldn't possibly understand the life I'd once led, most of which I considered extraordinary. I wanted to remain proud of my upbringing and elite education. Especially since I still felt so guilty for leaving.

On June 13, 2003, I was asleep, exhausted after teaching all week and driving seventy-five minutes to his house for a weekend visit. Afraid of proposing on Friday the thirteenth, Garry waited until two minutes after the clock struck midnight to ask me his burning question. Groggy and blurry-eyed, I happily agreed to marry him.

As if that wasn't enough excitement, Garry had secretly bought the gorgeous brick Victorian with a wrap-around front porch that we'd been drooling over for months. He kept the purchase a secret, citing endless reasons why we shouldn't buy it. But later on the day he proposed to me, Garry revealed the purchase agreement—which was $30,000 below the asking price! Within two months, we each sold our own starter homes and moved into our dream house. I couldn't believe I was living there.

Six months after Garry proposed, we got married. Guess where we held the wedding?

I cringe whenever I recall the unease I felt throughout the ceremony. Every bride wants to celebrate with friends and family. Since most of mine still lived at Grenville, it seemed logical—and cheaper—to hold the wedding there. I even asked two women who were Grenville staff members to be my only bridesmaids.

Getting married at Grenville turned out to be a mistake. Another misguided attempt to secure the validation I'd so often craved growing up. The December wedding was beautiful, just not enjoyable. I felt uncomfortable the entire time, as if I didn't belong. (Probably because I didn't.)

Almost a year later, I gave birth to a perfect baby. When, through a haze of indescribable pain and exhaustion, I heard the doctor announce, "It's a *girl!*" I was overwhelmed with relief and delight. Images of a future raising my precious daughter flooded my mind, erasing the agony of childbirth. The love I felt for my little Victoria nearly took my breath away. On that first night, just hours after her birth, I lay on my side and cradled her to my chest, softly singing Christmas carols to soothe her to sleep. Tears of joy slid down my face as I took in the wonder of her.

Parenting proved more difficult than I'd expected, especially since Victoria never napped. (I'm not exaggerating.) Regardless, I threw myself wholeheartedly into mothering and attempting to lose the horrifying thirty-seven pounds I'd gained during pregnancy. That was more challenging than ever before. I was so sleep-deprived that I craved sugar around the clock. I was terrified that I couldn't control my cravings. *Not this* again!

Eventually, I joined a local group of moms subjecting themselves to Baby Boot Camp and began the punishing process of reclaiming my value. Then, just before returning to work, I joined a local gym and let the familiar shame wash over me as the intake trainer weighed and measured my body. Several mornings a week, I'd rise at 5:30 a.m. to work out at the gym, then feed my baby, shower, get myself and Victoria ready, pack lunches, drive her to daycare, and commute forty minutes before the school day began.

Eighteen months later, when I shared the exciting news that I was pregnant again, my trainer exclaimed, "You're going to gain all the weight back that you just lost!"

Thanks for reminding me, I thought before wondering, *Did she really just say that out loud?*

Two years after Victoria was born, I gave birth to another perfect baby—this time a boy. His sweet face, framed by a full head of brilliant red hair, melted my heart all over again. It felt like my capacity to love doubled in size as I gazed at William. His big sister felt the opposite way, scowling in our first family portrait taken that day. (That photo remains one of my all-time favourites.)

My life felt complete. I had a dream family, a dream house, and my dream job. Everything seemed too good to be true.

Still, cracks were appearing. I couldn't shake a perpetual feeling of unease. It was nearly impossible to enjoy living in my new house, where I felt like an imposter. *Don't get used to this, Beth. It won't last. You'll have to move any day now.*

I craved a sense of belonging. After growing up in a community of hundreds of like-minded followers, I felt empty and isolated. It didn't help that I had no friends. When I left Grenville, I effectively cut ties with the only people I'd ever known. I was so used to the connection that bound us through faith and steadfast commitment, which didn't seem to exist in the outside world.

For a while, I went church shopping, desperate to fill that void. But each church's music and sermons seemed like dull milk toast compared to the ones at Grenville. Our services had been showstoppers, full of pomp and pageantry. There was nothing like them in the outside world. Plus, I couldn't stop crying. *What's happening? Why these tears?*

For several years, I dragged my little ones to an Anglican church where at least the lead musicians were good. I tried hard to forge a connection with the members there. But most of the time, the entire enterprise was fraught with turmoil. Just getting the kids and myself all dressed up was a huge pain. Especially when I was exhausted from teaching full-time and needed the chance to slow down on the weekends. (Fun fact: teacher parents never actually slow down on weekends.) It didn't help that Garry refused to attend church more than a few times a year. Then there was the inner torment I experienced every time I went to church. At best, I felt numb; at worst, I felt rage or grief. Tears threatened so often that I'd sit in the pew, wondering why the hell I was bothering.

The church conundrum was put on hold when William turned four and started hockey. His weekend practises made attending services nearly impossible. I decided it was a sign. Little by little, we morphed into the kind of family I'd judged my entire life. One that only attended church on Christmas and Easter. I worried terribly about the fate of our souls. Was I condemning my kids to Hell?

†

At work, I was overwhelmed by the pressure I put on myself. I figured every teacher felt that way. Every day, it seemed like I was required to guide thirty vulnerable children up Mount Everest on my first attempt. My heart would race all day, seemingly fuelled by adrenaline and fear. *What if they figure out that I'm not good enough? That I'm too haughty? That it's not God's will for me to be teaching?*

Without realizing it, I became an overcompensating, validation-seeking missile. My students were going to succeed, even if it killed me. Luckily, I instinctively knew that children do best when they feel encouraged, loved, and inspired. My goal was to generate as much fun and excitement during school as possible. My mind was always racing, concocting innovative ways to teach everything from phonics to probability. (Have you ever walked into a classroom where the eight-year-olds are grouped around card games, yelling, "Hit me!"?) As much fun as we had, the endgame was all about performance. My students were going to shine.

My need to impress my principals and the administration at the board level was desperate, and the fear that I wasn't good enough plagued me constantly. During my first performance appraisal meeting, I experienced my first-ever migraine, and escaped the principal's office just in time to vomit. When I contracted pneumonia during my first year of teaching, I was too afraid to use my sick days. Instead, I kept working, feeling like death warmed over, and coughing my lungs out. (As a result, I had recurring bouts of pneumonia for years, and even suffered a cracked rib and partially collapsed lung from my racking cough). Whenever I got the courage to take a sick day, I'd beg Garry to make the call. I couldn't handle the anxiety of telling my principal that I needed to miss a day.

Over the years, I'd lose the capability to think or breathe during one-on-one meetings with my principals. If they ever questioned me, panic would rise within me, tears would burst, and I'd hyperventilate, often in their presence. It was humiliating. I'd avoid my principals as much as possible, over-functioning to prevent potential judgement or criticism.

I like to think that the years I spent in overdrive benefited my students at least. They always exceeded my expectations on the dreaded provincial tests. I strove to bring out the best in them and help them discover their talents: singing, dancing, painting, playing sports, and even creating comics.

One of the most exciting discoveries early on in my career happened at a workshop about teaching Shakespeare's works to children. I was hooked instantly—and even better, my students took to Shakespeare like ducks to water. They loved the intrigue, the drama, the intense emotions, the plot twists. The class would take on all the parts, reading with such drama that they begged for more. Their journals came alive. Even boys who hated writing would depict the fight scenes with hilarious speech or thought bubbles. After recess, when I'd race back into the classroom, my students would chant, "Shakespeare! Shakespeare! Shakespeare!" and hold their books or journals above their heads in a collective begging session. I'd laugh, promising that we'd get back to Shakespeare once we finished whatever required subjects were on the schedule. At one point, I filmed the students chanting, figuring no one would believe me. (I still marvel at that precious footage.)

Soon, I was creating scripts, using original dialogue from *Romeo and Juliet*, *Twelfth Night*, and *A Midsummer Night's Dream*. The narrators were like hosts on *Entertainment Tonight*, delivering the latest shocking news, while reporters would stand on the scene, introducing the unfolding drama. It was a winning formula. To start, my students performed live at a Shakespeare festival for kids.

Next, I got the idea to turn their performances into movies. I'd never made videos before, but soon I was making forty-minute films, with pop music and green-screen technology for added pizzazz. I also started a Shakespeare club and invited students from other grades to join. During recess, my classroom would be full of kids practising Shakespeare. Students from other classes would greet me with, "Can I join your club? What play are we doing next year?" The delight they experienced was infectious, and I felt like I'd finally found my true calling.

For several years, instead of relaxing with my family during weekends and breaks, I'd sew costumes, paint sets, and edit movies. I was living life at the speed of a galloping racehorse. My students were featured on the front page of our local newspapers in all their Shakespearean glory. The director of education's media team filmed me and my students for his annual video report to the Ministry of Education. A representative from Canada's Shakespeare mecca even invited me to present at the annual Stratford Festival Teacher's Conference.

Soon after, I received a letter from my school board's director of communications that praised my accomplishments. The letter had been carbon-copied to Mrs. M—my principal—and the director of education. Through happy tears, I read his glowing words that filled me with unfamiliar pride:

> I am thrilled to write this letter to you because it is a written recognition of the tremendous work you do in your classroom every day of the school year. Beth, you are one of a kind in our school board. I say that with

complete respect and sincerity ... Congratulations for engaging your students at such a young age to make that connection to literacy that will benefit them for the rest of their lives.

It was all so exciting, and I got caught up in the whirlwind with a passion I didn't know I possessed. Whenever I thought I couldn't keep up, my students would surprise me with their astonishing enthusiasm, and I'd be compelled to push forward, my inspiration renewed.

I navigated those Shakespeare years with all of the passion I could muster, completely oblivious to the fact that soon, it would all come to a crashing halt.

†

Another issue reared its ugly head again shortly after I got married: my binge cravings. It seemed that my head was full of battles between opposing voices.

Beth, look at your gorgeous house! You have so much to be grateful for!
Yes, it's gorgeous, but I need chocolate right now.
Look at your adorable children! They're everything you ever wanted!
Yes, but I need junk food in huge quantities—immediately.
Beth, you have the career of your dreams! It brings you such satisfaction!
Yes, but I feel like there's not enough food in the world to satisfy me.

No matter how hard I tried, I couldn't escape the overwhelming urge to binge. As soon as the teaching day was over, the battle would begin. The forty-minute commute didn't help. Whenever I ate junk food, shame would take hold and plunge me into such excruciating despair that I needed more food to numb the pain.

Nothing made sense. Why, when my life seemed so perfect, was I still so plagued by the need to escape and self-soothe? I figured something evil was lurking inside me, determined to sabotage my life. So I turned to exercise, self-help books, and new diets. I locked up all carbs and gave Garry the key—and my credit card. But no matter what I tried, I'd end up bingeing and feeling such intense self-loathing that I couldn't cope. Every morning after a binge, I felt like I was waking up at the bottom of a deep pit of despair. The shame was so debilitating that I'd exhaust myself trying to atone for my gluttony.

Finally, I began to share my pain with Garry. Utterly mortified, I'd confess my sins to him. He tried to give me comfort and advice, but it was beyond him. One day, as I sat on the living-room floor, my head hanging in shame and my body racked with sobs, he kindly stated the obvious: "You need help, Beth."

A long, frustrating search for a counsellor began. To save money, I started with therapists who were available through work's employee assistance program. During the initial interview, I met with an intake supervisor to match me with a therapist. "I don't mean to alarm you, but I'm afraid that our EAP program won't meet your needs," the supervisor said. "You might need therapy for the rest of your life."

I thought she was being dramatic.

After trying several different counsellors, the final one told me, "Beth, I think you need expertise that I don't have. You have a complex history, and I believe you need a psychologist who specializes in eating disorders and trauma."

By then, I'd realized that finding a good therapist was as tricky as dating. After a few more dead ends, I found a clinic in Ottawa that was owned and run by a married couple who were both psychologists. It offered the lifeline I needed. After a battery of tests and interviews, I was diagnosed with PTSD and bulimia nervosa. These diagnoses were a relief, though I didn't understand the magnitude of the recovery that lay ahead.

What I genuinely needed was therapy twice a week. As it was, I could hardly afford to see a psychologist once a month. Still, I found immense comfort, compassion, and hope as soon as I started receiving expert treatment. During one of my first sessions, Dr. Jane said, "Beth, I'm not going to touch your eating disorder with a ten-foot pole. You need to stop trying to fix your eating. It's only a symptom of something much larger." While I didn't fully understand her meaning, it gave me such relief. *Is there a reason I binge apart from my hopeless gluttony?*

It quickly became clear that I had a long road ahead. Some days I wished I could move into my therapist's clinic. The weeks between visits felt like an eternity. My one-hour sessions flew by so fast that my psychologist hardly had time to help me address my day-to-day problems, much less peel back the layers of my past. Additional help was suggested, so I joined group classes that focused on bingeing. (We were ordered to eat a *lot*, which shocked me.) Soon afterward, I started seeing the clinic's psychiatrist, who would one day prescribe me anxiety meds. But that's a story for later.

All this treatment came at a cost. On top of the expense, I went from being afraid to take a single sick day, to working only part-time for six months: doctor's orders. It was humbling and scary. I didn't want to be a financial burden on Garry or be seen as a weak link at work. I was determined to heal—immediately.

Spoiler alert: that didn't happen.

Chapter 22
Shit Hits the Fan

In August 2007, when I was halfway through my second maternity leave, my mom called with shocking news.

Grenville's closing! It's gone bankrupt!

At first, a strange relief washed over me. Then worry struck. Over one hundred staff and staff kids still lived on campus. That meant a hundred people would have no jobs or housing. *It's not my concern anymore*, I'd remind myself. But I couldn't help fretting. My parents had accepted outrageously low wages for thirty-seven years in exchange for lifetime room and board. Now what?

Part of me empathized with the remaining staff. I kept my ear to the ground about a final closing celebration that was being planned. But the other part of me was tuning in to news from a very different channel.

Somehow, I heard about Factnet (Fight Against Coercive Tactics Network), a website where cult survivors shared their stories anonymously. Right after Grenville announced its closing, former students started posting on the forum in large numbers. Within weeks, thousands of posts were made under the category of Community of Jesus/Grenville Christian College.

What I found on Factnet stopped me in my tracks. Everything in my busy life came to a standstill as I sat, mesmerized by the words on my computer screen. Over the coming weeks I'd be continually pulled to the website like a force field, my overwhelmed brain spinning as I tried to take it all in.

Hundreds of survivors had gathered online, mustering the courage to share the pain they'd carried alone for decades. Everyone was looking for answers or searching for validation. In post after post, former students, writing under pseudonyms, uncovered the long-hidden abuses they'd experienced:

> I remember all the boys having to wake up in the middle of the night to suffer for the "bad attitudes" and "thought crimes" of a few of us. I was labelled one of the "worst children to ever grace the grounds of GCC" and "was solely responsible for bringing down the school spirit." I endured running around the track in the middle of many nights. The stars were the only happy thing. (hobart dishmachine)

> By the middle of my grade twelve year, though never breaking a single rule, I was beaten twice with the famous paddle, the second time while held down by three men and so deeply bruised, that the first person who saw me immediately vomited. (Dignity Quest)

> When FF [clearly Father Farnsworth] discovered I was gay, he continually referred to me as a mental defective and said being gay was an illness with a cure. FF convinced my parents to enroll me in a twelve-step "Become Straight" program. It was a year of incredibly painful hell-on-earth. I was treated worse than a piece of shit and made to feel that it would be better if I killed myself. In fact, FF told me that my family would be relieved if I moved away or died. (gayatgcc)

During my time at GCC I honestly never wanted to spend so much time in trouble. It made me very nervous at the time, to the point where I suffered from stomach ulcers, which I never had again after I left. Over the four years I was there, I felt that FF and other staff were trying to break me. The lasting effect of this treatment made me feel I was never good enough. (alwaysonD)

Letters were often read at the school. And they did not hide the fact. I remember FF standing in front of the whole school announcing how many times one student used the word "I" in the first page of her letter, then saying how self-centred this student was. (Tiny)

Repressed memories flooded my mind. Suddenly I was viewing the experiences I'd normalized with a new perspective, reading accounts of others' trauma while acknowledging my own.

If I hadn't been on maternity leave, I would have missed it all. In late August, teachers were already in their classrooms, gearing up for the next school year. But since I was off work, I continued skimming through the message boards like an addict.

When I read the following post, I started shaking:

Separating staff children from their families definitely happened at GCC. I always thought it was strange.

The biggest example I can think of is the day one of the staff kids was no longer with us. She had just disappeared from GCC, as though she had never existed. Rumours circulated that she had a "relationship" with a boy. As the months wore on it turned out that her parents had to relinquish their positions at GCC in order for her to come back from the Community. They got demoted in order to get their daughter back. It was SOOOO transparent to all of us at GCC what was going on. Especially when it was a member of FF's family who took over the relinquished position. To that daughter if she is reading this: you were being NORMAL. You did nothing wrong. I have always felt horrible about that incident and I had nothing to do with it other than that I was there, and paid attention. I have always wanted to say that to you. (tmw)

Someone had noticed my pain? I could hardly contain the relief as an unfamiliar sense of validation washed over me. I had no idea who had written it, but their words made a powerful impact. I kept reading, amazed by everyone's words. So many others had suffered like I had. My recurring nightmares also began to make sense:

I have nightmares that I'm not going to get to dinner on time or I can't manage to clean my room perfectly AND get the dorm duties done before flag raising. This is twenty years later! It's that constant fear of nothing ever being good enough which has now developed into some kind of obsessive-compulsive perfectionism. (former gcc grl)

My nightmares over the years (I left in '89) always revolved around being trapped and having no way of getting away and having no help. I am being terrorized and can't get away. (tmw)

With every post I read, my eyes opened wider, especially with the awareness of the damage that boarding students had sustained. Growing up as a staff kid, I'd always assumed they had it easy compared to me. After all, they got to go home on breaks and only attended Grenville for a few years.

The revelations on Factnet painted a different picture, though. Many teenagers who were normal kids when they arrived at Grenville had left shattered. Where they'd once had confidence, they were now full of self-loathing. Where they'd once had hope for their future, they were now crippled by self-doubt. Where they had once trusted others, they now felt closed off. Where they'd once had faith in God, they now struggled to set foot in a church.

Upon leaving Grenville, students had no way of processing what had happened to them. Most of their parents didn't believe the stories they'd shared. The brave kids who had run away from the school often found themselves on the streets, cut off from their families who wrote them off as spoiled brats, or worse. Many went off to university, where they lived so wildly that they eventually dropped out, then blamed themselves for ending up exactly as Grenville's leaders had predicted. Others seemed to have made it, but like me, they continued to experience psychological problems:

> I never found a therapist that could help me, so for many years I was stuck in survival mode and didn't even know how to find or trust anyone. Even when I had the opportunity to seek therapy, I have never been able to find someone that doesn't just sit there and listen in awe. Therapy has always seemed like me sitting there telling crazy stories that they can hardly believe. As far as life after leaving, it has included a series of abusive relationships, substance abuse problems to numb my pain, and being stuck in negative, failure thought patterns for years. I still have major issues trusting people. And I tend to have a complete shutdown response whenever I'm in a stressful situation. (dreamtruth)

Then I learned about several survivors who couldn't bear their pain any longer and had died by suicide.

The more posts I read, the more I understood how damaging our school had been. At Grenville, one often-repeated motto was, "We're going to break you down and build you up the Grenville way!" Now I realized that so many students had been stripped of their dignity, self-esteem, and peace of mind there. The public humiliations had traumatized those who had been singled out *and* those who had borne witness to them. A culture of paranoia had permeated our lives at Grenville, and every student had experienced it. The spy network had ensured that people were always in trouble, being accused of real or imagined sins. Disciplines had been cruel and unjust, and students had been treated like criminals with nowhere to turn. They couldn't even contact their parents. Their lives had been seriously impacted, even if they'd lived at Grenville for only a few months:

> When I first found this forum I was overwhelmed. Utterly stunned to learn there are so many of us out here suffering in so many ways from the abuse. For twenty-four years I thought it was just me and what I experienced was because of who I am. I taught myself that I was bad—too sensitive—too ugly—too everything that wasn't good. (purgatory)

> I am quick to jump on the defensive when people say certain things, such as "we need to talk" or "can you come to my office, I have something I need to speak with you about." I find those statements paralyzing. I do not go to church, and I avoid all forms of organized religion in every way, shape and form. (tmw)

> Grenville did not "fix" me. Instead, it "broke" me and certainly ruined my self-esteem, my ability to trust people and my opinions toward religion. I spent three years alone at GCC, without real friends, being told how to think and act and came out of that school in worse shape than when I went in. (Tinkerbell84)

The word *cult* also came up frequently. A connotation I'd once dismissed now revealed itself in all its ugly truth. When I researched the matter, I was struck by Dr. Michael Langone and Dr Louis Jolyon West's definition of a cult. Langone, the executive director of the

International Cultic Studies Association, and West, a psychiatrist and brainwashing expert, defined a cult as, "a group or movement exhibiting excessive devotion or dedication to some person, idea, or thing; and employing unethically manipulative techniques of persuasion and control ... designed to advance the goals of the group's leader, to the actual or possible detriment of members, their families, or the community." (West & Langone 1986, 119–120)

Yup. That sounds about right.

Dr. Steven Hassan, an expert on mind control, cults, and similar destructive organizations, opened my eyes further. His book *Combating Cult Mind Control* helped me see how closely Grenville and the Community controlled members' behaviour, information, thoughts, and emotions. For example, he explained that in authoritarian cults, regulation of an individual's behaviour includes control over their housing, clothing, jobs, schedules, rituals, and indoctrination. This is on top of the practise of public humiliation, punishment for conduct and sins, and the requirement to obey the leaders above all else.

When I considered the aspects of information control described in Hassan's book, there were endless similarities to how Grenville had operated on that front:

- "Cults deliberately withhold and distort information when recruiting." *Check.*
- "They limit access to information from the outside world since it's considered unhealthy and satanic." *Check.*
- "Members are forbidden to maintain contact with outside families or ex-members." *Check.*
- "Members are required to spy on each other and report misconduct." *Check.*
- "Information gained in regular confession sessions is used against members." *Check.*
- "Letters and phone calls are screened, and reading material is censored." *Check.*
- "Members are required to report thoughts, feelings, and activities to supervisors." *Triple-check.*

My mind reeled as I read examples like the following in which Hassan explained how cult leaders control members' thoughts and emotions:

> Cult leaders instill an "Us vs Them" mentality. Members are taught they shouldn't think for themselves, and they should accept the doctrine. There is excessive use of prayer, singing in tongues and chanting to block thoughts. Feelings of shame, guilt and unworthiness are promoted. Members are taught that there is no happiness or peace outside the group. Emotions are kept off balance. Members live with a constant fear of discovery and punishment by fellow members and leaders. Relationships are controlled and sexual feelings are suppressed. Regular confession of sins and wrong attitudes are required—which are then used against you. People are praised one minute, and tongue lashed the next, and are often punished for imagined sin. (Hassan 2015, 115–124)

The more comparisons I made, the more my eyes opened. It was like I could see clearly for the first time, and the view sickened me. I'd been raised in a destructive cult that had forced its beliefs and practises on hundreds of unsuspecting teenagers, many of whom were profoundly damaged as a result. This knowledge haunted me.

More and more truth continued to emerge online. It was as if Grenville's closing was finally giving former students the courage to speak. They craved connection, validation, and accountability. It became clear that the school could no longer ignore the collective pain and suffering it had caused. The question was, would they try to sweep it under the rug?

A grand closing weekend was planned for September of that year. Grenville billed it as a celebration where former students could gather, reminisce, and thank God for all the school had accomplished.

What people wanted was a public apology. Everyone online started speculating: *Do you think they'll apologize at the closing?* Most agreed that Grenville had little choice by then.

But who would apologize? And would it be sufficient? People would ask one another online if they were going to the ceremony. Some boldly said they wouldn't miss it. *Over my dead body*, others declared.

Many showed up for that fateful weekend. I was still nursing William, so he accompanied me as I navigated those halls that were so familiar and yet so foreign. Having lived at the school for three decades, I felt compelled to greet everyone I recognized. Grenville had taught me to be sociable. But that weekend, I didn't feel at ease. With every meeting, I'd wonder, *Are you a Grenville defender? Or were you victimized, too?* I also noticed hushed conversations everywhere, as though alliances were being drawn.

The tension at the school was palpable. I could tell the staff who lived there were on high alert, trying to protect the school's reputation. I also sensed that they didn't want to get anywhere near the controversy. One conversation with a former staff kid—whom I thought I could trust—told me everything I needed to know. She brushed off the online maelstrom by saying, "It's all a bunch of exaggeration. Students were never abused."

Well, that's the end of our friendship, I thought.

I chose my discussions carefully after that. At one point, I bumped into another former staff kid who was so visibly shaken that he couldn't bring himself to enter the school's buildings. We were instantly on the same page, overwhelmed by the ugly truth that was emerging. He told me, in hushed tones, that there would be a meeting in Brockville the following day for anyone interested in discussing a class action lawsuit.

My stomach dropped as I considered attending. *Has it come to this? If true accountability isn't taken, a lawsuit might be inevitable.*

That night, after a grand banquet and the kind of live entertainment only Grenville alumni could pull off, the dining room hushed as former principal and headmaster Ken MacNeil approached the podium. He looked subdued as he began what I hoped would be a momentous speech. Of it, I only remember nine words: "If we contributed to your hurt, I am sorry."

Huh? Is that it? It only approached an apology, and I felt completely let down. Where was the genuine admission of wrongdoing? Why did he make it seem like those who were hurt were somehow at fault?

Others also felt like MacNeil had missed the mark. Some took to the media. Soon after that weekend, our school was featured on front-page news across the country. Many survivors were interviewed, sharing stories of their abuse. But the interview that hit me like a gut punch was with Rev. Gordon Mintz, a former teacher and the school's final headmaster. In *The Globe and Mail*, he was quoted as saying that the "allegations of abuse were without foundation."

I felt gutted. *Why did he lie? Why the cover-up? He knows better!* Mintz had been at Grenville for over two decades and he had squandered the opportunity to take accountability, to show a shred of empathy. His words enraged me.

I wasn't alone. Others on Factnet had plenty to say:

> Do you know, "Rev" Mintz, who the father of lies is? Do we need to ask the Church Lady? Introduce you to the ten commandments? (papillon)

> Who are you kidding Mintz? You always told me to own up to things and be a man people would be proud of. It's your turn now. (bossman)

> Gord Mintz. Where do your convictions lie? If you continue to actively attempt to cover up the truth, I think you need to reconsider your role as a minister. (quietgrl)

The burden of my new perspective weighed heavily on me. I couldn't sit by and do nothing anymore. After more front-page headlines exposing shocking allegations about the cult leaders, I felt compelled to take a stand.

We began with the Anglican Church. At least forty of us requested personal hearings at the diocese in Kingston. There I met with the bishop, my priest, and a few church higher-ups to tell them about the abuse I'd experienced and witnessed. Not surprisingly, doing so triggered a lot of painful memories. *Why did I think I could handle a three-hour meeting surrounded by clergy?*

Soon after, I was struck by the following heartbreaking account on Factnet, written by a mother who had sent her daughter to Grenville. Once the scandals broke, she'd also accompanied her daughter to see the bishop. Her words opened my eyes even further:

> I can't express the agony which I felt when I sat with my daughter in the presence of Bishop Bruce, the executive and lawyer for the Diocese of Ontario. I thought I would vomit, became shaky and perspired, and felt like I was in a time warp. Everything was in slow motion as I heard my child describe the emotional and mental cruelty which she endured directly at the hands of FF and some of his staff. She was never allowed to keep friends. As soon as she felt close to someone and felt she could confide her fears to them, FF would address and berate her and tell her that she could no longer be in their company.
>
> I love my daughter more than life itself and had to sit with her while she told these men how FF tore her down, told her that no one could love her, that her family wished to be rid of her because she was such a bad person, that she was so damaged, even God could not love her.
>
> I was physically sick as was my daughter when our session was over, and both emotionally broken down. I feel for every one of you who has the courage to talk to the bishop, the newspaper and the police to share your stories. (familylove)

Skeptical that the church would do anything significant of its own accord, I joined conference calls with others who were considering a class action lawsuit. I spoke for hours on the phone with those who felt we had a case. With every conversation, the scope of the abuse and damage kept widening, and my jaw dropped further to the floor. Soon, three law firms were interested, and we were assured that our case was strong.

One of our potential lawyers had filed the Cloud class action in 1997 on behalf of all former students of the now infamous Mohawk Institute Residential School. In December 2004, the Ontario Court of Appeal had certified the Cloud class action with 80,000 potential claimants. After six months of negotiations, all parties had agreed to the largest abuse claim settlement in Canadian history. Of course, for those victims who, as children, had suffered through Canada's cultural genocide, the damages awarded were only the first step in an impossibly difficult process of healing and reconciliation.

Still, that win shed light on the type of systemic abuse that had been swept under the carpet for so long. It forced the government and the churches involved to take accountability for their part in the students' horrific treatment. It also gave voice to the traumatized, whose suffering would last a lifetime and affect generations to come.

Honestly, I didn't think our case could compare to the trauma suffered by the residential school survivors. But the lawyers we spoke with assured us that what they were hearing about Grenville was, in its own way, just as egregious.

A steering committee was formed. Our lawyers patiently answered the burning questions so many of us had during conference calls. Who would be named in the lawsuit? How much could this cost us? What about religious freedom? Was our abuse even illegal?

We were told that Grenville had breached its fiduciary duty of care—a serious violation that would be the cornerstone of our case. (Grenville owed a fiduciary obligation to its boarding students, since all control was handed over to the school by the parents of both paying students and the parents on staff.) Our lawyers couldn't hope to prove that the school's religious practises were abusive in and of themselves because religious freedoms cover a multitude of sins. *Huh. How ironic.*

Our lawyers also explained that a class action is a very slow process and could take years. Even just getting our case certified by the Ontario Superior Court of Justice would be a huge victory. There was also the chance that it might never make it to court, so we needed to seriously consider our motives. The journey wouldn't be easy, we were warned. The lawyers had seen plaintiffs who later wished they'd never come forward. So many obstacles would be in our way, including the cost of hiring representation.

But I'll never forget the hope Loretta Merritt, one of our potential lead lawyers, offered. She spoke of the power of validation that could be gained from being represented in court. I could tell that she cared about abuse survivors and recognized the value of being heard. She also told us about clients who had healed after being acknowledged by the courts. Settlements and payouts were, of course, distant possibilities. But I was convinced that if Grenville victims were to have a hope of closure and recovery, the justice system was our only resort.

We were tasked with drafting statements of experience. I wrote mine through intense tears, hating every minute of that daunting task. Each word was a painful reminder of a life I'd subconsciously buried. At that point, I couldn't dig very deep into my trauma. Still, the act of acknowledging the systemic abuse that took place at Grenville was a massive step for me.

During that time, I got reacquainted with many other former students. It shocked me how much Grenville's closing was derailing their lives. Seemingly successful adults were falling apart and needed to take extended leaves from work. It was like Pandora's box had been opened, and many couldn't escape the fallout.

One of these students had attended Grenville twice. Jacqueline spent one year there in kindergarten, but her mom pulled her out once she started having nightmares about Hell. Then she returned for grade twelve as a boarding student. Even though I was in her grade, I never had a clue what she suffered that year. And when Jacqueline called me up after the school's closing, she admitted she was afraid to do so. She'd kept her distance during grade twelve because I was a staff kid.

I laughed. "Don't worry. I'm afraid of most former staff kids too!"

We talked for hours that day, and we've been doing so ever since. Jacqueline wrote her statement of experience and shocked me with the details she recalled. Hers was forty pages long and represented one year at Grenville. My eight-page submission to represent thirty years paled in comparison. But that was all I could muster at the time.

When the legal team asked me to be one of the five representative plaintiffs, I was terrified and full of self-doubt. *Can I take this on? I'd be standing for everyone. Risking my financial future. Risking my relationships. Risking my peace of mind.*

Despite my fear, I felt a growing sense of conviction. My intuition kept saying that this would be the path to my healing. Sure, it would require bravery, but it would also force me to face my demons. So I took a leap of faith and said yes.

With that decision, I knew I'd be destroying countless friendships. I might even have to cut ties with family members. But I was prepared for that. Our relationships already seemed beyond repair. Earlier that year, when I asked my mother to watch Victoria so I could go to the hospital to give birth to William, she'd said she needed to pray about it and get back to me. As usual, her life at Grenville trumped anything happening in the lives of her children.

Not surprisingly, my parents were deeply upset by my decision. My brother Garth cut off all communication with me. Out of hundreds of former Community members, Grenville staff, and staff kids, I kept ties with only a handful.

At the same time, I gained a purpose. The opportunity to help forge a path toward collective healing felt like a gift. No matter the cost, it seemed to me a vital cause.

†

Our statement of claim was issued in the Ontario Superior Court of Justice in Toronto on January 17, 2008, seeking damages for psychological, physical, and sexual abuse. The defendants in the action were the corporation of Grenville Christian College, the Anglican Diocese of Ontario, Charles and Betty Farnsworth, and Al and Mary Haig. In the action, we sought a declaration that the defendants breached their fiduciary obligations owed to the plaintiffs in the operation of Grenville Christian College. We also sought compensation for breach of fiduciary duty, negligence, battery, and intentional infliction of mental suffering.

I had no idea how much this lawsuit would impact my life, or how it would drag on for years and challenge me more than I could imagine. It's a good thing I couldn't have predicted any of that. I'd never have said yes if I had known.

Chapter 23
Edge of Sanity

I spent the following years living on the brink of insanity, though no one would have known by looking at me.

For starters, helping spearhead a multimillion dollar lawsuit felt constantly overwhelming. As a representative plaintiff, it became commonplace for people to share their traumatic stories with me. I listened with shock and despair, adding each new account to my growing burden.

I met Vinny at a gathering in Toronto soon after we launched the lawsuit. A handful of us gathered in an upscale bar after we left the law firm. I was sitting there, battling with my doubts, when Vinny and I started chatting.

I asked him when he attended Grenville. The fact that he arrived in 1973, just months before the Mothers first arrived, got my attention. "Did you notice a change in the school after their arrival?" I was so curious to know if it was all in my head.

"Everything changed! By the fall of 1974, Grenville felt like a different place," Vinny said. He went on to describe how bizarre he found the light sessions. "On several occasions I was taken into a room and interrogated by a group of staff members. I never had any idea what I'd done wrong. They kept trying to find weakness in me and break me down." When he mentioned a huge light session that took place after the two-headed calf was born, my jaw dropped.

Memories came flooding back. "Vinny, do you mean I haven't dreamt that whole situation?"

"No, I remember it like it was yesterday. I was in the barn when a two-headed calf was born. Later that day, we were all called into the chapel. The first thing they said was that God had sent us a sign. We were being punished for the sins at the school. It was scary; they put so much fear into us. It ended up being a mass confession. One by one, students stood up and publicly declared their sins. After the meeting, which lasted forever, we were not permitted to talk to anyone for twenty-four hours."

I could picture it all. The mass meetings. My fear of the two-headed calf. And of Satan entering our school.

Vinny continued, "Then there were the disciplines. Once my punishment lasted for around three months. Every morning, I was sent to the barn at 5:30 to feed the animals and shovel manure before breakfast. After every meal, I was on dish crew. To this day I don't know what I did to get this discipline. I suppose it was to keep me away from the other students."

I imagined Vinny, a confused sixteen-year-old, and I knew exactly how demoralized he must have felt. But what he said next shocked me.

"Things only got worse that year. One day, during a light session, I was ordered to tell on my friend who had been smoking. I refused to rat him out. So they told me that God was directing them to punish me with the paddle. They ordered me to drop my pants and underwear in front of them, then to bend over and hold on to the chair in front of me. I was terrified. At that point, Mr. Ortolani swung the paddle like a baseball bat onto my bare behind. I still remember the sound it made, as if it happened yesterday. The pain was indescribable. I could no longer stand after the second hit, so another staff member, Mr. Childs, held me up while I was struck six more times. My skin felt like it was on fire, like they held a torch to it."

His voice broke as he added, "I can still feel the burning to this day."

Tears pricked my eyes as I took in his story. While I had always lived in fear of the dreaded paddle, I was stunned at what I'd missed behind those office doors.

"Vinny, I'm so terribly sorry," I managed, knowing my words weren't nearly enough. Curious, I added, "How did you cope? What happened next?"

"Well, after the beating, I ran away with my buddy in the middle of the night. We trekked through the dark forest and found the train tracks, but discovered there was no way to jump onto the passing trains. So we followed the tracks to Brockville and caught a bus to Parry Sound, a 500 kilometre trip. We hid at a friend's place for a few nights before contacting our parents. It took me almost two weeks to get home. When my parents saw the remaining black and blue marks and purple welts, they finally agreed to let me leave Grenville—but only if I agreed to return for two weeks to finish the semester."

I marvelled at his courage and told him so. "What was it like when you returned?"

Vinny almost laughed as he recalled those final weeks. "It was terrible. I was pressured by the headmasters into staying at the school until June. But my mind was made up. I still have a letter I wrote to my parents during this time. The last sentence of the letter reads, *See you in 381 hours and 15 minutes.*"

"You still have that letter? That's incredible!" He chuckled and assured me he'd made copies. Vinny went on, "Almost fifty years have passed. Yet there has never been a period in my life since leaving Grenville that I have forgotten what they did to me. Now that I'm an educator myself, I wonder—*how could someone do this to a student?*"

I shook my head. "I've been asking myself the same question." We both sat in grim solidarity, gazing out at the busy bar, lost in thought.

†

The collective pain of our past was so heavy I could hardly bear it. So instead of dwelling, I turned to the only thing I knew: escape. Instinctively, I spent every waking minute on a kind of high-speed treadmill, frantically trying to outrun my crippling anxiety. *Just keep racing! Whatever you do, don't let the pain catch up with you!*

Goal number one remained earning my worth. Therapy could barely begin to unravel my insatiable need to impress. Working in a school didn't help, either. I didn't realize how much it was triggering me all the time. I worried that my administrators and colleagues were secretly criticizing everything I did.

My worst fears were realized when my principal decided to shut down my Shakespeare program.

Three years after I joined the lawsuit, I made the grave mistake of confiding in my principal. Mrs. M had seen me crying far too often to ignore the issue anymore, and I felt I had to explain why I was such a mess. She seemed sympathetic and invited me to vent in her office whenever necessary. A few times, I called her in tears from the side of the highway, and through ragged breaths, explained that I was too distraught to teach. She would reassure me that my class would be covered while I took a few minutes to calm down.

I was far too trusting, it turns out. One April, without explanation, Mrs. M informed me that I would be teaching kindergarten the following year, and that my Shakespeare program was over.

I sat there in shock, failing to find words to express my despair, confusion, and outrage.

Incomprehensibly, all my contributions to the school didn't seem to matter. Mrs. M refused to change her mind, no matter how much I begged her to reconsider. From that day on, she refused to meet my eyes in the hallways and instructed me not to tell the parents or students, saying the information was confidential. I had no idea what Mrs. M had against me.

For the final three months of the school year, I experienced intense panic attacks at work. Tears would stream down my face regularly. I guided my kiddos through their testing and their final triumphant Shakespeare performances with a constant, painful lump in my throat and the feeling that I couldn't breathe. I didn't make the connection at the time, but Mrs. M's treatment of me felt like I was back at Grenville. It was like being pulled off the stage, being denied my grades, being forced into Discipline for no reason, and being dumped inexplicably.

I couldn't imagine why she'd turned against me. Only one thing was clear: I couldn't remain under her leadership.

It broke my heart to transfer to a new school without saying goodbye to my students. In despair, I packed up all of their precious Shakespeare writings, the costumes, backdrops, props, and video equipment, and moved it into storage, where it remains to this day.

Years later I would discover why Mrs. M shut down my Shakespeare program. It appeared to be from a place of pure spite. She was a devout member of the church in Brockville that Father Farnsworth and several other staff had joined once Grenville closed. She was also a close friend and next-door neighbour to former Grenville staff who were staunch defenders of the school. I'm guessing that she'd heard me described as public enemy number one. The motives for her inexplicable actions were never confirmed, but I learned my lesson. After her, I never trusted a principal again.

†

Once my Shakespeare program was shelved, I felt compelled to create new projects. At my new school, I made parody videos with primary students. The year "Gangnam Style" was all the rage, I wrote lyrics for my students and painstakingly filmed hours of footage during recess. "Working Student Style" was so well received on YouTube that I did similar parodies for several years. While I'm proud of the end products, I cringe at the desperate need for validation that motivated me.

My psychologist tried hard to get me to slow down. "Beth, these kids are only in grade one! All you have to do is teach them how to read and enjoy school." I could hardly comprehend her advice, though. I couldn't even conceive of relaxing.

In addition to my fear of administration, I never really felt comfortable around my colleagues. I assumed no one really liked me, though I went out of my way to be collegial. Even collaborating was tricky for me. I preferred to do everything myself rather than deal with other teachers' opinions and differing approaches. Every meeting threatened me like a potential light session.

Occasionally, my emotions would get the better of me. At best, things just got awkward. Like in the staff room when I declared that I was sick to death of skinny colleagues openly discussing their diets. "I'm paying thousands of dollars to a therapist who's trying to convince me that my size doesn't matter!" The room went uncomfortably silent.

At worst, when I got triggered, I'd shake with sobs, hyperventilate, and be incapable of speech. "Are you OK, Mrs. Granger?" my students would ask. "What's the matter? Why are your eyes so red?" I'd have no choice but to take unsteady breaths, dry my eyes, push down my pain and carry on. It often felt like I was acting in a marathon series that never ended—and sometimes I couldn't act my way through it. Emergency calls to my psychologist would result in me being ordered off work so that I could try to recover and regulate.

†

Despite the money I was spending on therapy, I continued to binge. It was my most shameful habit, and I was desperate to stop. I couldn't accept the advice my psychologist kept giving me. "Beth," she'd say, "you'll probably binge for the rest of your life. Be grateful that you're not an alcoholic, a drug addict, or worse. The sooner you accept yourself, the sooner the constant desire to binge will subside."

But instead of accepting myself, I frantically tried to fix myself. *If only I could stop bingeing, everything would be perfect!*

I've always been an overachiever. But I've never worked harder at anything than I've worked to end bingeing. And I've never failed so epically at anything, either. In addition to therapy, I never stopped seeking solutions. I paid thousands to an Ottawa bariatric medical clinic after learning my neighbour had lost thirty pounds there. (That only made my bingeing worse.) Without telling Garry, I hired a physical trainer at GoodLife for $3,000 and lost only fifteen pounds, all of which I gained back. I purchased several workout programs from Beachbody and drank their expensive protein shakes every morning for years. Each group challenge I tried would see me lose weight only to end up bingeing more. At one point, I hired an online binge expert who promised to help me conquer my problems. But her approach was to restrict trigger foods, which backfired big time.

I did successfully lose weight several times. Those episodes would catapult me into brief forays of false self-esteem. I'd post selfies that projected my glowing health and happiness. I'd embrace new activities reserved for the thin version of myself, like riding horses or going to the beach. I'd buy beautiful clothing and bask in my fleeting confidence. And whenever I was in this empowered state, I'd vow never to eat sugar again.

But no matter how much weight I lost, I'd always end up bingeing. The same sense of emptiness, like a void inside me that needed to be filled, would wash over me every night. Then the cravings would start, and I'd begin my battle against them. I'd distract myself in every possible way. But it never worked. The incessant voices in my head would yell, *Eat something! You need food! You're starving! Hurry up! Eat!* If I took one bite of anything, my resolve would crack, and I'd shovel in whatever snacks I could find. Then, after eating a shocking amount, I'd trudge up to bed and lie there, drowning in shame, begging for the oblivion of sleep.

Exercise seemed my only defence against binges. For years I moved heaven and earth to work out daily. But during the drive home, I often couldn't control the cravings. Hating myself, I'd pull up to a drive-through and order more calories than I'd burned off. The self-loathing would spike, and it would be all I could do to stop myself from launching into an epic binge. The next day, I'd wake up in the pit of despair, struggling to face another day. The only thing fuelling me was my need to atone for my gluttony.

Working out always made me feel better, and I truly enjoyed it. But the effort it took to fit in these workouts was monumental. One day I complained to a friend who exercised only occasionally. She asked sincerely, "Have you ever considered bariatric surgery?"

My heart sank. I couldn't believe she'd said that. *Am I that fat?* (I was size sixteen at the time, and very fit.) How could I have worked so hard to fix myself for so many years, only to have a close friend suggest drastic surgery?

Other suggestions I received were just as unhelpful:

"Have you tried brushing your teeth, so you won't want to eat after dinner?"

"What I do is I savour one square of chocolate so slowly that I find I don't need any more."

"If you are hungry at bedtime, just drink a glass of water!"

I couldn't imagine being able to stem the tidal waves of cravings with such lame tactics. *How is this so easy for everyone else?* I'd wonder time and again.

My anxiety levels were also off the charts. I'd feel breathless with fear all the time. Eventually, I agreed to try medication. My psychiatrist started me on one prescription after another, explaining some potential harms and benefits each time. After trying several different problematic meds, she suggested Ativan. It instantly took the edge off my anxiety and helped calm my racing thoughts. The best part was, it didn't have any troubling side effects. Or so I thought.

What I didn't realize was that Ativan is a benzodiazepine. It's now only recommended to be taken in the short term (two to four weeks max), even for patients with chronic severe anxiety. The internet is currently full of warnings against the long-term use of benzos. Cautions I never heard about until it was too late. I truly trusted my psychiatrist, and, in her defence, most practitioners are only now learning about the dire problems with long-term benzo use.

After about ten years on the meds, I noticed I was experiencing acute memory problems. I couldn't remember the names of my homeroom students, even after teaching them daily for months. I couldn't recall whether I'd read books or seen movies I'd previously enjoyed. At work, my job became increasingly difficult, as I forgot more and more important details. Sticky notes littered my classroom, reminding me of things I didn't want to forget.

What is wrong with my brain? I kept wondering. Afraid to find out, I just soldiered on, feeling like I was about to shatter.

The fact is, I was parenting and teaching full-time while managing complex PTSD and a chronic eating disorder *and* shouldering the ongoing responsibility of undertaking a class action lawsuit. The combined burden took its inevitable toll.

Chapter 24
The Wheels of Justice Turn Slowly

Our lawsuit moved forward at a glacial pace. Every year or so, we representative plaintiffs were required to attend court proceedings. Each event felt like ripping off the bandage of an open wound. The personal cross-examination sessions were the most challenging. In 2008, 2011, and 2015, each of us was grilled for hours by the defence. I don't know how I found the courage to endure those triggering ordeals. For weeks leading up to each session, I'd be sobbing on the commute to work.

Since I was so afraid to take time off from work, even to attend court proceedings, I never had the opportunity to process the trauma. I'd teach right up to the day before, travelling last minute to Toronto—a six-hour drive—and be back in the classroom as soon as it was over. Somehow, I white-knuckled my way through it, reminding myself, *If I can survive three decades at Grenville, I can survive anything!*

†

When I joined the lawsuit, I was only beginning to understand how I'd been impacted by Grenville. Initially, I didn't think I'd actually been abused. At one point, I was in a car with Lisa—the other female representative plaintiff—and Jacqueline, who also helped spearhead the lawsuit. We were travelling to Toronto for the first of several cross-examinations. Feeling sick with nerves, I asked, "What if I can't remember details? Everything feels like a blur from high school. It's like my brain has blocked it all out! Also, I don't think I was abused. If they only want to hear my personal experiences, what do I have to offer? So many others had it worse than I did."

Jacqueline and Lisa gasped. "Beth, are you serious? Is that what you really believe?"

"Well, yes. For me, it's been so normalized. It's difficult for me to even distinguish abuse from the ordinary routine." Then I launched into various stories about how I became immune to the daily restrictions, light sessions, and disciplines. When I told Jacqueline and Lisa about the toothbrush incident during Boot Camp, they were both rendered speechless.

"What?" I asked.

Almost laughing, Jacqueline replied, "Beth, even if you can't remember everything, you have more than enough stories to make a huge contribution to this lawsuit. All you must do is tell your truth."

Eventually, I came to understand how that simple anecdote revealed so much about my trauma. First, there was the absurdity of needing to get permission to obtain a new toothbrush. Then there was the fact that no decision could be made without praying for God's will. Finally, there was the internalized shame of being unable to discern God's voice and my assumption that I was too sinful to hear from Him. No wonder I had issues.

†

Looking back, I can see that the lawsuit was much harder on me than I was willing to admit, even to myself. Since I was the only representative plaintiff who had lived at Grenville as a staff kid, I felt an immense burden to represent everyone. This only intensified whenever I was privy to someone's personal story of abuse. With each conversation, email, or Facebook post, I was continuously overwhelmed by the extent of the damage inflicted on the students.

One day, I was sitting in Union Station, awaiting a train. I'd just endured another legal proceeding and I was feeling the usual exhaustion and uncertainty. *Is all of this pain worth it?*

Then my phone dinged. It was an email from a former student who had attended Grenville in the seventies. She was sharing her statement of experience with me. Not sure if I could handle reading it just then, I hesitated. *I'll just take a peek,* I thought.

Her story grabbed my attention and I couldn't put it down. Liz had arrived at Grenville as an innocent, smart, enthusiastic fifteen-year-old. Within days of her arrival, she was pulled into a private light session. Liz recalled that event:

> The first statement out of Mrs. Haig's mouth was, "You are not a virgin, are you?" I was flabbergasted. The accusation came out of nowhere. "Oh, come now," she went on. "You can tell me." I was still a virgin, though. I'd never even had a boyfriend. But no matter how much I tried to set Mrs. Haig straight, she wouldn't believe my truth. I left that meeting with a target on my back.

I gazed up at the elaborate arched ceiling in the station's great hall, trying to stop my blood from boiling as I pictured someone treating my own teenage daughter like that.

With a pit in my stomach, I kept reading as Liz described the next weeks of misery before she ran away. She and a friend barely escaped into the woods behind the school, the staff hot on their heels. In the darkness they followed the railway tracks to Brockville, then hitchhiked on Highway 401. I cringed, imagining all kinds of worst-case scenarios for these young girls as they travelled with strangers on their twelve-hour trek back to Hamilton. But running away didn't solve her problems. Her family just sent her back to Grenville, where she was put on harsh Discipline for three weeks.

> The enforced silence and strenuous labour were a shock. I was treated like an outcast, shamed, isolated, and shunned. It only got worse from there.

After Thanksgiving break, Mrs. Haig demanded to know what contrabands I'd brought back from home. When I denied having any, Mrs. Haig grabbed me by the front of my blouse and slammed me against the wall, pressing her face close and screaming at me, calling me a liar.

After a locker search turned up nothing, I was so frightened that I blurted out a secret: I'd written a letter to my friend back home and it was hidden until I could safely mail it from town. I was afraid of Mrs. Haig finding the letter, because in it I described having a crush on two boys.

Flashbacks from my own life kept flooding my brain and my heart went out to young Liz. Still, I wasn't expecting what she wrote next.

After dinner that evening, the students had free time while the staff and their children attended a meeting in the chapel. I was in the red lounge when Sid, a staff kid, told me Mrs. Haig had read my letter aloud to the entire gathering! Then she asked, "With a show of hands, who thinks Liz is a prostitute?" Apparently, everyone except three teenage staff kids had condemned me. Sid swore me to secrecy, since he could be disciplined for telling me.

My blood ran cold. I couldn't comprehend that my personal correspondence had been opened and read aloud. What a violation! I ran up to the payphones on the main floor and collect-called my mother. I was nearly hysterical, telling her what happened. Suddenly, Mrs. Haig grabbed the phone from me and ordered me to go to the dorm. She then told my mother I was upset because they had found contraband in my locker. Mrs. Haig assured her that they were taking care of the situation and that there was nothing to worry about.

Over the next two months, I was ostracized, put on silence, and severely disciplined. I endured constant light sessions until I broke down and agreed with their cruel accusations. I was supervised full-time by Miss Newman and Miss Case, who were constantly browbeating me. "You're a sinner, a whore, you need to repent." They would continually read the Bible and pray over me. I also endured repeated interrogations by Charles Farnsworth who asked me for sexually explicit details about my thoughts and actions.

I was told that in the book of Proverbs, whores had their heads shaved. They couldn't exactly shave my head, but Miss Newman took me into town to a hairdresser and told the woman to cut off all my long hair. I came away with a haircut as short as a boy's.

By this point, my cheeks were wet. Tears of sorrow, grief and rage. *How could they do this to her? Or to anyone?*

Then, in late February, Mrs. Haig declared, "Liz, you've changed for the worse. You're going to need to go back on Discipline." To prove my sinfulness, another locker search was conducted, and they found birth control pills. I couldn't call my mom, who had divorced my dad and moved overseas. So Mrs. Haig told my dad that I was using the pills because I was promiscuous. (He wasn't aware that a doctor had prescribed them to alleviate menstrual pain.) She explained that I was no longer welcome at Grenville, and my dad took me home in disgrace.

I left the school with my self-esteem in shreds. For decades I've endured extreme anxiety, depression, panic attacks, and nightmares.

I looked up from my phone, barely noticing the busy travellers racing by as my heavy heart replayed Liz's haunting story. It was at once so familiar and so shocking, I could hardly take it in. Liz had only spent six months at Grenville and here she was still trying to heal, forty-five years later. Her story seemed to be shouting at me, *Remember, Liz is only one of many!* I squared my shoulders, and renewed my resolve. Staring up again at the majestic ceilings of Union Station one last time, I reassured myself. *Beth, you're doing the right thing.*

†

As the class action dragged on, I was often surprised at how aggressively the Grenville supporters attempted to protect the school's reputation. Back in 2007, when Factnet exploded with revelations, alumni with opposing perspectives would frequently battle it out online. The defenders' posts were often so toxic that I avoided commenting altogether. I understood that not everyone had been damaged by Grenville. Some people—often former prefects who had been groomed, indoctrinated, and rewarded by the leadership—swore the school was the best thing that had ever happened to them. They weren't about to acknowledge their roles in some abusive spy network.

Understanding why some disagreed with the lawsuit didn't make the vitriol any easier to take. We were accused of exaggerating our difficulties for attention and financial gain. Of course, the representative plaintiffs got the worst of the harassment. Hurtful attacks with words like *whiny bitches* and *poor-me losers* cut deeply even when they weren't directed at me.

What continually shocked me most was the level of deception to which Grenville's defenders would resort. People I'd once respected were outright lying under oath and on TV interviews. When I read the transcripts of affidavits and cross-examinations of the school's former leaders, I couldn't believe they were denying the truth.

In 2011, Don Farnsworth—Father Farnsworth's son, who had been a teacher, dean, and administrator at Grenville for decades—testified that when students were in trouble, it "might result in what was called a 'day of discipline,' which usually meant working in the kitchen. Punishment might be increased to three consecutive days of Discipline but would seldom go beyond that." He later added, "It is simply untrue that students were forbidden to speak while on Discipline. That was never the case in all the years I was at Grenville."

What the actual fuck? I thought, my blood boiling.

Similarly, former headmaster Ken MacNeil testified under oath that the suggestion is utterly false that students on D were put on silence. Further, he recalled "many instances in which students who were being disciplined would be speaking to one another or to staff members. The conversations were friendly and warm." Ken also claimed that he and his wife made all decisions about their children, as any other parent would. "At no time did the broader GCC community force us to do anything with our children without our approval."

One day I stumbled upon a YouTube video of an exposé by the show *Chronicle* (Channel 5 Boston) that was produced in 1993, called "Community or Cult?" Several former members of the Community were interviewed, exposing all kinds of abuse that had taken place. When Mother Betty appeared to discuss the allegations on camera, she lied repeatedly—and with great conviction.

When asked if children were forced to live away from their families, Mother Betty laughed and assured the reporter, "We don't remove children from their families. All children live with their biological parents." When asked if children were interrogated for hours about their sins, she said, "I've never interrogated a child and if anyone tried to do that here, it would be quickly stopped." And when asked why people would make up such stories, she explained, "This seems to be the age where personality disorders lead some to perceive situations in an entirely different fashion than what really took place."

What? I kept thinking as she lied again and again. That was when I realized that exposing the truth about our abuse wouldn't be easy. Even through the court of law, I'd need to strap in for the fight of my life because the leaders of Grenville and the Community weren't going to take our quest for justice and accountability lying down.

What made it all sting even more was that in my cross-examinations, I'd been scrupulously honest, at the expense of my reputation. In the interest of transparency, I exposed my greatest disgrace to the lawyers interrogating me, answering every one of their questions truthfully, no matter how painful. When I'd told them I'd been expelled and sent to Cape Cod in part because I'd shoplifted, I felt shame threaten to drown me all over again. I knew I didn't have to expose that detail; I'd never been caught stealing, and I hadn't needed to expose it when I was sixteen, either. But I'd told the lawyers everything because I'd been too scared to do otherwise. After all, I was under oath. To me, that mattered.

However, that sense of truth didn't seem to matter to my former leaders. And that infuriated me.

At one point, I tried discussing this with my parents. I explained the ways our former leaders were lying to cover up the ugly truth. They looked stricken, and I hoped they would see what we were up against—and that maybe they'd understand our mission better. Instead, my dad sighed and said, "Beth, I can't talk about this. I just can't."

I kept the lawsuit to myself from then on. Once again, I realized that within my family, I was still very much on my own.

†

Class action lawsuits feel like they move forward in slow motion. Especially if they concern historical abuse. It took over a year to obtain a Mareva injunction, which meant Grenville could pay only approved business expenses. Any proceeds from the sale of the property must be held in trust by the defendants' counsel.

Next, we had to apply for fiscal backing from the Class Proceedings Fund. So, for the first year of the lawsuit, I lived in a state of limbo, waiting for the opportunity to plead our case. I figured that if they took us on, fate would be giving us the go-ahead.

Nearly two years after the lawsuit began, we received the wonderful news. The Class Proceedings Committee had decided to fund our case! They had carefully considered the strength of our lawsuit and the scope of the public's interest, and agreed that we were worth the risk. If we lost, they would pay our litigation costs.

With that news, I felt certain of my fate. Win or lose, I was all in.

Our class action didn't get certified for six years. For the first four years, we fought to satisfy all five requirements under the Class Proceedings Act. Unfortunately, our first certification attempt was denied on May 23, 2012. In his decision, Justice Perell ruled that we must dismiss our action against the Anglican Diocese of Ontario, as their church was not responsible for Grenville's day-to-day operations. Therefore, the Church hadn't breached a fiduciary duty to the students. Further, he denied certification on the basis that, in his opinion, a class action wasn't the preferable procedure.

This was a mighty blow. We reluctantly accepted the need to drop the Anglican Church as a defendant. But our lawyers assured us we had a good chance of winning an appeal for certification.

Almost two years later, our lawyers argued before three judges in the Ontario Superior Court of Justice Divisional Court. As I sat in the historic, imposing courtroom at Osgoode Hall, I held my breath and willed the judges to properly consider our case.

It only took them one month to make their ruling. On February 24, 2014, Justices Kiteley, Rady, and Whitaker ruled in our favour, unanimously holding that our case be certified as a class action. We were finally on our way!

The next few years involved more cross-examinations, more court proceedings, and more press coverage. In 2015, CTV's W5, Canada's popular investigative show, decided to produce a sixty-minute exposé on Grenville. Andrew, a representative plaintiff who was a major driving force behind our lawsuit, called me a few weeks before filming was to begin and tried to convince me to be interviewed on camera. He was very persuasive, and I felt compelled to agree, despite my misgivings. I didn't want to let anyone down. But I was tied up in knots of self-doubt.

At the time, I'd suffered another series of nervous breakdowns after some triggering events at work. The fact that I was barely coping made the idea of being featured on national television feel impossible. Even worse, I worried that my latest diet wasn't enough. *I can't stand to be filmed looking like this!* I also thought I had nothing valuable to offer in an interview.

In the end, the documentary was filmed without me. W5's "In the Name of God" was broadcast in February 2016. My body trembled as I watched friends and former classmates bravely expose their pain on camera. Tears flowed down my face as Joan Childs, one of the most powerful leaders next to the Farnsworths, discussed the abuse. "They aren't exaggerating," she said with conviction and sorrow. "They aren't making these things up. As sad as it is, these things happened." She confirmed all the allegations, including the sexual abuse. I could hardly believe it. This woman I'd feared for decades was brave enough to join our side.

Sadly, I wasn't surprised to see Don Farnsworth on the show, defending the school. He compared our allegations to fish stories, which was insulting, to say the least. He seemed to be parroting his father's denials, some of which had been published before Charles had died in 2015. In the W5 documentary, Father Farnsworth was quoted as saying, "We have been accused of many things that I never knew of and never heard of. I honestly think some of the people have gone delusional. Some of the things they said happened, some of the accusations of sexual abuse by me. They just did not happen."

The documentary's impact was profound. Our private Facebook group was flooded with stories from survivors who were only just coming to terms with the trauma that had followed them since Grenville. With every account, I'd think, *Will these stories ever stop surprising me?* So many former students reached out, wanting to connect, be heard, or find healing. I'd always respond with compassion, taking on the burden of their pain as if it were my own.

Two more years passed before we were called to attend a mediation meeting to negotiate a possible settlement. It was an opportunity to bring closure to the litigation without the ordeal and risk of a trial. Our presence was requested as a symbolic show of our resolve to take the litigation all the way to trial if necessary. We were also tasked with providing instructions as the mediation progressed, that would be in the best interests of the whole class.

As the two-day meeting approached, we didn't have much hope, especially after reading the defendants' mediation brief. Our lawyers warned us that it took a very harsh position against us representative plaintiffs, our claims, and the entire litigation. We were also cautioned that Don Farnsworth would be in attendance.

As the date drew closer, I'd suddenly cry at the drop of a hat. *What's going on with me? Get a grip, Beth!* But I couldn't snap out of it. I felt like a proper basket case and couldn't handle teaching at all. Just picturing seeing Don Farnsworth was sending me into a near-constant state of panic.

Luckily, Jacqueline, a vice principal at the time, helped set me straight. "Beth, you need to book the whole week off. There's no way you can handle going right back into teaching the day after this upcoming ordeal." And so, after ten years of being a representative plaintiff without booking time off to recover after each stage of litigation, I contacted my doctor and made the necessary arrangements.

The mediation in Toronto in December 2018 turned out to be an exercise in frustration. By the end, we were nowhere near a mutual agreement. Deciding we'd rather risk losing at trial, we refused the defence's final offer. At least we'd have the opportunity to be heard and acknowledged, and to hold our abusers accountable. There was still hope that we'd gain a sense of justice and closure.

Surprisingly, ninety-five per cent of Canadian class actions never go to trial. I never imagined that we'd be the first historical abuse class action to ever make it that far in Canada.

Chapter 25
Breakdown

As the lawsuit plodded forward, I tried to keep it out of the forefront of my mind as much as possible. This tactic often worked during the waking hours. I was so busy that I couldn't spare it much thought. During my sleep, it was a different story. I'd have nightmares every night about Grenville or the Community, then wake up shaken and exhausted. Then I'd do my best to shake off the haunting memories as I tackled each day.

My therapy at the time often involved finding new ways to distract from my relentless anxiety and binge urges. Dr. Blouin kept encouraging me to reconnect with my lost interests. One day, she asked if I had any artistic talents lying dormant. Immediately, I thought of singing. It had been over fifteen years since I'd flexed my musical muscles.

After examining the repertoire of several ensembles, I set my sights on the Ottawa Choral Society. They regularly performed with the symphony orchestra at the National Arts Centre. The idea seemed thrilling. I shared my ambition with my dad, telling him about their upcoming lineup of Orff, Brahms, Mendelssohn, Duruflé, Lauridsen, and even a Pops concert of Hollywood hits. He seemed impressed before advising me not to audition. "You won't be able to handle performing music at such an advanced level," he cautioned.

That remark stung, but instinct told me he was wrong. My friend Wendy gave me excellent advice: "Just remember you're there to offer whatever talent you can contribute." My audition went so well that the director asked me where I'd been hiding. *How much time have you got?* I thought, nervously laughing off his question.

As singing became a positive part of my life, I felt such a well of emotion. Tears would stream down my face whenever I drove, singing along to masterpieces from my past. I couldn't tell if they were tears of sadness or joy. All I knew was that now there were no light sessions, no mind games. Just the thrill of making glorious music with a hundred other dedicated singers. To my delight, I found I was extremely well prepared. The training I'd received at Grenville allowed me to handle the repertoire with ease.

Three months later, I auditioned for a solo part in the Christmas concert. At the time, I didn't realize that such an opportunity would be rare. (For typical concerts, the OCS hires superstar soloists like Maureen Forrester, Ben Heppner, and Measha Brueggergosman, to name a few.) I'm so glad I seized the day, despite my fear. I got to hear my voice soar in front of a packed Christ Church Cathedral in Ottawa. Even better, Julie Nesrallah, our acclaimed guest soloist, told me afterward, "Girl, you've got pipes!"

I still get goosebumps from that memory.

Without question, adding music back into my life was therapeutic. Singing built my confidence and often helped me refrain from bingeing. But it didn't lessen my anxiety. In truth, my life only became more chaotic. Juggling my demanding career with parenting, William's hockey, Victoria's dance, my choir, fitness classes, and household duties was nearly impossible. It really was madness, especially since Garry did shiftwork. Nevertheless, I felt I had no choice. Above all else, I was afraid to lose control around food. I couldn't afford to slow down.

Sometimes my therapist suggested meditation. "I can't do it!" I'd insist. "It feels too much like praying." She understood this and moved on to other ideas. But the truth was, I couldn't handle facing the trauma simmering beneath the surface, waiting to erupt.

Eventually, in 2019, my attempts to outrun my past came to a screeching halt.

By January of that year, I'd been taking three Ativan daily for almost ten years, and my memory issues were getting worse. It was so bad, that I finally googled the problem. My heart raced as I skimmed through articles about the risks associated with long-term use of benzodiazepines:

> Those who had taken a benzodiazepine for more than six months had an 84 percent greater risk of developing Alzheimer's than those who hadn't taken one. (Merz, 2014)

> Benzodiazepines generally should not be prescribed continuously for more than one month. (Johnson, 2013)

> Even for younger people, benzodiazepines cause acute cognitive impairment. Increased risk of dementia is another major concern with long-term use of benzodiazepines. (McKeehan, 2016)

Why didn't I do my research? I thought, panicking as I read warning after warning. I'd been under the impression that I'd be on Ativan for the rest of my career, which was another decade. Could I handle teaching without meds?

I told my psychiatrist my concerns. She agreed that it was best if I stopped taking Ativan, but that I'd need to taper off to avoid withdrawal symptoms, ideally cutting my daily dose by one-third every two months so I could adjust. That sounded good to me. Feeling hopeful—and fearful of what life would be like without Ativan—I resolved to taper off and spend the rest of my life med-free.

The first few days after the initial taper weren't so bad. I felt weird, and kind of disoriented. *I can handle this*, I kept telling myself.

Within a week, though, I felt like a human possessed. My anxiety was so acute that my skin felt like it was crawling, and my muscles were involuntarily clenching. I couldn't stand to be around my beloved students. It felt like they were an infestation of rats, all clawing at me simultaneously. One morning in the classroom, I snapped. Tears streaming, I ran to the office and begged the principal to cover my class. He kindly obliged and told me to take the rest of the day off. I couldn't possibly conceive of the journey that awaited me as I left his office.

My symptoms were so severe that I called my psychiatrist for an emergency appointment. I told her what I was experiencing: heart palpitations, the inability to catch my breath, panic attacks, persistent vertigo, crying over everything, and much more. I also told her how the simplest tasks were overwhelming me. How I was so dizzy that I was falling over. How I couldn't concentrate on anything or form coherent sentences. How I'd lost the desire to do anything, even things I enjoyed.

My psychiatrist ordered me off work until the end of June. I couldn't imagine being off work for so long. But I didn't argue. Something was terribly wrong, and I couldn't possibly handle working.

My first thought was, *I'll take this time off to get healthy! I'll have time to exercise and maybe I'll finally stop bingeing and lose weight!* I was so clueless.

Over the next few months, my symptoms got worse. I could barely function. One day, I experienced a panic attack while driving on the highway. Victoria was in the car with me, and I'd already been driving for forty minutes to take her to a dance competition. Suddenly, I felt like I couldn't breathe, and started gasping for air, like I was hyperventilating. Alarmed, Victoria grasped my hand and held on tight. Then the tunnel vision began. Terrified, I felt like my car was going at Mach speed and was about to crash. Fear gripped me, and I started crying. I cringe now, wondering how my poor daughter handled it as I cried, "I'm so scared! I can't do this! Oh God! Oh God!"

After what seemed like an eternity, I pulled over at the side of Highway 401. Pulse galloping, I got out of the car and tried to catch my breath. But as soon as I pulled back onto the highway, the symptoms returned with a vengeance. I barely made it to the next exit.

A few weeks later, I drove on the highway again, thinking I was getting better. After fifteen minutes, the same thing happened, this time with

William in the car. I'll never forget the terror of relying on my twelve-year-old son to grip my hand for dear life while bravely coaching me to breathe and hang on.

This kind of panic would happen every time I attempted highway driving. It got so bad that I couldn't even handle merging into traffic. For well over a year, I avoided highways altogether.

Another withdrawal symptom I couldn't stand was akathisia, or the constant urge to move. I felt a persistent restlessness that propelled me to want to pace, rock while standing, or clench my muscles. Often, I pictured my body undergoing a Hulk-like transformation. It felt like every muscle was exploding. As a result, resting was out of the question. The only thing that provided relief was aggressive exercise. But the loud fitness classes I'd once loved now overwhelmed my senses. So, I took to walking. No matter the weather, I'd head out for an hour-long walk, at least twice a day. I walked so much that within a year, I developed chronic foot and knee pain.

I'd walk with tears streaming down my face. I'd walk with dizziness so acute that I was afraid of falling over. I'd walk with muscles that begged to be clenched. I'd walk until my feet hurt so badly that I'd call Garry to pick me up.

Eventually, I joined a few Facebook groups for people going through benzo withdrawal. It helped to know I wasn't alone. I also learned that tapering is dangerous and that I should have done it more slowly. Many people never manage it. On top of the symptoms I was already experiencing, benzo withdrawal can cause life-threatening symptoms like seizures, suicidal thoughts, and psychosis. And when you taper too quickly, you can experience protracted withdrawal symptoms that can last for years. Worst of all, most doctors and even psychiatrists aren't aware of the dangers of benzo use and withdrawal.

Over time, it seemed like my brain could barely function. I couldn't speak without taking long pauses to find words that would never come to me. I couldn't handle reading—not only books, but also social media posts and even recipes. Using a computer was also out of the question. Even checking email overwhelmed me.

In addition, I was paranoid about returning to teach. After two months off from work, I was assigned to teach kindergarten the next school year. This was despite the fact that I'd frequently made it clear to my principal that I'd happily teach any grade *except* kindergarten. Now, when I pictured myself surrounded by thirty little ones, my stomach would clench in terror. No matter how much I wanted to recover and get back to my career, it seemed fate had other ideas.

Soon, I accepted that I was nowhere near capable of teaching any grade. And I had no way of knowing when that would change.

My doctors urged me to apply for long-term disability so that I wouldn't have to return to work in the fall. If successful, I could get 50 percent of my pay for up to two years. The application process would take months, however. It was humbling and scary. But I knew I had to try.

During all this uncertainty, something even more frightening was looming. Our lawsuit had finally been scheduled to go to trial in the Ontario Superior Court of Justice. We were notified that it would begin on September 16, 2019, and would last approximately five weeks. Once I learned the news, I could hardly take it in. After dragging on for eleven years, we were finally about to have our day in court.

The fact that I was such a basket case didn't help matters. *How on earth will I handle being questioned for hours on the witness stand? In front of a judge and a full courtroom?* The very idea terrified me. Still, a small part of me was eager. We'd been fighting for so long. Come what may, I hoped our stories would be heard.

†

I still had a lot to learn about class action lawsuits. Our lawyers explained that in a regular lawsuit, going to trial is the final stage. It's where both the question and the consequences of wrongdoing are determined. With a class action, the process is split into multiple trials.

During the first stage, the Trial of Common Issues, we'd be tasked with proving that boarding students at Grenville experienced a series of common issues in a framework of systemic abuse. The school's actions, policies, and practises had to be shown to be below the legal standard of care applicable over the time period, and that this wrongdoing amounted to breaching the duty of care Grenville legally owed to its students.

The difficulty remained that religious practise isn't justiciable. Even if we could prove that Grenville was operating like a cult, this isn't illegal. Freedom of religion is a constitutionally protected right, allowing believers the freedom to worship without limitation or interference. I knew we had a steep uphill battle before us.

If we succeeded at this trial and the judge ruled in our favour, the next trials would address the consequences of Grenville's wrongdoing, including what damages would be owed to the students and how those damages would be assessed. But if we lost the common issues trial, our lawsuit would be dead in the water.

As the trial date drew closer, my worries about testifying intensified. First, I was concerned about the simple act of formulating sentences, which I was having difficulty with daily. How would I speak coherently and effectively on the witness stand? Second, my short-term memory was terrible. I couldn't remember if I'd fed my dogs five minutes after I'd done so. But during the trial, I'd be asked questions about what happened decades ago. Since the lawsuit had begun, I'd been plagued with the knowledge that my memories of life at Grenville were vague at best. It was like they were trapped inside a locked safe, and I didn't have the key. I'd answered hundreds of questions during cross-examinations over the years, but was always frustrated by my lack of memories. Now, I'd be in hot water if my answers contradicted any of the responses I'd given in 2008, 2011, and 2015.

Still, a tiny spark of hope flickered. Hope that no matter how difficult the process was, I'd experience the healing power of being heard in court. Hope that our abuse might be taken seriously, our painful truth might be acknowledged, and true recovery might begin. Hope that our abusers might be held accountable, and that our case might serve as a warning to others who still commit abuse in the name of God.

That hope prompted me to prepare in earnest the summer before the trial. Instinct told me to start writing. At that point, I couldn't tolerate a computer screen. A dollar-store journal offered the next best option. Every day, I forced myself to sit still and remember. It was the first time since leaving Grenville that I took the time to relive memories. The process was excruciating. I felt like a child again, terrified, with no one to love me. I felt the despair of living without my parents and the shame of constantly being accused of sin. Tears streamed down my face as I uncovered one painful memory after another.

It felt like a geological dig. Every day I unearthed one more layer. Every attempt to uncover the past gave me a new glimpse of my childhood. My understanding of how messed up my upbringing had been grew clearer. My mind had blocked out memories of trauma for a reason. The more I let myself remember, the more pain I felt and the more I'd spontaneously cry. And, the more I wanted to escape—or binge.

Even still, as our trial loomed closer, I doubted whether Grenville was all that bad. Would the court think we were a bunch of whiners? Would we seem like a gang of disgruntled rich kids who didn't enjoy our privileged boarding school? Would my experiences be dismissed, since I was a staff kid and my parents lived on campus? Did I have anything valuable to contribute?

Had I even been abused?

Luckily, I had the help of my psychologist. Every few weeks, I'd share my journal with her, allowing her access to my latest memories. While she read, my body would shake as I sat in her plush armchair, worrying about her reaction to what I'd written. *I wonder, am I boring her?*

As usual, my worries were irrational. My psychologist was appalled by the stories I was sharing. Even though I'd been seeing her for twelve years, we'd only scratched the surface of my trauma. I'd been so busy trying to cope with life that I couldn't handle delving into the past. If it weren't for the looming trial, I wouldn't have dared. Fortunately, she continued to assure me that I had sustained a level of trauma that often destroys lives. "Beth, you have complex PTSD. Quite frankly, it is shocking that you've been able to accomplish as much as you have till now. The fact that you're currently severely psychologically disabled in the context of extreme and prolonged childhood abuse is not at all surprising."

I clung to her validation like a life raft.

Another way I prepared for the witness stand was by listening to audiobooks, podcasts, and recordings about cults. I wanted to articulate how much our minds were purposely controlled at Grenville. I also wanted to understand and recall the teachings I'd absorbed in my youth. To that end, I forced myself to listen to recordings of the Mothers' teachings. Many of them were digitized by a former Community member who had shared them online. My mom also found a collection of the Mothers' tapes in her basement. As I listened to the voices of my past tormentors, my body would immediately tremble, and my head would feel as heavy as concrete. These women had had so much power over me that I'd never questioned their commands. No matter how painful it was, I was determined to consider the indoctrination I'd received so long ago, so I paid attention.

After every recording, I'd be so dizzy and disoriented that I could barely focus. After suffering through more than ten recordings, I quit. The Mothers' voices had tormented me enough. And now I finally understood how indoctrinated we'd been by the leaders, whose goal was to tear us down and break our spirits. Only once we felt worthless, could we become true servants of God. *That explains a lot*, I thought.

A few weeks before the trial started, I received copies of my previous cross-examinations. Our lawyers suggested we refresh our memory so we could remain consistent on the witness stand. The transcripts for my sessions alone totalled 476 typed pages. For over a week, I poured over the documents, crying as I reviewed every probing question. It didn't help that I could barely stand to read or look at screens. I was also confronted with the fact that my understanding had expanded since the past depositions. Some of my previous testimony was lacking in detail or perspective. Before that summer, much of my teen years had remained a blur. Resolved to fix that during the upcoming trial, I allowed more memories to surface through my daily journaling.

I was fully aware that as a plaintiff, my memories couldn't be considered relevant unless I'd experienced them firsthand. Since I'd lived at Grenville for nearly three decades, I felt an intense burden to use my experiences to shed light on the systemic abuse that had occurred there. The defence would try to paint the picture that my experiences were unique, since I was a staff kid. In effect, they'd try to negate my pain. My goal was to prevent them from doing so. I was determined to show that most of the harmful things I'd endured had also been experienced by boarding students.

Though I couldn't discuss other people's experiences on the stand, I was affected by the stories of those whom I'd be representing. More than ever, people were posting about their trauma in our Facebook group. I also received private messages day and night. Every word added to my growing burden. *How can I possibly represent all these people?*

Luckily, I wouldn't be alone. Our lawyers had chosen eleven more witnesses to testify in addition to us representative plaintiffs. One of these was François, who sent his statement to me days before the trial. His story gave me the extra boost of courage I needed to face the courtroom. I couldn't stop thinking about it. François had been one of those students who left a lasting impression on me. He stole the show every time he set foot on the stage. I never could have guessed the private torment he was suffering at Grenville. Imagine being gay while Father Farnsworth was preaching that homosexuality was worse than murder! François wrote:

> I learned to watch my back constantly while repeating the mantra, "The only place I'm safe is in my head." As a gay teenager, I was particularly frightened of being found out, humiliated, and expelled. "You'll end up living on the street," the leaders would threaten. Against my will, I found myself believing the message that gays were disgusting filth. I would lie in bed, begging God to cure me of my homosexuality and my filthy, pathetic, sinful ways.

My heart hurt reading that. I had spent years unlearning the homophobia that was central to my upbringing. But I'd never really considered how destructive it was for all the gay students in our midst. (At the time, it hadn't even occurred to me that there were gay students at Grenville!)

François was nothing if not observant. I chuckled at the way he compared the abnormal behaviour of staff kids and prefects to Stepford wives. He was shocked by our impossible positivity and how we seemed so comfortable disciplining other students. I also appreciated his description of Father Farnsworth, which I thought was bang on:

> His penetrating sideways stare was icy, and his perpetual grin always got more joyful when he was humiliating a student. He radiated a kind of charisma that posed as genuine care and concern for those students who did his bidding, but I wasn't fooled. I sensed the monstrosity of that man hiding behind the mask. I was right to be wary of him.

Then François's account took a disturbing turn. He experienced our headmaster's hypocrisy and predatory nature first-hand. I'd heard many rumours, but I was afraid to confirm them. I had always attributed Farnsworth's fixation with sexuality to his desire to purify us. François revealed a more sinister preoccupation.

> I'll never forget the day he sexually interrogated me in his office. That day, I narrowly escaped expulsion and sexual assault.
>
> In my first year, I developed a crush on a senior student, whom I'll call Aiden. Once he graduated, I sent him love letters. I never received a reply, so I eventually moved on. Then, in my fourth year, out of the blue, Aiden mailed me a letter with a pamphlet for a Christian gay conversion therapy group in Toronto. Not being a complete

moron, I put the ridiculous letter aside and didn't think much about it.

Here I stopped and marvelled again at the way we suffered in isolation at Grenville. Coincidentally, I had also had a secret crush on Aiden. I was transported back to a light session about another letter I never received. Some eagle-eyed staff member intercepted it and turned it in to the authorities. In it, Aiden's only attempt at flirting involved inviting me to a Christian summer camp called Circle Square Ranch. Of course, I was ambushed for having fuelled Aiden's lust. I shook my head at the bizarre memory before jumping back into François's story.

Two weeks later, I was called to Father Farnsworth's office. He told me that he had received a letter from Aiden, who was worried about me living in sin.

At that moment, a huge adrenaline rush came over me. I imagined being expelled and my father disowning me. I had to think fast, or things would get disastrous.

Instinctively, I started regurgitating a bunch of "Jesus speak" to get myself off the hook. "Yes, Satan was trying to manipulate me when I was confused for a few years. But since then, I've prayed and opened my heart to Jesus. I haven't written to Aiden in a couple of years. That was just a phase. I've grown out of it and into Christ's presence."

This didn't appear to satisfy Father Farnsworth, who launched into an intense interrogation. He wanted to know all my most private sexual thoughts and fantasies. Had I masturbated while thinking about Aiden? Did I have dreams about him or other boys? Did I fantasize about girls too? What went on in my fantasies? His relentless questioning made me feel dirty and violated. Only the fear of expulsion kept me cooperating.

All I wanted to do was get out of Father Farnsworth's office. He went on to tell me that my feelings were normal. As if to make his point, he moved from behind his desk to sit next to me, then told me that when he was a teenager about my age, an incident had happened. He had been sitting on a park bench, and an older man sat beside him and touched his leg. Father Farnsworth then asked me if I wanted him to show me how the man had touched him.

I could tell where this was heading. Panicking, I jumped up and tried to diplomatically wiggle my way out of the office. I repeated more Jesus talk, saying things like, "It's OK, I believe you. I know I just need to pray and keep Jesus in my heart. This phase in my life is over and Jesus has shown me the light. Also, I don't want to be late to [whatever activity I conjured up at that moment]."

Father Farnsworth got up and moved back to his desk chair, acting serious again. He told me that the letter I'd received from Aiden could destroy the reputation of me and my family. I was ordered to retrieve it from my dorm and turn it in to him for safekeeping. He would hang on to the incriminating evidence until after I'd graduated. This felt like blackmail, and for the rest of the year, I felt threatened with an extra layer of anxiety.

I remember walking out of his office speechless and dizzy, like a hole had been punched out of me. Again, my Grenville mantra haunted me: "The only place I'm safe is in my head." But even that no longer seemed true.

I finished reading his statement with an ache in my chest. *Will our pain ever end?* I was also struck by the irony of his mantra. Sure, François might have felt safe inside his head, at first. But certainly not for long. Grenville ruined all sense of safety; even—or especially—inside our heads. We were left with minds that attacked from the inside.

Chapter 26
The Reckoning

To say that the trial was life-changing would be an understatement.

Before it, any attempts to heal from my past could be compared to ER visits. All the therapy and meds were like desperate attempts to temporarily patch me up so I could be on my way.

In contrast, the trial was like invasive surgery, where bones are fractured and moved and units of fresh blood are pumped in. The kind of procedure that requires months, even years of recovery, and where there's the risk of infection if the patient tries to rush the healing process.

The trial most likely affected each of us differently. Former students flew thousands of kilometres to attend. Judging by the tear-stained faces during recess, it was clearly a painful process for many. But there was also a powerful sense of validation. It was empowering to have black-robed advocates leading us into battle. At the very least, our stories would be heard and taken seriously.

I could write an entire book about our lawsuit and fill over half of it with stories from the 2019 trial. Since it's now a matter of public record, anyone can read all 2,627 pages of the transcripts. So instead of rehashing the entire ordeal, I'll focus on the moments that left an indelible impression on my memory (impaired as it was).

†

I wasn't scheduled to testify until the third day of the trial. That didn't diminish my nerves on day one, though. Luckily, I was surrounded by supporters. So many Grenville survivors showed up that we couldn't all fit on the plaintiff side of the courtroom. Some days, we needed extra chairs to accommodate everyone who attended on our behalf.

On that first day, I sat on the edge of my seat, willing our lawyers to succeed. When Loretta Merritt delivered her opening statement, I hung onto her every word. My breath slowly steadied as she confidently laid out our case. She finished as strongly as she began:

> "This case is not like other abuse cases that have been certified as class actions. In most cases, the systemic negligence is the institutional failure to uncover the abusive acts of a few bad apples. This case is different. Here the systemic nature of the behaviour is much worse. It involves a system of intentional acts done for the purpose of breaking the spirits of the children and autonomy of the children in order to remake them in the Grenville way, meaning obedient and subjugated, in other words, good Christians as the leadership defined that to mean. In this way, the case is more akin to the Indian Residential School Settlement Agreement where the [schools'] mission was the assimilation of First Nations children.

> "The issue here is not whether the Community of Jesus or Grenville Christian College were cults. The purpose behind their policies, patterns, practises of behaviour are not issues Your Honour needs to decide. The issue is whether these practises, patterns, and policies fell below the standard of care. We anticipate our friends will call witnesses to say that their experiences at Grenville were different than the plaintiffs' experiences or that their exposure to the institutional culture was not impactful to them. Again, the individual experience of harm and extent of harm is not material to this action. We say

the evidence will show that certain policies, practises, and patterns of behaviour were not only in place, but purposely applied throughout the class period; and these policies we will show through expert evidence were improper, abusive, and below the standard of care required and a breach of the duties owed."

In addition, Loretta explained that the court would hear from two expert witnesses on our behalf: Dr. Paul Axelrod, a retired university professor of educational history and policy; and Dr. Rosemary Barnes, a psychologist. She also stated that the defence wasn't going to call upon expert evidence—and that "no reasonable expert would testify that what went on at Grenville was appropriate."

Next, the defence's lead lawyer made his opening remarks. The more he spoke, the more fear and frustration gripped my body in its familiar vice. He described the school, in all its beauty with its excellent reputation, and illustrated its elite status by name-dropping several high-profile members on its board of advisors. He also mentioned several of the defence witnesses whose successful lives would thwart our claims. Once he concluded, it sounded impossible that systemic abuse had occurred at Grenville:

> "When you hear the evidence the defendants present, you will seriously wonder if these people went to two different schools. And when you hear how many students were satisfied with their experience and education and felt no abuse, you'll wonder how there could possibly have been a systematic abuse towards the class as a whole."

Our team had our work cut out for us. For eleven years, we'd been fighting to prove not only that students had been abused at Grenville, but that the abuse had been systemic. This would continue to be the crux of the matter. I knew the defence witnesses were former administrators, prefects, and students whose parents were important donors to the school. *I hope this judge isn't fooled by their testimony,* knowing it was entirely possible.

One of our most important witnesses was Joan Childs. Our lawyers scheduled her to speak first because her testimony laid down the foundation for our case. The fact that she was a member of the leadership's inner circle was critical.

Even though I knew Joan was on our side, I couldn't believe she was willing to expose all the ugly truth she knew. She'd previously spoken out against Grenville publicly, but I still couldn't relax in her presence. Along with the other former leaders, Joan had terrified me so much that my body kept shaking whenever she was near. In fact, on the first day of the trial, I politely declined an invitation to eat lunch with Joan and her daughters to avoid being triggered.

All that changed after Joan finished her epic testimony and cross-examination. She held nothing back. Taking responsibility for her part in the abuse, she bravely exposed the harm she knew Grenville had caused. Her words had the effect of exploding open the vault of secrets we'd fought for so many years to crack.

In detail, Joan explained how Grenville became associated with Mothers Cay and Judy. She revealed what being a vowed member of the Community entailed for the school's staff and how the Cross life—which included light sessions, live-in retreats, the Mothers' teaching tapes, and letters of confession—all began after taking a public lifetime vow. She also confirmed that the following trial exhibit was a small excerpt of the vow ceremony:

> I express my obedience to you, Jesus, through my yieldedness and submission to the Community of Jesus and to my spiritual mothers, Mother Cay and Mother Judy.
> I am nothing without you.

Additionally, Joan clarified how light sessions were at the centre of our communal living and how the "Community of Jesus Vow Service"—a twenty-seven-page typed booklet—illustrated the concepts that formed the cornerstone of living in the light. Headings such as Admonish,

Chastise, Conversion, Correct, Discipline, Obedience, Submission and Yieldedness painted a clear picture of the life we were expected to lead.

Joan went on to explain how staff were treated to all kinds of discipline if they didn't conform—and she provided many examples. They could be put on silence, forced to move, fired, demoted, forced to work without salary, and compelled to endure continuous light sessions. Those meetings were intense, and often included physical violence. Once, Joan lobbied for teaching staff to be granted study time during the summer, instead of cleaning all day. As a result, Mary Haig slapped her across the face for not being submissive.

Joan explained that staff members also treated the students in the same way:

> "It was direct confrontation. So, if we felt a student had a bad spirit, if we felt that they were haughty, jealous, or trying to be the centre of attention, we would speak to them about it, using those terms. If there was a bad attitude in the student body, we'd call all the students together and say, 'There's something wrong here. You all need to look at yourselves and see how you're a part of the problem.' We didn't hit anybody in those school sessions. We didn't throw things in their face. We just yelled at them and humiliated them."

When it was revealed that Joan had been a member of the A-team, I leaned forward, hoping she'd reveal what went on in those secret meetings. I wasn't disappointed. Joan told the court that the team met with Charles Farnsworth daily and talked about everything that was going on in the school:

> "As one of the A-team administrators, a lot of staff would report to me on every light session, every issue that they were dealing with another staff member. It would be attitudes. Or whether they're seeing their sin, whether they have repented, how they responded in a light session.

Charles wanted to know details about everything. So, if there was something going on with a staff member, he would expect me to get a report about them either from their spouse or even their older kids, from friends, from who they lived with, and then I would pass those reports on to Charles."

Joan's words hit me like a ton of bricks. She'd confirmed what I'd suspected all along: I'd been brought up within a network of spies. *No wonder I'm always paranoid!* I thought.

When Joan was asked to explain the rules at Grenville, she went beyond the written rules stated in the student handbook. Her explanation clarified what I'd been grappling with for decades. Tears streamed down my face as she revealed what I'd never understood:

"There were unwritten rules that we just all knew. Prefects were expected to be perfect. Staff kids were expected to be perfect. They would be expected to report on anything they saw in a student that didn't quite feel right. An unwritten rule was, 'Don't be too good at something.' If you're too good at something, you're going to end up being pulled from it. An example of that would be a student chosen to be the lead in a Gilbert and Sullivan performance and two weeks before the performance, after months of practise, they would be pulled out of it because it wasn't good for them to be doing so well, and so somebody else, usually a staff member, was put in their place. So, it was anything that caused a student to look like they were doing well or enjoying themselves. It doesn't make sense, but that's what it was."

Tears stung my eyes as Joan's words washed over me. I pictured my younger self, so desperate to please, but feeling so doomed despite—or because of—my talents. *It wasn't all in my head. They really did target people like me.*

Joan then described the excessive discipline so often used at Grenville. Having been in the inner circle, she had a distinct perspective of the way the paddle had been used:

> "Charles was in charge of the paddle. He had it under his desk. He loved his paddle. He would take it out and he'd hand it to the dean of men and say, 'This calls for a paddling,' and it could be anything. It could be a major thing, or it could be just an attitude. There was no policy because it changed depending upon how Charles felt about that student."

Joan also revealed how girls were targeted for being temptresses and pulling on the boys with their lustful bodies. She told the court how Father Farnsworth would meet the girls in the dorm (in their pyjamas) to warn them against luring boys into sin:

> "Prior to those kinds of meetings, Charles would meet with the administration, and he'd say, 'I'm going to the dorm tonight. I'm going to meet with the girls … they need to know that they pull on boys, that they're whores, they're prostitutes.' It was just part of what we believed."

As Joan spoke, I remembered those meetings. All hundred of us huddled together in fear on the floor of the blue lounge, in our pyjamas or nightgowns. I'd dreaded those gatherings, but I'd attended so many that I'd almost forgotten they had happened. It was one more memory of something abusive that I'd normalized.

During Joan's cross-examination, the defence repeatedly tried to disarm her. Yet she stood strong in her truth, even when it was ugly. At one point, she was asked about questionnaires Grenville had sent to the families of fifty-five students. While several parents had voiced their strong objections to practises they deemed harmful at Grenville, the defence was quick to point out that "7.9 out of 10 described their children as 'generally happy'."

We gasped when Joan explained the reason for this. "Well, I can comment on that because I was a part of crafting the survey. We picked very carefully who we sent those to."

The defence lawyer wasn't happy about that. "Well, what are you saying? That you were lying and deceiving?"

"Yes."

"Wow. You must be very proud of yourself."

"I'm not proud of myself at all." Joan's voice was grave.

The defence tried another tactic. "I'm going to suggest to you that that is not true about these questionnaires, is it? You didn't pick and choose parents?"

"Yes, we did," Joan reaffirmed.

The lawyer went on to press Joan about her claims that Grenville didn't celebrate excellence. He wouldn't accept her testimony that students weren't allowed to do well. But Joan held her own against the barrage of attempts to get her to change her statement. Eventually, she said this:

> "I can say that in many, many cases, students were not allowed to receive the honours they should receive, to prevent them from the sin of haughtiness or thinking themselves to be great. It's not black and white. We strived for excellence. We were thrilled when our kids did well: students, staff kids, everybody. And we would advertise that, and we would be very proud of it. But that does not take away the fact that a kid who maybe won at a debate or was the best cross-country skier was then corrected for their haughtiness. They would go on a team trip, and they'd win, and they'd call home and we'd be so proud and excited, but the whole trip home they would be yelled at for their haughtiness."

Yes! Yes! Yes! Struggling to keep myself together, I silently cheered Joan on while the defence questioned her motives, her integrity, her honesty, and even her faith. I held my breath, waiting to see how she'd fend off each attempt to destroy her credibility. To put it mildly, the defence lawyers terrified me.

Minutes after Joan finished on the witness stand, I found myself weeping alone in the lobby, overcome with emotion. It felt like Joan's testimony had broken another dam inside me, and the pain I'd been carrying for decades had burst forth. I kept picturing myself as a frightened child, so full of shame. *How did I survive that?*

But as I cried, I felt a shift inside myself. For the first time in my life, a strong wave of self-compassion washed over me, and I glimpsed what it might be like to be free of self-loathing. *None of it was my fault. I didn't stand a chance at Grenville. Look what I endured!*

My tears refused to let up, though. I cried alone for several more minutes, mopping my face with the heels of my hands. As I was curled over, rocking back and forth, the arm of a kindred spirit grasped my shoulders and held me tight. It was Loretta Merritt, offering her support. I forget what she said to me, but I'll never forget that she was crying too. Her compassion was the most precious gift, and I'll always cherish that moment.

Between Loretta's empathy and Joan's courageous testimony, I gathered the strength I needed to face the long days ahead. Joan's truth, painful as it was, was as illuminating for the judge as it was for those of us still desperate to understand why we were so damaged.

Later that day, our lawyers ushered me and the three other representative plaintiffs who were present into a private meeting. My blood ran cold when I saw the look on Loretta and Sabrina's faces. With trembling voices and tears welling, they told us that our fifth representative plaintiff, Tim Blacklock, had suffered a fatal heart attack while boarding the train that morning. He'd been heading to the trial from his hometown of Kingston, Ontario.

What? Tim is dead? Is this for real? I was instantly gutted. Tim had been so friendly and supportive, shouldering the agonizing pressure all five of us had been feeling. Yet, his stress had proven unbearable. Literally.

Despite our shock and grief, we needed to decide how to proceed. At one point, Lisa, one of the other representative plaintiffs, said, "Tim will never forgive us if we don't forge ahead." With heavy hearts, we all agreed to carry on. Our battle took on a new sense of urgency.

Tim, I thought, *rest easy. We'll fight this for you.*

†

Over the next few weeks, fifteen witnesses testified for the plaintiffs, including Dr. Rosemary Barnes and Dr. Paul Axelrod. As I listened to each expert speak, I wanted to pinch myself. Hearing their testimonies felt like receiving a lifetime of therapy in one jam-packed session.

Dr. Barnes compared Grenville to the Native residential schools and explained how total institutions tend to impose conditions of disconnection, degradation, and powerlessness upon children in their care. Once the sense of unchecked power of those in authority is established, an atmosphere of insecurity and fear pervades the institution. If punishment is imposed arbitrarily or excessively, children need not experience it directly to be affected by the fear that they may be next.

Dr. Barnes also addressed how being on Discipline was abusive when it involved cruel and inappropriate treatment including menial, physically harmful, and degrading work for days at a time. She testified that the forced isolation of students from their peers amounted to spurning, a form of abuse in which children are belittled, degraded, shamed, singled out for punishment, or exposed to public humiliation. In addition, the arbitrary nature of Discipline made everything worse. There was no written policy or protocol about the nature of the work, the length of time or limits on what students could be asked to do, no avenues of appeal, and at times, no regard for student health and safety.

Both Drs. Barnes and Axelrod testified that Grenville's use of the paddle fell below the standard of care because it was applied arbitrarily, and that there was an absence of policy and record-keeping. Students were physically and emotionally injured by the excessive use of the paddle, and there were no checks to prevent an abuse of power.

According to Dr. Axelrod, the practise of humiliating students publicly for behavioural or attitudinal issues was "unheard of in other educational venues." Dr. Barnes also gave evidence that the public humiliation sessions amounted to spurning. She described the adverse impact of involving other students in this type of conduct towards their peers, which forced others—like prefects—to violate their values. Exposing students to such coercion causes shame and self-loathing.

At one point, Dr. Barnes testified that the practise of taking children to the boiler room to show them the flames and comparing it to Hell was a practise that met the criteria for a form of abuse known as "terrorizing." This involves placing a child in unpredictable or chaotic circumstances and setting rigid or unrealistic expectations with the threat of loss, harm, or danger.

Dr. Axelrod gave expert evidence that Grenville's teachings concerning sexuality were harmful, abusive, and out of keeping with Ontario's standards of sexual education. To that end, Dr. Barnes described the phenomenon of sexualized abuse, which can cause emotional trauma. Examples of sexualized abuse that occurred at Grenville were requiring sexual confessions; berating students for inciting lust; the vilification of homosexuality; using derogatory terms such as *temptress, sluts,* and *whores*; and preoccupation with sexuality and sin. Dr. Barnes also explained that requiring girls to bend over to check for cleavage was abusive. So was humiliating students over expressions of romantic feelings towards their peers.

At Grenville, many students felt they couldn't share their abuse with their parents. Dr. Barnes explained why this occurred. In total institutions, children who are maltreated by adults in authority experience many complex barriers to communication, including fear of punishment, fear of not being believed, and fear of failing to meet parental expectations. Students also feel guilt over their parents spending significant sums of money on tuition. Matters are made worse when authorities instruct the students not to disclose their troubles, since letters and phone calls are often monitored. Finally, most teenagers lack the language to communicate—much less understand—the psychological impact of their abuse.

To me, the experts' testimonies felt like rain after a long drought. *If we don't win, at least we have the gift of their opinions.* I hoped it wouldn't be lost on the judge that the defence called no expert witnesses to plead their case.

†

Court cases don't unfold according to schedules. I was supposed to take the stand on September 18 but had to wait an agonizing five extra days. Listening to other representative plaintiffs get grilled by the defence nearly did me in. Knowing that they'd make every attempt to disarm us didn't make it any easier. I was a wreck during Andrew Hale Byrne's cross-examination. It was like twenty years had disappeared and I was right back at Grenville, witnessing his public humiliation and chastisement. Tears streamed down my face as he bravely fended off the defence's attempts to discredit him.

I don't know if I can endure that treatment, I thought. *Do I have the strength? Or will my brain go blank? Will I fall apart and embarrass myself?*

I hardly slept that week. Worst-case scenarios plagued my mind day and night. It was almost a relief when I was finally called to the witness stand.

I was sworn in on Monday, September 23, 2019. For years, I'd hoped that if I finally got to testify in court, I'd feel empowered. And I suppose I did feel emboldened, especially on day one. I sensed that it was my moment, and I didn't want to hold anything back. But what I didn't expect was that I'd be under interrogation for the better part of three days.

My lawyer asked many open-ended questions, and I took advantage of the opportunity to include as much relevant detail as possible. I was determined to illustrate how far-reaching the Community's practises had been and how they had affected the lives of boarding students. In one instance, when I was asked to compare the practises and experiences at Grenville to the Community, I spoke for so long that the judge interrupted me and suggested a lunch break. When she apologized for the interruption, I asked if I could finish my thought. She agreed, and I continued, making sure my point was clear.

Though fuelled by determination, I was terrified. Mostly, I was afraid that my mind would go blank, and I'd waste this precious opportunity. As the hours dragged on, I found it increasingly difficult to think. My head felt like it was encased in concrete, and dizziness was taking over. I forced myself to focus, willing myself not to omit important evidence.

If my goal was to add detail to the testimonies I'd given over the years, I suppose I was highly successful. What I didn't consider was how viciously the defence would attack me for doing so.

My cross-examination began on Tuesday morning and didn't end until Wednesday afternoon. It was a torment more gruelling than I could have ever predicted. When the defence got started with me, I was already desperate to be finished. I'd been on the stand for an entire day, and my brain was fried. Still, I knew the worst was yet to come. I expected the defence lawyer to twist my words, back me into corners, trip me up, and destroy my credibility. It wasn't until their questioning began that I realized how torturous the process felt—and how it was all too similar to a light session.

I'm safe in this courtroom, I'd remind myself. *The judge is impartial. The lawyers are professionals. No one can hurt me.*

No matter how much I tried to self-regulate, I couldn't escape the excruciating pain of being interrogated by lawyers whose job was to break me down. I forced myself to keep going when what I wanted more than anything was to get the hell out of that courtroom. Whenever I broke down crying (which happened several times), the judge would kindly ask if I needed a break. I always declined, saying that I wanted to get the process over with.

Despite the pain, I paid especially close attention to my interrogator's every word, willing myself not to get tricked. It didn't take long for me to catch on to his strategy. One thing that helped was that his approach angered me so much. For three decades, I'd been so demoralized that I'd never stood up for myself. I wasn't about to let that happen again. Especially not in this courtroom.

That spark of anger was the fuel I needed. I refused to let the defence lawyer put words into my mouth. Or to agree with his attempts to retell events according to his agenda. Or to allow him to discredit me. And with his every question, I infused my answers with more incriminating testimony.

The defence had several red flag phrases: "Ms. Granger, I'm suggesting …" or, "Wouldn't you agree that …" or, "In 2008, when you testified under oath …" They all sent alarm bells off in my brain. Whenever I heard them, I braced myself myself for his next attack. At one point, he said:

> "Ms. Granger, I'm suggesting that you're attempting to rewrite history here in this courtroom to advance the class action, contrary to the truth of what actually happened, that you testified several times to under oath in the past. Isn't this all a rewrite of history … to colour the proceedings to make things look so much worse than they really were?"

He repeatedly objected to the additional details in my testimony, and I had to set him straight every time, as I did here:

> "Sir, I've explained that I've done a lot of preparation to come into court. It's been very painful. I had to sit and write down flashbacks over the last several months and I have recalled a lot more. And respectfully, the last three examinations I was only answering what your team asked me. It was just scratching the surface of the thirty-year experience."

The defence also seemed determined to separate my experiences from those of the boarding students. They constantly tried to get me to agree that things were so much worse for me than for the boarders. I knew that if I agreed with that perspective, they'd easily disregard my experiences as one-offs, not examples of the systemic abuse so pervasive at Grenville. It felt like the questioning continually led me into territory filled with landmines. Here's one such exchange:

Defence: Generally, you had it much worse than the non-staff kids, as there was no escape over the summer, over long weekends and holidays; that fair?

Me: Grenville was so abusive you didn't have to be there for very long to be abused.

Defence: Well, you can hardly speak for all 1,350 members of the class, can you?

Me: Well, I was there for the entire class period, and I saw students being regularly abused.

Defence: There were many more light sessions for you and the other staff kids over the summer and Christmas break than there were over the school year; true?

Me: Yes.

Defence: And you were known by all the non-staff kids as a staff kid; right?

Me: Yes.

Defence: And for that reason you had no other kids to confide in while you're at Grenville?

Me: It was hard to make friends.

Defence: OK. And you felt very alone and isolated as a staff kid?

Me: I did.

Defence: And that was an aggravating factor in your mental suffering; wasn't it?

Me: It was one of the many factors.

Defence: You had no close friends at all at Grenville; did you?

Me: Well, Grenville specialized in separating students and separating friendships. That was not unique to staff kids.

Defence: What is the answer to my question?

Me: I believe I just answered it.

Defence: You gave a speech that didn't respond to my question.

Me: Should I repeat myself?

Defence: No, that would just be giving the same speech.

Additionally, the defence tried to destroy my credibility by catching minute discrepancies between my testimonies and affidavits from 2008, 2010, 2011, and 2015. If any of my 2,213 previous answers varied even in the slightest from the ones given on the stand, the lawyer pounced, suggesting that I was fabricating memories. This included whether I testified that girls were *called* bitches in heat versus *acting* like them, and why I'd stated that girls were forced to have their hair cut short when I hadn't specified until 2019 that it had happened to me. Even the adjectives I used to describe practises like Discipline and light sessions were scrutinized. And the defence didn't let any inconsistency go unnoticed:

> Defence: You said a number of times yesterday and again today, just now, "I was at the Community of Jesus for seven months." And if you look at the transcript from 2008, page 87, question 430.
>
> "So, you were sent down to the Community of Jesus. How long were you there for?" You answered: "I stayed for six months." Do you remember giving that evidence?
>
> Me: Yes. For a long time, I thought it was six months and then as I was reflecting recently, I remembered I left at the beginning of February and didn't come back till the end of August, which is effectively seven months. So, I have tried to clarify that.
>
> Defence: The horrors just keep on expanding the longer into this we go; isn't that fair?
>
> Me: Seriously?
>
> Judge: Just answer the questions.

Another defence tactic that caught me off guard was questioning posts I'd made in the private Facebook group for Grenville alumni. (How they infiltrated that page, I'll never know.) During the months leading up to the trial, I'd posted occasionally, sharing insights and sparking dialogue. This wasn't unusual for me. In one instance, I'd posted photos I'd taken of the Mothers' teaching tapes that my mother had found in her basement. I'd also shared a YouTube video that explained cult dynamics very well and invited discussion. To my surprise, the defence attacked me for these posts, suggesting I was gathering incriminating evidence that had nothing to do with my experiences:

> Defence: I'm suggesting that you've conflated what you've heard on those tapes very recently with what you think you were taught at Grenville.

> Me: I was in no way confusing them. I was reminding myself and refreshing my memory because if you heard these tapes, you would certainly repress what you listened to from a young age. And it was not confusing. No, it reminded me and confirmed the connection between the Community of Jesus and Farnsworth's teaching.

Then, to press my point further, I leaned into the mic and said, "This one's called 'Be Needy, Be Wrong, Be Alive'."

The lawyer went on to suggest that by posting the video about cults, I was fishing for information to prove that students were abused at Grenville. Evidence that, according to him, I couldn't possibly have witnessed for myself:

> Defence: I'm suggesting, Ms. Granger, that this demonstrates that you didn't have a clue what was going on with the non-staff kids at all, in terms of what they were experiencing.

> Me: I would not be in a very painful, difficult trial right now and have endured eleven years of this if I hadn't been convinced that students were damaged at Grenville. It's because of the students that I've come forward since 2007.

The lawyer didn't let this point rest, though:

> Defence: In poring over the Factnet and Facebook Grenville site stories, I suggest that you've become emboldened

by these to perhaps recall more light sessions and Discipline involving non-staff students than you have actual firsthand knowledge of.

Me: I disagree.

Defence: Well, you already said you had no idea of the extent of suffering going on at the school around you when you were there.

Me: In 2008 when this first got started, I had very little understanding of the extent to which I was abused and the people that I grew up with were abused and the students who were abused. And it has taken a lot of therapy and a lot of work on my part to even be able to cope with the kinds of damages that happened to me and to be able to come up with an understanding of what was happening all around me.

When the defence lawyer suggested that I was lying about the extent to which I'd shoplifted as a teenager, he nearly broke me. The shame of revealing that transgression in open court was already agonizing. *Why did I ever mention shoplifting in the first place?* I thought. *I was never caught or charged or convicted. They never needed to know that.*

On day one of my testimony, I'd explained why I'd been sent down to the Community at age sixteen. In my explanation, I'd said that I'd been so afraid of going to Hell that I'd confessed to shoplifting the sports bra and the chocolate bar. However, I omitted that I'd also stolen a novel while house cleaning, a detail I'd revealed in earlier testimonies. The lawyer jumped on this error, suggesting I intentionally omitted it to understate my culpability.

Suddenly, I was back at Grenville, being publicly humiliated and shamed. I could hardly breathe, feeling the sting of the court's judgement and the onlookers' criticism as if it were acute physical pain. But that spark of anger within me was still flickering. Somehow, I mustered the courage to speak up for my younger self:

> Me: When a child steals when they're in high school, should it be that they are torn to shreds and sent away out of the country so they cannot attend school for the next seven months, or indefinitely?

> Defence: All right. And did you ever consider that you could have been arrested and charged and prosecuted as a youth offender? Did that ever cross your mind when you're feeling sorry for yourself about this?

> Me: Every possible shame and type of consequence was well communicated to me at that time.

> Defence: All right. But they didn't have you prosecuted. They didn't turn you over to the police, did they?

> Me: No, sir.

As the minutes and hours of my cross-examination wore on, the torment became increasingly unbearable for me. Every utterance the defence made struck me like a physical blow, as though his words were instruments of torture. Everything in me wanted to quit. I kept silently begging him to stop.

Whenever the court took a recess, I'd fall apart. Tears would stream down my face. Friends would gather around me, telling me I was doing well. I'd respond, "It's too much. I can't do it anymore. I really don't think I can keep going." Even eating lunch was too overwhelming. But somehow, my team would prop me up with encouragement. So, with leaden feet, a body shaking from stress, and a head too heavy to focus, I'd trudge back to the front of the courtroom and subject myself to more interrogation.

When court finished for the day on Tuesday afternoon, the defence lawyer told the judge he'd need me again the next day. I collapsed internally. The truth was, the cross-examination was triggering me more than anything I had experienced since leaving Grenville. I left the witness stand thinking, *If I had any clue it would be this awful, I never would have agreed to this.*

Since I was still under cross-examination, I wasn't permitted to speak to my lawyers. But apparently, they were worried about me. Months later, Jacqueline told me that Loretta had cornered her that Tuesday, saying, "Whatever you do, make sure Beth gets back on the witness stand tomorrow. They would like nothing better than for her to quit. But if she does, her entire testimony will be inadmissible."

Jacqueline was my rock throughout the trial. For some ridiculous reason, I had planned to attend the trial by myself. I didn't want to burden my husband, who was understandably stressed about our finances. Just days before the trial began, he had tried to forbid me to attend for longer than the four days my Visa points would cover. That's when I lost it.

Shouting with a force that I had never uttered before or since, I scream-cried with an intensity that shocked even me. Through hysterical sobs, I made my needs known. I was going to that trial, and I would stay for as long as I was needed. He could take care of the kids and I was not going to apologize for relying on him.

To my husband's credit, he received the message loud and clear and he held down the fort back at home. Even better, Jacqueline instinctively understood that I needed her. Since the lawsuit launched, she had become the best friend I was never allowed to have. Without my asking, she took precious time off from her job as a high school vice principal to attend all five weeks. Together we found accommodations at Airbnbs, hotels, and even in her daughter's university residence. Without her, I wouldn't have made it through that ordeal. Jacqueline's encouragement and strength helped me keep returning to the stand of torment.

My final day of cross-examination was more of the same, including more questioning about why I sometimes couldn't specify exactly how certain abuse had played out. Each time, I'd feel panic rising. *How do I explain that many of my memories are still a blur?* I'd think. *That I've blocked them out. That I dissociated through much of high school?* Here's one such instance:

> Defence: You never experienced anyone yelling or screaming at you during any of these private light sessions, did you?
>
> Me: They were yelling. They were also speaking very sternly. It is a blur and it's not something I like to remember. In fact, I have repressed a lot of it, and I would disassociate during those light sessions as well.
>
> Defence: Everything's a blur with what went on during that time, even today, for you, isn't it?
>
> Me: No, it's not all a blur.
>
> Defence: It's largely a blur, isn't it?
>
> Me: A lot of it is, but I was there for almost thirty years, and I normalized it.
>
> Defence: I'm suggesting that you're filling in gaps with fabricated evidence. That you actually do not have an independent recollection from thirty years ago.
>
> Me: I am being as honest as anyone possibly can with my abilities of memory.

I've never felt such intense relief as I did when the defence finally said, "Thank you, those are my questions." It was even sweeter relief than having just given birth—without an epidural.

That cross-examination remains such a terrible memory that I can hardly bring myself to think about it. Even to write this book. I'd completely underestimated how painful it would be to endure an experience that would so thoroughly retraumatize me. It took me almost three years to get the courage to read through the transcripts of the trial. When I finally did, I was surprised at how well I'd spoken, under the circumstances. Somehow, I'd found a bravery that amazes me to this day.

After my cross-examination was over, our lawyers hugged me, and I basked in their genuine validation. That evening, after Jacqueline and I ate dessert for dinner (obviously), we got word that the defence was offering to settle. My testimony must have made quite an impact. But the amount they proposed was so low that we declined. At that point, our days in court were worth far more than what they were offering.

Several more witnesses spoke on the plaintiffs' behalf over the next week. (In total, we had sixteen witnesses, including Tim Blacklock, whose earlier depositions were submitted as evidence before he died en route to the trial.) Tears spilled down my face as they each bravely took the stand. Each one of them spoke of abuse that was so familiar yet so shocking. I had no idea that these former students—some whom I'd idolized as a child—had been so traumatized. Their experiences formed unique pieces of the puzzle that depicted the common issues students suffered at Grenville. All of them had left the school broken in some way and had been struggling their entire adult lives to heal from the damage.

Our lawyers chose our witnesses selectively. That way, a wide range of mistreatment that was common among the entire class would be shared. The worst abuse wasn't even presented, since this was a common issues trial. So with our witnesses, we'd hardly scratched the surface. Still, I hoped the judge had heard enough of our painful truth.

✝

One of the hardest parts of the trial was listening to some of the defence witnesses disregard the fact that they were under oath. I understood that some chose to recall only fond memories of their time at Grenville, so I was expecting their version of events. However, I wasn't prepared to hear the outright lies some of them would tell.

Unsurprisingly, Don Farnsworth seemed determined to protect his family's reputation, even if it meant stretching or denying the truth. I had to keep myself from exploding by taking detailed notes. (The margins of my journal were littered with expletives.) For some reason, Don downplayed every connection between the Community and Grenville. When asked what role the Community played in the school, he answered, "We might use them for advice from time to time, but they had no direct impact."

No direct impact? Images flooded my mind then, of retreats with the Mothers when they upended our lives and jobs. Of light sessions, disciplines, rules, and behaviours that mirrored the practises modelled by the Community.

In response to Don's remarks, our lawyer Loretta showed him official Ontario Corporation documents that listed Mother Cay, Mother Judy, and later Mother Betty as directors of the Grenville Christian College Corporation. They were dated 1984, 1986, and 1992. The direct impact was there, in black and white.

Bizarrely, Don also tried to distance Grenville's association with the Anglican Church. When asked if the school flew an Anglican flag, he answered, "No, there was never an Anglican flag at the school."

What? My tolerance for his lies was done. As soon as the court recessed, I grabbed the first Grenville yearbook stacked next to our lawyers. When I flipped to the first page, what did I see in full colour? The front steps of the school, flanked by three flags—including the Anglican one—flapping in the breeze. Loretta then presented this evidence to the court when she resumed Don's cross-examination.

Then there was Don's version of Discipline. According to his testimony under oath, when a student broke a rule, and it was a first offence, they'd be informally spoken to about their behaviour. Further problems might result in what he called a day of Discipline. He went on to say that, "Punishment as a general rule might be increased to three consecutive days of Discipline but would seldom go beyond that."

When Don insisted that students were never put on silence during Discipline, my blood boiled. In his 2011 affidavit, he'd stated, "It is simply untrue that students were forbidden to speak while on Discipline. That was never the case in all the years I was at Grenville." While on the stand in 2019, he confirmed, albeit slightly haltingly, that statement. "I'll just say that's what I remember."

Why is he misrepresenting facts that everyone witnessed? I thought.

Strangely, according to Don, there were also no rules against same-sex intimacy at Grenville. And when Loretta asked him if students were allowed to have sexual relations, Don answered cavalierly, "We just never came across it."

This infuriated me. By that time, it was well-known that Don's younger brother Robert had been accused of having sex with several teenage boys in the dorm when he was a staff member. In 2016, his arrest for sexual assault and gross indecency at Grenville made local headlines. And after a gruelling court case for his alleged victims, he was acquitted at trial. Still, the fact that Don was now stating under oath that the school had never come across homosexuality was beyond the pale. I kept thinking of friends who had undergone a form of gay conversion therapy while at Grenville. Friends who had been told by Father Farnsworth that they were worse than murderers, and then spent their lives drowning in shame.

The defence's next witness was Gordon Mintz, the school's final headmaster. In 2007, Gordon had been quoted in newspapers saying there was no truth to the allegations of abuse. Since then, he'd become a chaplain in the Canadian Armed Forces and risen through the ranks to lieutenant colonel. I couldn't believe that he'd jeopardize his career by appearing in court to defend Grenville twelve years after the controversy exploded.

Gordon seemed unfazed about publicly defending a school that had allegedly abused so many students. Since the mid-eighties, he'd worked at Grenville in maintenance, then as a teacher, then as a dean before becoming headmaster. So he knew very well how students had suffered. Yet here he was, joining forces with Don to defend the school's reputation.

The picture that Gordon painted of life at Grenville was a rosy one. When asked how long Discipline was likely to last, he answered, "One or two days, at the most, unless it was something very serious … in general, it was a day or two." He also said he couldn't recall what *Hotel D* meant or where it had been located.

The dean's apartment where you lived was only steps away from Hotel D where the boys on Discipline slept! I thought, incredulous. *You can't recall that information?*

Gordon went on to whitewash Grenville's harsh disciplines and rules. When asked about the rule prohibiting students from listening to music, he testified that Walkmans were forbidden because the adults didn't want students to stay up late.

"So, it had nothing to do with rock music being the devil's music?" Loretta pressed him on this point.

Gordon replied, "Correct."

"So, why would a student have an Iron Maiden t-shirt confiscated? Because a t-shirt can't keep anybody up late, can it?"

"That's a good question."

"Well, that student was told because it was rock music and that was the devil's music."

"Well, that's not a situation I was involved with so I couldn't speak to that."

My head was spinning. Everything remotely related to rock music had always been strictly forbidden. *How can a so-called man of God lie so effortlessly in court?*

During his cross-examination, Gordon was asked about former students he allegedly abused directly. In every case, he downplayed or denied the allegations, repeating again and again that he couldn't recall.

Other defence witnesses acted as if they'd never boarded at Grenville. Julie, a former prefect, testified that she couldn't remember any light sessions, even with the entire school. According to her, there had been zero abuse at Grenville. The only meeting she remembered was with all the prefects, when they were informed that because of their bad attitudes, they'd all lose their prefect pins and had to earn them back. According to Julie, this punishment was justified.

Lucy, a former prefect who attended Grenville from 1985 to 1988, had nothing but good memories of her time there. She denied every allegation made by the plaintiffs' witnesses. According to Lucy, she had a boyfriend and never got in trouble for it. When asked what she remembered from the school-wide assemblies, she said, "They were usually inspirational. Father Farnsworth would talk to us about life in general, or career goals, or being a better person. I remember always leaving feeling good and inspired."

"So in your recollection, these public assemblies, no student was ever stood up or singled out?" our lawyer Sabrina pressed.

Lucy confirmed that no one was ever singled out.

Lucy, don't you know you're under oath? I thought.

Eventually, Lucy admitted that dating was against the rules. She was then asked why she was allowed to break the no-dating rule while she was a prefect. She said, "Remember, it was a normal high school, and we were allowed to be normal people, and normal people end up liking other people. Nobody enforced that rule."

What the actual fuck? I wanted to scream.

Just when I thought I couldn't tolerate any more fabrication, Emma, who followed her sister Lucy onto the witness stand, described public assemblies with Father Farnsworth: "I remember being commended as a student body for having done well, or particular students being commended on their success, or doing well in school." When asked if there were discussions of sin at any group meetings, she said, "Not that I remember."

Like Lucy, Emma had been a prefect in grade thirteen. She had glowing memories of the good times at Grenville, but her recollections ended there. Under cross-examination, she said she couldn't remember the school ever enforcing the no-dating rule and claimed she had no memory of students being forced to stand up to be corrected in front of the school. Emma couldn't even remember students being in trouble for having bad attitudes or sins like haughtiness. According to her, there were also no dorm searches, and she got away with keeping medication in a locked drawer.

Emma also made it clear that she respected and admired Father Farnsworth. "[He] was somebody that touched my life in a very positive way. He provided lots of wisdom and guidance, and helped me become a more confident, strong individual to be successful in life. I thought he was a great person."

By the time all thirteen witnesses for the defence had finished testifying, my anxiety was off the charts. *What if the judge believes their version over ours?*

Fortunately, many of the defence witnesses corroborated the common issues to some extent. Some truthfully recalled aspects of the school's discipline, rules, and practises that echoed the plaintiffs' descriptions. They just happened to have fared better than others. The fact that the defence witnesses remembered Grenville in a positive light didn't negate our claims. As Dr. Barnes had explained during her testimony, some people remain unscathed by systemic abuse, even when they're exposed to it.

Before the court recessed on the trial's last day, lawyers from both sides made closing statements. Kleenex was passed around as Sabrina summarized the evidence presented by our sixteen plaintiffs. She then came to this decisive conclusion:

> "On the totality of the evidence produced at this trial, we respectfully submit that Grenville failed to meet their fiduciary obligations. They failed to provide an environment for their students free of emotional, physical, and sexualized abuse and maltreatment. Their policies and practises in fact created this unsafe environment and they allowed their religious beliefs and devotion to their counterculture lifestyle and their so-called Christian mission to supersede their purpose as an educational institution in the best interest of their students. Grenville's systemic negligence towards the class was oppressive, high-handed, and harsh. Grenville was indifferent to the consequences of its policies and practises employed

with its students. An award of punitive damages is appropriate to not only denounce this conduct but to deter similar conduct at large in the future."

I left the courtroom in a daze, feeling a strange mix of relief and pride. Once our team was outside, a few of us gathered around for a group picture. There we were, bonded by a shared purpose. I stood at the back, my face puffy and tearstained, lit with an exhausted but triumphant smile.

We knew the judge would have six to twelve months to make her ruling. There were no guarantees that justice would prevail. But I knew that win or lose, we had forced those who were responsible to take accountability. More importantly, as Sabrina had stated so well, we had harnessed the power of the justice system to deter similar conduct at large in the future.

The trial had been much more difficult than I'd anticipated. But that's what made it so rewarding. I left that experience with zero regrets, full of hope that the judge would rule in our favour.

Chapter 27
The Aftermath

After the trial, I returned home to continue my recovery. There was no escaping from that. My psychologist kept reminding me that the trial had been like surgery. My body had been riddled with the infection of unprocessed trauma. Now, I was like an open wound, full of toxicity that had to drain and heal, no matter how long that took.

Two months later, my insurance company granted me up to two years of long-term disability. Relief flooded through me, even as I worried about my eventual comeback. Just the thought of classrooms freaked me out so much that my brain refused to let me dwell on it. Every time I pictured any aspect of teaching, it was as if two metal doors in my mind would slam shut. I sensed my subconscious telling me, "Not now. Maybe, not ever." While this knowledge gave me immense grief, I had to accept it. I was in no shape to return to work. My mental health was in tatters.

Recovery can be lonely. I've been living in a permanent kind of limbo, healing in isolation for years. Nearly all my social life happens online. Still, anyone viewing my occasional posts would have no clue what my life is really like.

Allow me to set the record straight.

A considerable part of my recovery has involved walking. Photos of my outdoor treks that I've shared online may imply that I'm full of serenity and joy, surrounded by such beauty. What I didn't share was the monumental effort it took to get myself outside in the first place. That as soon as I woke up, waves of unease would swell into a tsunami of anxiety if I didn't exercise first thing. This was often accompanied by a feeling of despair and apathy so powerful that I could barely imagine being active. I often found myself shaking with sobs, unable to put my sneakers on. Then, throughout my exercise, I forced myself to keep going, no matter how dizzy I felt.

Exercise was the only thing that took the edge off my anxiety. When the gyms closed during the pandemic, I panicked, even though I hadn't been enjoying fitness classes since I'd started tapering off Ativan. I couldn't stand the noise, the intensity, the feeling of disorientation. Being in crowds sent me over the edge. There was no joy in the movement I'd once loved. I'd cry in the middle of classes, which was embarrassing.

COVID-19 led me to discover the Ferguson Forest, nestled in my hometown. As I walked its trails in 2020, something about its atmosphere made my tears flow in earnest. Years and years of pent-up pain began to release, one step at a time. It was like waking up in a new, welcoming world free of stress and expectation. Before then, I'd had little appreciation for nature and its calming beauty. Now, I can't cope without my regular forest visits.

Sometimes I post photos of my forest walks. But I don't include the pain behind the camera lens. People see the gorgeous trees, the deer, the sparkling water, the vibrant wildflowers, and the soaring Canadian geese. They don't realize how often I cry while walking. How I'm often confronted with painful memories that hit me out of the blue. Or how I'm soaking up the tranquility of the forest like a plant dying of thirst.

†

When I share photos of my paintings on Facebook, no one knows the story behind them. I turned to painting to try to quell my breathless anxiety. For over a year, my heart was always racing. According to my Fitbit, my heart would rush at 110 beats per minute while I was folding clothes or brushing my teeth.

Despite my crippling self-doubt, painting became my solace and a big step in my healing. My Grandma Gillis had been an oil painter of some renown. I'd always admired her incredible work. It turns out I inherited some of her gifts. I couldn't believe how much I enjoyed painting and how natural it felt. And the best part? My heart would slow to a healthy seventy beats per minute while I painted. It was miraculous.

Since I began, I've built up quite a portfolio of my acrylic renditions of landscapes, flowers, birds, even dog portraits. I look at them in wonder. *How did I manage that?* Still, I often hesitate to share my paintings online. While I'm proud of them, it's impossible to explain their role in my healing. How painting forces me to be still, calm, and quietly creative. How much I need to do this so I can learn to breathe and allow my nervous system to recover.

†

Occasionally, I post photos of my three Cavaliers asleep on my lap. While Harry, Hermione, and Ron are the cutest, most cuddly dogs on Earth, it took me almost two years off work before I could relax enough to nap with them.

One day I told my psychologist, "Sometimes, while I'm walking in the forest, I feel like I'm fighting a battle between opposing impulses. I feel compelled to run or do push-ups while simultaneously looking for places to lie down and nap. And it doesn't help that I'm usually crying."

"Are you still drinking caffeine?" she asked.

"Yes. I drink it all day long."

"What?" She looked alarmed. I think she expected that I'd taken her advice to quit years before. I hadn't.

When I quit caffeine cold turkey in January 2021, I entered a new phase of recovery. On top of the initial headaches, I'd need several naps a day. It was like my nervous system finally had a chance to calm down. Between short bouts of household chores, I'd sit on the couch, and all three of my dogs would pile on my lap. Minutes later, we'd all be sound asleep, oblivious to everything else.

Eventually, I cut out the morning naps. But ever since quitting caffeine, I've needed to sleep for two to three hours each afternoon. I get an overwhelming wave of exhaustion, dizziness, and the feeling of walking through quicksand. That's my cue to climb into bed and under my weighted blanket. I sleep soundly and dream about Grenville and teaching. When I wake up, I have enough energy to feed my family before my next rest on the couch with my dogs.

Living this way is humbling and strange. I spent my first fifty years living on high alert. Racing at top speed, always feeling like I wasn't going fast enough. I couldn't even nap on the rare sick days I took. Now, it's a whole different story. I crave peace and quiet. When I have to miss a nap, I pay for it with acute dizziness and exhaustion. It turns out that you can't outrun unprocessed complex trauma forever.

†

Don't get me started with selfies on social media. Anyone looking at my smiling photos would never guess the intensity of my unrelenting body shame. Or the lengths to which I've gone to conquer my issues with food. No one viewing my profile pics would guess that I've prioritized recovery like a full-time job. That I've turned to endless audiobooks or podcasts on body image and binge-eating recovery, listening with an insatiable thirst for knowledge and hoping to understand myself better.

The road to recovery from a lifelong eating disorder is complex and excruciatingly slow, even with therapy, expert coaching, and all the determination in the world. By 2020, I was sick to death of craving, bingeing, and drowning in self-loathing. It didn't help that for years I'd followed the advice of too many so-called experts whose guidance only fuelled my eating disorder.

When I turned fifty, I resolved to find a way to stop bingeing, come hell or high water. Ever since, I've done intense work to heal a lifetime of diet-related trauma. Still, there's further ground to cover. It's frustrating to discover that there's no one-size-fits-all in eating-disorder recovery. There doesn't seem to be an expert who has all the answers. At least, I haven't found one yet.

In 2020, I invested in a masterclass called Stop Fighting Food, created by a woman named Isabel. Her message that binges are a natural response to years of dieting and feeling deprived around food was game-changing. She explained that trying to control binges by restricting foods only makes binges worse. She also clarified that even if we were no longer restricting, our binges would continue to occur if we remained under the influence of diet mentality and fatphobia. Even our fear, shame, and self-judgement are powerful triggers for binges. The relief I felt by listening to Isabel is hard to quantify. I felt seen, understood, and validated. I also felt hope unlike any I'd felt before.

I listened to Isabel's lessons and coaching calls day and night. Whenever I could, I joined live calls and bravely asked for her help. Isabel kept urging me to surrender my desire to control: "You cannot be out of control with food unless you are trying to be in control in the first place." She challenged me to accept my body, my food, the fact that there's no magical fix, and no wagon to fall off. "You won't win," she said, advising me to stay out of the boxing ring with food. "Even if you do, you'll lose by getting battered and beaten and crazy trying to hold back the force of food's power."

Yup. I know that's right.

As difficult as it was, I followed the advice of Isabel and others like her and gave myself permission to eat everything. This isn't easy for someone who's afraid of weight gain. I attempted to accept my size and heal from my relentless body shame. I listened to podcasts like *Maintenance Phase* and *Go Love Yourself* and read books like *More than a Body* by the Kite sisters and *Anti-Diet* by Christy Harrison. I joined another online support group run by Joni in Australia, helping women find peace by processing their diet-related trauma. I filled many journals with my fears, worries, and frustration. I shared my struggles with strangers during Joni's group coaching sessions. Little by little, I began the work of deprogramming from decades of fatphobia.

The scariest part of recovering from diet mentality was allowing weight gain. I was required to battle this fear head-on. No amount of superficial body positivity can heal this deep trauma. I had to go back to my childhood and relive every memory of fat shaming. Every cruel word, every light session, every mention of my gluttony. I wrote about it in my journal, processing traumatic memories with tears, meditation, deep breathing, hypnosis, coaching, and more tears.

I've made a lot of progress in my eating-disorder recovery. Admittedly, I still experience powerful urges to binge, especially at night. It often feels like an aching emptiness that can never be filled. The good news is, I'm learning to observe my urges, rather than acting on them. I'm currently following advice from Kathryn Hansen's book *Brain Over Binge* and feeling optimistic. More importantly, I've learned that I don't need to feel ashamed of my eating disorder. It was never my fault. One thing's for sure: I'll never attempt to diet again. I also have a great deal of self-compassion that I never had before. Shame used to fuel every attempt to fix myself. Now, I approach my struggles with curiosity and kindness. I'm hopeful that someday I'll feel comfortable sharing full-body photos of myself on social media. Just as I am.

†

Once in a blue moon, I share photos of family gatherings. We all smile and appear to be so close. The painful truth, however, is that my family was broken beyond repair by our cult leaders. I'm trying to salvage our relationships, but most of our interactions are triggering. For the most part, we've been living separate lives. In the rare event that we get together, at least two of my brothers are missing. During the past twenty years, only two photos have been taken with all four siblings.

Garth has faithfully kept his vows to be a monk at the Community. When I became a representative plaintiff for the class action lawsuit—which indirectly implicated the Community—my brother cut off all communication with me. I love my brother Garth. He's an intelligent, thoughtful, and loving soul. But now he's lost to me. We agree on basically nothing. That was confirmed when I last saw him in 2016. (Guess who got his vote in the US presidential election that year.)

Then there's Rob, my youngest brother. How do I describe his situation? In many ways, my life has been a cakewalk compared to Rob's.

In fact, when I considered joining the lawsuit back in 2007, it was primarily on Rob's behalf, not mine.

As far as I know, Rob is still alive, but just barely. He was abused for the first twenty-one years of his life before leaving Grenville without any coping skills. Ever since he left, he's been battling to survive. When a debilitating depression sidelined him, he tried to end his life and landed in the psych ward. Then, when bipolar mania set in, he was incarcerated for public mischief and destruction of property. He's bounced between the psych ward and jail for the past two decades, dealing with homelessness and substance abuse on top of his mental health challenges. It's been trauma stacked upon trauma.

I'm always braced for terrible news about Rob. His mental illness has intensified so much that it's hard to find hope. And I blame Grenville for this. Of our four siblings, Rob had the most potential. His poetry makes me cry. His prose puts my writing efforts to shame. Once every few years, Rob will stabilize, and I'll catch a glimpse of the man he might have been. From jail, when he's sobered up and properly medicated, sometimes he writes poems and letters to me that are full of his brilliant and hilarious insights. But those moments are fleeting, and I've learned to cherish them like precious gifts.

When I think about Rob, I'm enraged with every Grenville defender who hasn't acknowledged the harm so many students suffered. The former leaders who defended the school in court proved they couldn't care less about the lives damaged by the school. They seem content to obstruct the progress of a class action that could help victims who barely survived. Rob needs expert treatment. He needs housing, hope, and love. He needs to know he isn't worthless. I've fought this lawsuit for myself, for hundreds of damaged survivors, and especially for my little brother. I only hope my efforts won't be too late.

†

I used to have a Room of Shame. Right off the kitchen, it contained everything from hockey gear to teaching supplies, cleaning equipment, games, toys, or clothing to sell. Every year or so, I'd clean up the clutter and post before and after photos. After two years of recovery, I finally mustered the energy to tackle the room once and for all. Garry was so sick of the mess that he pitched in. I was a tearful, shaky mess throughout. But within a week, we transformed that Room of Shame into a functional home office.

I proudly shared photos of that transformation. What I've never shared was that my most profound healing has taken place in that room. Once I set up that office, I felt a pull toward writing.

Several signs pointed me in that direction. First, Jacqueline kept urging me to write my story. I thought she was over-eager. *I mean, what's so interesting about my life?* Then, one day, my psychologist told me that I should write a book someday. She felt that the process would be healing.

Around that time, Facebook ads for a memoir writing course created by Canadian author Alison Wearing started popping up in my feed. I followed my instinct and signed up for her course. It was a revelation. Long-buried recollections would flood back whenever I attempted an assignment. It was like my memories were stored in a fortress full of locked rooms. The course encouraged me to open one door after another.

The writing process was transformative. A powerful sense of purpose took hold. I discovered the benefits of writing, which propelled me to keep going despite my difficulties. I'd start with a shred of a memory, and as I wrote about it, the details would reveal themselves to me, as if by magic. Powerful emotions also surged almost out of nowhere. Tears would flow freely as I wrote. Thank goodness for Ron, our ruby Cavalier. He'd sleep on the floor next to my desk, and whenever I began crying, he'd wake up and demand to lick away every tear.

Writing about my past hasn't been easy. Especially while dealing with the cognitive impairment resulting from BIND (benzodiazepine-induced neurological dysfunction). At first, I could only handle writing for twenty minutes at a stretch. Also, my word recall was appalling. Luckily, Alison's course suited me well; it led me back into my past in baby steps. I never felt overwhelmed by the enormity of my history.

Each task allowed me to sample my story by focusing on one bite at a time. Once or twice, I shared an assignment with my classmates online. The feedback was incredibly motivating. "I can't wait to read more!" or, "What happened next?" or, "Your story must be written!"

It took me several months to finish Alison's course. Every day I'd write for about an hour. Once I felt too mentally, physically, and emotionally drained to continue, I'd take a nap. Without sleep, I'd turn into a crying, shaky mess. My naps had become an essential part of my healing. And writing made them even more so.

By the end of the memoir course, I decided to tackle my story from beginning to end. I didn't get caught up in dreams of publishing. All I knew was that writing about my past was intensely healing. If I ever wanted to recover completely, I'd better keep at it.

I've been writing in my former Room of Shame ever since. It's ironic that I'm repairing a lifetime of shame in that room.

Chapter 28
Revelations While Writing

Writing a memoir is not for the faint of heart. Especially when you have the sense that your story is not your own. That your words might resonate with hundreds, maybe thousands of others. So I kept at it for years, despite the triggers, tears, and exhaustion. It seemed the only way to turn my pain into purpose.

Writing, like recovery, is lonely. Sometimes I'd wonder, *Will this story matter to anyone?* Then, I'd talk to others whose experiences at Grenville were as devastating as they were inspiring. With stories like the following haunting me, I kept on writing, not just for myself, but for my fellow survivors.

I started by peppering my parents with questions to better understand my early childhood. Luckily, they had accepted that there was no escaping from our painful past. Over time, and through many difficult conversations, not only did they finally choose to support the lawsuit, but they encouraged my writing. To their credit, my parents answered everything I threw at them. We spent one memorable weekend at a campsite, revisiting those decades at Grenville.

I finally heard my dad's side of the story when he ran away from the Community. He has forgotten a lot about life at Grenville, but the incident from that summer is seared into his memory.

> "I don't think I'll ever forget the August of '87 when I attended that first Master Schola retreat. One reason I

went was to learn all about pipe organs so that Grenville could acquire one. I had arranged to meet the organ tuner in the Community's empty church before the retreat's first dinner. He had first-hand knowledge about organs that were for sale. While we were there, I asked him all kinds of questions and the organist demonstrated various sounds with the numerous pipes and pedals.

"After the first retreat dinner, someone tapped me on the shoulder and ordered me to report to the kitchen. Mothers Cay and Judy were waiting for me by the door to their private elevator. I can still picture their stern faces.

"To my shock, the Mothers blasted me. They were enraged by my audacity to meet the organ tuner—an outsider—without their knowledge or permission. They were appalled by my haughtiness and determined to obliterate my ego. Accusations were hurled at me, the kind that wound deeply and are never forgotten. I stood there, immobilized by their vicious attack, completely caught off guard.

"Once the Mothers were finished, I was so devastated that I could barely breathe. I spent the next few hours too distraught to speak, think, or sleep. Finally, at 2:00 a.m., I grabbed a few necessities and snuck out of the dorm, blindly following my instinct to get the hell out of that place.

"I walked all through the night along Old King's Highway. At daybreak, I came upon a bus stop and scrounged enough money to buy a ticket to Boston.

Upon arrival, I called my dad and asked for help. He wired me money to purchase the fare to Buffalo, NY, where he met me. Then he drove me back to his home in London, Ontario.

"That following week was a time of torment. I agonized over my future, weighing my options, grappling with my confusion and despair. Ultimately, I made the choice to return, with my tail between my legs."

It took a while for his words to sink in. Then my blood began to simmer. "They treated you like a criminal for your desire to learn about pipe organs? At a music retreat? Dad, do you realize how fucked up that is?"

For once my dad didn't object to my cursing.

In addition to answering my questions, my dad agreed to scour his vast storage for confession letters he had once written. (Finally, his hoarding of Grenville paraphernalia came in handy!)

What he shared was a revelation. Here are excerpts from the letter my dad wrote to Father Farnsworth once he chose to return to Grenville:

I come to you to beg forgiveness. I want to say something which I can't articulate very well—a heart cry. Please listen to me. I cannot continue to live as I have been living in my grin-and-bear-it existence all these years. I cannot continue to live in Hell so that when I die, I can go to Heaven.

You say that my problems are not unique. But I hope there are not many others here whose hearts are filled with terror after hearing a staff meeting being announced. I hope there aren't many others who, when they see you coming down the hall, panic until they can think of something to say that might divert attention away from correction. I hope there aren't many others who, after finishing a task as routine as, for example, playing a postlude on the organ, breathe a sigh of relief that they have made it through an entire workweek alive. Mine is a truly hellish experience.

Charles, you are my priest, and my father in God. You say often that you love me, or that I've succeeded at this or that. Yet you qualify such expressions of commendation by saying that my successes are only by the grace of God. I myself am miserly in my praise. My oldest son, who has spent the last two years at RMC trying—consciously or unconsciously—to please me, and who, during that time, has done nothing to disgrace either himself or us, was rewarded for his efforts by my saying to him that he was welcome to visit us only by invitation. That he should no longer consider our home as his.

In spite of everything, we have four beautiful children—at least according to the world's standards. But they are growing older, and I feel as though I don't know them. I am even afraid to touch them other than in a formal greeting. For years I did nothing with them, or for them, except what I was required to do. And now I have few fond memories. My career meant everything, and my family meant nothing.

My love for my family gets twisted and distorted into something that hurts them terribly when I try to deny my natural instincts to do what I think is acceptable. Nevertheless, were I to leave them now, I would be doing further, likely irreparable, damage.

I know you have already relieved me of my musical responsibilities, and I deserve no consideration from you. I beg you to let me stay. But I also beg of you, even if God doesn't change my heart, please love me, and help me in spite of who I am, for I cannot carry on as I have for the past fifteen years.

The price my dad paid to return to Grenville was steep. He was ordered to apologize to the leaders in person. Ken MacNeil escorted my dad back to Cape Cod, where the Mothers informed him that he'd have to give up music as a consequence of his haughtiness. This meant that my dad, the heart of Grenville's musical program, was no longer allowed to teach music or direct the choir, the band, the orchestra, or the musicals. He wasn't allowed near a piano. Even the students were told he wasn't allowed to enter the music room.

I never knew how close my dad came to breaking his vows. Thirty-five years later, he told me he stayed only because he didn't want us kids to lose the benefit of an elite education. What he hadn't considered was that by staying, his kids would be broken far worse than he'd ever been.

†

I can count the number of former staff kids who are still my friends on one hand. Most cut ties after I joined the lawsuit, including my only bridesmaids. So I treasure the few friendships that remain intact. Even so, it's taken years for us to start discussing our past with one another. I guess it just seemed like a topic too painful to touch. After I began writing my manuscript, my friend Dawn revealed an experience which stunned and, frankly, enraged me.

As we sat at her dining room table reminiscing, I pictured Dawn, a star athlete in high school who I'd always admired. She was four years older than me and by the time she graduated from high school, staff kids were being pressured to stay for life. I remembered those light sessions, but I had no idea what it was like for those who, like Dawn, risked leaving.

Dawn laughed as she told me that the first time she escaped the school was during the middle of a light session. "What? Tell me more!" I begged.

"It was one of the ones when Father Farnsworth was putting the fear of God in us. You know, warning us that we would get pregnant, become prostitutes, alcoholics, and go to Hell if we left. He also started shaming staff kids who had already left, including my only brother, who was in university. This upset me so much that I got up to leave. Then Father Farnsworth yelled: 'If you walk out that door, don't ever come back!' So I packed a bag and took a train to Toronto, with nowhere to go."

"Dawn! You badass!" I marvelled at her courage as she recounted how she navigated the next week in a strange city, before reluctantly returning to finish high school. Sadly, her next words didn't surprise me at all.

"During the final months of grade thirteen, I was put on Discipline repeatedly. Father Farnsworth took every opportunity to instill fear and guilt in me. I'll never forget when he pushed my face right up against the window of the woodchip boiler. I shook with fear as I felt the extreme heat on my face. Father Farnsworth held me there while yelling in my ear that I would become a prostitute and suffer the flames of Hell if I left Grenville."

"Oh Dawn, I'm so sorry," I managed, as my own memories resurfaced. We sat for a while in silence before I asked, "What happened after grad?"

"Somehow, I graduated with honours and was accepted to Queen's University. However, the transition to the outside world proved harder than I anticipated. On one hand, I was excited to be free from Grenville, but I couldn't shake the fear and guilt overwhelming me.

"By the end of my first year at Queen's, I felt so confused and torn that I reached out to the Community of Jesus for guidance. The leaders suggested that I leave university to live and work in their sisterhood. Out of desperation, I agreed."

"You left Queen's to join the sisterhood?" I shook my head, horrified at the strength of our collective brainwashing.

"Yup. For over a year I was moved back and forth between the Community and Grenville, trying to find my place. They didn't seem to know what to do with me."

I smiled, recalling Dawn's fierce independence, which wasn't even immune to the coercion. But what she revealed next stopped me in my tracks.

"The second time back at GCC I had to undergo an AIDS test, which was mandatory for students and staff by then. A few days later, I was summoned to Father Farnsworth's office. With only the two of us behind closed doors, he informed me that I had tested positive for AIDS."

"Wait, what?" I couldn't believe my ears. Dawn confirmed it and added, "He didn't stop there." Horrified, I braced myself for more.

"Farnsworth then proceeded to ask me many sexually invasive questions: 'How many men have you slept with? Have you had oral sex? Anal sex?' He seemed to be taking pleasure in the interrogation. Of course, I felt embarrassed, awkward, and violated."

I interrupted, my anger taking over. "Shouldn't you have heard that news from a doctor? Isn't that a breach of confidentiality?" I had many more questions, but I bit my tongue while she continued.

"I wondered the same thing but was too afraid to voice my misgivings. So I accepted the news and submitted to the treatment that followed. While I waited for the results of a second test, which somehow took weeks to materialize, I was forced into quarantine. I was moved into Father Farnsworth's guest bedroom. Whenever I came downstairs, I had to wear latex gloves. I was told not to touch anything in the house—especially their dishes—without the gloves on and not to touch anyone. I also continued my daily cleaning duties at the school and had to sit alone at the back of the dining room during meals. It was beyond humiliating.

"One morning Father Farnsworth asked me what I would do if my second test came back positive. Had I been thinking about living my life with AIDS? His question troubled me so much that somehow, I woke up in that moment. Was all of this a twisted power play?"

Yes! It was! I wanted to scream. But I let her keep talking.

"After I finally tested negative, I found the courage to leave for good. A friend from Kingston offered to pick me up. My mom wasn't even allowed to say goodbye, and a staff member physically blocked her from reaching me. I'm still haunted by that memory. So is my mom.

"I jumped into the car and didn't look back. After that, I tried to keep in touch with my mom, but the letters I sent were confiscated. Mom was rarely allowed to visit me in Kingston, and when she did, she had to be chaperoned by another staff lady."

By now Dawn and I were both crying. I was overcome with grief and anger over what she'd endured. "How did you cope? Did you ever see a doctor?"

"Well, the entire ordeal terrorized me. I couldn't bring myself to confirm the results independently. I spent the next three decades wondering. *Did I ever have AIDS? Had Farnsworth lied?* Instead, I resigned myself to living with intense fear and shame. I guess it's no wonder that I've battled suicidal thoughts for years."

My mind was blown by Dawn's story. It has haunted me ever since. I'd always considered Dawn to be a happy, confident woman. I guess like me, she's a good actress. Sadly, she's often told me that she feels like a broken woman with very little self-esteem. Being psychologically abused since childhood will have that impact.

†

Karen's story was yet another eye-opener. She flew all the way from Vancouver to attend the 2019 trial in Toronto. I couldn't help but notice her tear-streaked face during those days in court. My heart went out to her at the time, but I really had no idea what she had experienced, even though we graduated one year apart. Months later, my curiosity got the better of me and I asked her about her story. At that point, Karen had just begun to write about her memories in a journal. So she sent me twenty-nine pictures of handwritten pages. What I read left me shaken.

Imagine being so traumatized that you can't remember cycling a distance of over 3,000 kilometres! There's a lot more to Karen's story, but even this fact paints an alarming picture. Karen's life was severely impacted by the trauma she sustained at Grenville. This was most evident in her experience with one of the teams that cycled across Canada in the school's most epic publicity campaigns. To me, it seemed that bike team members were held up on a pedestal for the rest of us to emulate. When I learned the ugly truth from Karen, my past envy seemed absurd, and my heart broke as she set the record straight. Here are some excerpts from her journal entries that impacted me the most:

> I can hardly bear to recall the memories of that hellish year on the Trans-Canada Cycling Team. In fact, many of them are blocked, even after years of therapy.
>
> No one knows what we went through. Sure, other students saw us red-faced and drenched in sweat, barely able to walk after our gruelling training sessions. What they didn't see were the constant light sessions behind closed doors. Our coaches would blindside us with emergency team meetings. Pulling us from classes, meals, or church, or waking us in the middle of the night to terrorize us. We would be verbally abused for anything: perceived underperformance, perceived overperformance, and everything in between. Our entire team was often accused of having an evil spirit. Individuals were attacked for being too competitive, haughty, lazy, rebellious, even slutty. One time, Mr. Ortolani was in a rage like nothing I had ever seen before. He launched out of his chair so fast that he came within inches of hitting me, his spit spraying my face as he yelled.
>
> There was a lot more that other students never knew. They didn't know we were punished with extreme physical training. Even if we collapsed or vomited, the coaches forced us to continue training faster, harder.

Then we would have to join the rest of the school for all the usual evening activities, dreading the next horrific light session about what had happened at training that day.

Other students also didn't know we were routinely isolated. I was forbidden to socialize with anyone other than the female staff or Community kids on the team. I would be disciplined if I was seen spending time with my former friends. We were ordered to never discuss with *anyone* what took place on the team.

In addition, no one knew about our restricted diets. I was only a size twelve, but the coaches continually told me I was fat, lazy, weak, and dragging the team down. They told me what I was allowed to eat, withheld food, and made me train harder to lose weight. During that intense year, I was always starving. In desperation, I began hoarding any food I could steal, I took diet pills, and bulimia took hold of me. I began exercising in the middle of the night to punish myself.

On top of that, other students didn't know what it was like to be indoctrinated like we were. Our team had to attend separate confessional religious ceremonies in a hidden chapel at the school every night before compline. With other staff members, coaches, and students, we had to pray and confess out loud in front of portraits of the Mothers. Anything I confessed during these sessions was fair game for future light sessions.

I was in a constant fear state. It wasn't safe to trust anyone. I became withdrawn and isolated. The adults were trying to break me, and sadly they did. During light sessions, I would dig my nails into the soft skin of my hands, causing welts that sometimes bled and lasted for days. Dissociating like this removed me from the attacks. It felt like I was floating outside myself, watching it happen, but sounds were muted like I was underwater. They couldn't hurt me there.

The trip across Canada was a waking nightmare. Most of my memories come in random flashes. I recall daily light sessions in restaurants or hotel rooms, sometimes in the middle of the night. Before, during and after every ride I endured verbal abuse. I would cry while cycling and be forced to ride despite injury, fatigue, or illness.

A few traumatic events are seared into my memory. We started out in British Columbia. I was the first cyclist to ride through the avalanche tunnels in the high Rocky Mountains and I was not prepared. Carrying a lot of speed on a downhill and wearing sunglasses, I suddenly went from bright sunlight into pitch darkness. I was terrified, blinded and deafened by the echoing sound of eighteen-wheelers rushing by me. When my bike hit a pothole, the front tire blew out, and I fought to maintain control. I thought I was going to die. Terror gripped me as I braced for the inevitable crash.

After what seemed like an eternal struggle to stay upright, I abruptly burst out into the sunlight. Somehow, I pulled myself over to the guard barrier on the edge of the road, that was meant to protect vehicles from plunging down the cliff. Shaking uncontrollably, I collapsed on the barrier and waited for the support van to come to my aid. I was alone on the side of a cliff, with huge trucks flying past me, in traumatized shock. I still remember the push and pull of the vehicles passing me as I sat sobbing, waiting for help. My front tire was shredded, and the rim was damaged. I couldn't believe I had survived.

No one came to my aid. *No one.* Finally, after over half an hour, I knew I had to save myself. Struggling to stand, I lifted my destroyed bike to my shoulder and headed into the dark hell of the next tunnel. Shaking and exhausted, I staggered through the darkness, terrified by the trucks rushing by. When I limped back out into the sunlight, coaches and teammates were waiting for me on the roadside. Instead of being met with compassion, the coaching staff bombarded me, their faces red as they screamed.

"How dare you stop in the tunnel, putting everyone at risk!"

"How dare you keep everyone waiting!"

"Do you know how stupid that was?"

I stood there in mute disbelief as they railed at me. When a teammate finally noticed the damage to my bike, there was no care, no concern, no empathy. I was never invited to explain myself. There were never any apologies for the coaches' verbal tirade. Later, I was put on Discipline and isolated for several days.

I can only recall flashes of other parts of the trip. At one point, I cycled in prairie winds that were so strong that all the bikes were blown off the top of the transport vans. I'll also never forget the cold rainy morning when I was cycling near Thunder Bay, Ontario. I watched in horror as my riding partner was sucked in by the draft of an eighteen-wheeler speeding past her. Elisa came within inches of being run over.

I have photos showing that when we made it to Toronto, we were welcomed like heroes at the SkyDome. VIP sponsors gathered in Trevor Eyton's skybox to watch our team cycle into the stadium. Photographs show us riding in the infield, handing a huge cheque to the Juvenile Diabetes Foundation, and one of me and a teammate being interviewed by media outlets while on the pitcher's mound. Each picture fills me with foreboding.

Our glory was short-lived. Something really, really bad happened in Toronto, though my brain refuses to recall the details of the light session. I have this huge feeling of dread, and I feel sick to my stomach. Otherwise, I have no other memories of the rest of that trip through Canada. It's like they've been wiped out completely.

Chapter 29
Victory (with a Side of Loss)

On February 26, 2020, I received a life-changing email. The first line read, *For your reading pleasure. WE WON!!!!* Loretta Merritt had forwarded Justice Leiper's seventy-five-page ruling in which she sided with us on all counts.

With shaking hands, I texted my fellow representative plaintiffs. *OMG!! DID YOU HEAR?!!* My body trembled as waves of emotion swept over me. I could hardly contain the overwhelming relief and joy, even as tears flowed freely. It was as if I'd been holding my breath for over a decade, and now I could finally exhale.

I spent that evening on the phone with Jacqueline and Lisa as we pored over the epic ruling, each of us taking turns reading Justice Leiper's words aloud. It felt surreal. *Am I dreaming? Did we really win?*

Not only did we win, but we were gifted the most precious validation in the form of Justice Leiper's words. The following excerpt is taken from the final pages of her report:

> I have concluded that the evidence of maltreatment and the varieties of abuse perpetrated on students' bodies and minds in the name of the COJ values of submission and obedience was class-wide and decades-wide. The plaintiffs have established that this conduct departed from the standards of the day. The school created a place

to mould students using the precepts and norms of the COJ. It obscured its more extreme practises from its patrons and parents. It failed to keep records of the more extreme disciplinary practises. It had no written policy on its disciplinary practises. It required the appearance of happiness, enforced by strict discipline. Grenville insisted on the highest possible standards for its own benefit and reputation to continue to obtain enrolment. The hidden cost for many students came in the form of lack of privacy, physical and emotional stability, autonomy, and well-being.

Grenville knowingly created an abusive, authoritarian, and rigid culture which exploited and controlled developing adolescents who were placed in its care. In doing so, it caused harm to some students and exposed others to the risk of harm. This meant that the headmasters profited from their positions, reputations, status, and control over a cowed student body.

Grenville's founders knew they had created a counter-culture—they had a preferential place in the culture and did not hold themselves to the standards they expected of others. There were no light sessions for the headmasters, in spite of the espoused value of living in the light. Without any accountability, either by reporting to a board or to written established policy, the headmasters were the absolute masters of the Grenville domain, indulging in acts of petty cruelty and doling out disproportionate physical and emotional pain to vulnerable or less-favoured students.

The finding of systemic negligence is a finding that the defendants' conduct deviated from established standards on a class-wide basis. I need not know with precision the number of students affected to make a finding that punitive damages are appropriate in law in this case. The principles drive that conclusion.

Finally, the fact that Grenville is no longer in existence does not remove the policy aims of applying punitive damages. These policies include denunciation and general deterrence in the public interest. This goes beyond sending a specific message to the administration of the school. Given the findings in this case, I conclude that it is important to denounce conduct which can affect the health and emotional well-being of individuals throughout their life. The duties owed to the developing children by educational institutions must be upheld: the failure to abide by the standards can assess a tremendous social cost to individuals, their families and to other institutions. Such failure can also erode public trust in private educational institutions which must meet the standards and abide by fiduciary obligations and duties of care towards students.

I hadn't dared to dream of this kind of acknowledgement. Sure, we'd only won the first trial, and we had a long way to go before damages were determined. But this victory was monumental. The judge had truly heard us. She recognized the severity of the abuse we'd endured. More importantly, she acknowledged the importance of ruling in our favour as a matter of public interest. I'd wanted our case to be a cautionary tale, and Justice Leiper acknowledged that.

Our jubilation was short-lived. The defence quickly announced they'd appeal the decision. They found fault with each of Justice Leiper's conclusions. Around that time, the pandemic had shut down our country, and the world. Everyone was reeling from the difficulty posed by lockdowns and disease lurking in our midst. We were told that the appeal wouldn't happen for quite some time, with courts closed and cases backing up.

I spent the next year trying to put our lawsuit out of my mind. But dread would creep over me every time I thought about it. *What if the defence wins on appeal?*

Finally, the appeal hearing was scheduled for May 4, 2021, on Zoom. Three new judges from the Court of Appeal for Ontario would preside over it.

For two months beforehand, my dizziness worsened. It was so debilitating that I couldn't turn my head without falling over. My brain couldn't seem to handle any more Grenville stress. With the appeal came all the usual fear and doubt: *Will the other judges side with us? Will they think we were exaggerating?*

Attending the proceedings from the comfort of my home was a silver lining. None of us were being called for testimony this time, either. It was only a battle between our lawyers. Our legal team warned us that the defence had hired a hotshot lawyer who specialized in appeals. From my perspective, he specialized in tormenting me—and misrepresenting the truth. Whenever he wove his warped version of reality, I felt like I was being tortured all over again. Even so, I forced myself to listen as the defence proposed his twisted arguments. He tried to point out that Grenville couldn't have known its treatment would harm students (*Wait, what?*) and that most of the abuse wasn't systemic. He also repeatedly made incorrect leaps in logic. For instance, he said that girls were never paddled, meaning at least 50 percent of the class didn't experience physical abuse.

I sat there fuming, desperate to raise my objections. *Just because we didn't present a female witness who testified about being paddled doesn't mean girls weren't beaten!* Our witnesses had only scratched the surface of the abuse that had taken place at Grenville.

All day long, I ate my homemade chocolate chip cookies in anguish, which didn't help matters. By the end of the proceedings, I was a nervous wreck in a sugar coma. It wasn't my best day.

The appeal also stirred up all kinds of drama online. During the lead-up and the aftermath, Grenville survivors joined in the typical frenzied posting that always coincided with our court proceedings. As always, some Grenville supporters tried to discount our collective pain. I couldn't handle seeing alumni getting re-victimized by the school's defenders. At one point, Don Farnsworth went so far as to post, *My father abused no one.* His words triggered so much rage and despair that I cried for two days. After thirteen years of litigation, he still refused to acknowledge the truth.

When Mel, a former staff kid, stood up to Don with this brilliant post, I let out a loud whoop:

> DON FARNSWORTH, you say you "wish you could communicate in a way that would help all of us to come to terms." The best way would be if you stopped communicating altogether with students processing their trauma from Grenville. As long as your "terms" exist in a world of denial and lies, you continue the abuse. It has gone on long enough. The fact that you are on this space talking to students in this manner is appalling. Many of us have had to accept that our parents abused and traumatized young students put in their care. And many of us feel the weight of being complicit. Unless you come to any acceptance of this truth, please stop.
>
> You ask for details and then you say the details are lies. You ask for conversation and all you do is minimize and attack and accuse. You cannot redeem Grenville. And your posts filled with anger, judgement and disdain are evidence against you. Where are all the other staff rallying to Grenville's defence with you? Nowhere. They are silent. I don't respect their silence, but it is far preferable to your noise. I know I am not alone when I beg you to stop.

The fallout from this drama was intense. Within days, the organizers shut down the forum. It was a permanent solution that stopped the fights but also wiped out the evidence of a decade of discussion, healing, and connection.

†

The abuse exposed during our first trial had only represented the tip of the iceberg of what had gone on at Grenville. Since it was a common issues trial, our lawyers could only highlight the kind of mistreatment that was commonplace at the school. Over the years, I'd been privy to stories of abuse that were much worse than mine. Some of my close friends had been sexually abused, and their lives had been damaged beyond repair. They were so broken by their experiences that they couldn't even bear to discuss them.

Shortly after the appeal, we got wind that *The Fifth Estate* had chosen to make a new documentary on Grenville. Knowing that a new exposé by Canada's premier investigative documentary series was in the works gave me a boost of optimism. I clung to that hope as we waited for the judges to consider the appeal's merits.

Producers from *The Fifth Estate* contacted me several times, trying to glean background information. They asked me for an interview, but I was full of misgivings. My story had already been told in court. I hoped they could find former students with different stories to tell. Also, the thought of being filmed sent me over the edge. My psychologist agreed. I was in no shape to be interviewed on camera.

In the end, I needn't have worried. Several survivors agreed to be interviewed, including Michael and Grace, two of my closest staff-kid friends. In addition to the standard mind control, they reported being sexually abused by the Farnsworths. The process was going to be agonizing for them, and I did my best to help them endure the months of reliving, interviewing, and filming. Their courage humbled me. I knew their interviews would make a tremendous impact, exposing abuse that previous attempts at criminal charges had failed to prosecute. Still, it was heartbreaking to watch the toll the process took on them.

On the bright side, I received the second-best email of my life just days before *The Fifth Estate* segment aired. Our lawyer Sabrina wrote, *I am so happy to pass along the Court of Appeal decision to you all. We won!!*

I could hardly process my relief. I knew that despite the triumphant headlines and the outpouring of excitement, the defence could still appeal their second loss to the Supreme Court of Canada. I dreaded this, as it would string out our litigation for many more years.

Happily, we waited only fifteen days. On November 10, 2021, we were notified that the defence wouldn't be applying for leave to appeal. Our win finally sunk in then. We had won a landmark case! It was now the first class action involving historical abuse, and the first one dealing with systemic negligence, to win at trial in Canada. It dawned on me that our efforts might genuinely make a difference. And in my head, I was designing Grenville survivor t-shirts. (Mine read, *#HaughtyAF*.)

The next day, *The Fifth Estate*'s documentary "School of Secrets: New Revelations from Inside the Cult" aired on prime time. As I watched it, I held my breath. Sometimes I cheered. Other times, I cried. My heart broke as my friends shared their private, painful memories on screen.

That documentary was a significant step toward our collective healing. Within months, over a million people viewed it online. It not only highlighted previously hidden sexual abuse but also uncovered strong connections between Grenville and the Community, confirmed by CBC through powerful footage, interviews, and documents. This was especially gratifying because the Community's legal spokespeople had been vigorously denying any role in the abuse that took place at Grenville. At one point in an interview, their Boston-based lawyer said, "I know you have a take. I happen to think it's grotesquely unfair and that it's hugely sloppy. It's preposterous, and frankly it should be offensive to anybody who cares about fundamental fairness."

Easy for him to say, I thought. *He never lived at the Community.*

The Fifth Estate also exposed how Gordon Mintz, Grenville's final headmaster, had recently been given command of the Canadian Forces

Chaplain School. Back in 2019, two former students had lodged official complaints to the Chaplain General of the Canadian Armed Forces about Gordon. One of them, Brad Merson, reported being cruelly targeted by Gordon at Grenville. Each whistleblower received emails informing them that investigations had been launched. Two years passed, and nothing was ever done.

The Fifth Estate changed that. Especially when the chief of staff to the Chaplain General told the show that unless Mintz faced criminal charges, no action would be taken by the military. This upset so many viewers that an online petition was launched, and the military was flooded with letters of outrage. Less than a month after the documentary aired, a CBC article reported that Gordon was no longer in charge of the Canadian Forces Chaplain School and was leaving the military altogether, per the Department of National Defence.

Tragically, Brad Merson's life had already been broken beyond repair. In March 2022, Brad reached out to me for guidance in writing his impact statement for our lawsuit. Overwhelmed and triggered by the process, he struggled to record the years of mental illness he'd endured since leaving Grenville. I tried to help, but I became worried when he didn't answer my texts. You can imagine my grief when I heard that Brad had died by suicide in May 2022.

†

On January 20, 2022, a CBC article announced, "New sex abuse allegations target son of former headmaster at now-closed Christian boarding school." Since *The Fifth Estate* exposé, more victims had come forward about Grenville. Shockingly, one of them reported being victimized by Robert Farnsworth as a child at the Community. The other had been in grade eight at Grenville when the headmaster's son allegedly assaulted him. In both cases, the leadership was made aware of the incidents and never alerted the police.

One of the victims, who wished to remain anonymous, said, "I'm speaking out today because I know that someone who sexually assaults little kids, who doesn't hesitate to take away their innocence at the age of six, or seven, or eight … will never stop. Not until he's … locked up." The article concluded by saying after *The Fifth Estate* report revealed new allegations of sexual assault against Robert Farnsworth, the OPP announced it would review its entire investigation into Grenville. (Sawa et al., 2022)

I'll believe it when I see it, I thought.

While it was gratifying to know that action might be taken, I was aware of the toll this process had taken on my close friends. Ever since the show had aired in November, they had been inundated with #MeToo messages. Michael and Grace helped everyone as best as they could and were instrumental in furthering the investigations in the media and with the police. But consequently, their already fragile health deteriorated further. Awareness was being raised, but at what cost?

Meanwhile, I was fighting another battle of my own.

In October 2021, my two years of disability ran out. Both my psychologist and my psychiatrist firmly agreed that I wasn't ready to return to work. They reassured me that with my history, I'd be granted long-term disability. Despite this, I was terrified that my insurance company wouldn't agree.

As part of the process to determine my eligibility, I had to undergo extensive testing by a Toronto psychologist hired by my insurance company. For two days, I was bombarded with questions that made me feel like my brain was going to explode. Anyone who's been through benzo withdrawal would understand. Tears streamed down my face as I struggled to answer thousands of questions that assessed my cognition, memory, and mental health. It was humbling to have so much trouble working through relatively easy tasks. The testing assistant watched stoically as I repeatedly became overwhelmed. Most of the time, I felt like a dizzy, foggy blockhead.

When it was over, my file for the insurance company was two inches thick. I was told that it would take four to six weeks for the psychologist to prepare her report. I went home, relieved that it was over and hoping the doctor would agree with my specialists.

Living under the threat of losing my financial security was excruciating. I could hardly bear the uncertainty. Even though my testing was completed on October 15, 2021, the psychologist's results weren't ready until January 28, 2022.

It wasn't worth the wait. My LTD claim was denied. Even worse, I learned that the so-called expert determined I was malingering (a.k.a., faking my poor results). She even claimed that I didn't have PTSD and suggested that I'd benefit from treatment for borderline personality disorder.

Her labelling me as a liar sent me over the edge. Suddenly, I was right back at Grenville, being falsely accused and sentenced. This triggered a maelstrom of physical and psychological issues. For days, I was a weepy, violently dizzy mess. I couldn't sleep or exercise. Anxiety threatened to paralyze me. Over the ensuing weeks, all I could think about was hating my body or how much I craved food. I constantly wanted to eat my way into oblivion.

It took me a month to rally myself and summon the will to file an appeal. I felt unequal to the task and despaired of ever being granted compensation. Still, I had to try. My head swam as I endured phone calls with insurance representatives and lawyers. I was tasked with writing a letter of my intent to appeal, in which I had to plead my case. Along with that, I had to solicit letters from my specialists to refute the findings of the insurance company's psychologist. My doctors rose to the occasion brilliantly, each preparing comprehensive reports jammed with evidence explaining my diagnoses, my trauma history, and my current inability to work.

On March 3, 2022, I sent my appeal documents to the insurance company by courier. I was told I'd have to wait at least three months for a decision.

And so began my life without a salary. It didn't help that Garry had retired and was on a reduced income. Or that gas prices and inflation were skyrocketing. At the same time, Victoria was in competitive dance and preparing to graduate from high school. How would we put her through university? How would we even pay for our cars, and housing, and insurance, and groceries, and vet bills, and …?

For months I braced myself for the insurance company's fateful inhouse decision. Trying not to hope or worry too much. When the ruling was made on October 25, 2022, I had no reserves left for the final blow: my appeal was denied.

Words cannot adequately describe my devastation. All my worst PTSD symptoms reared their ugly heads like a terrifying Medusa. Dark thoughts swirled like menacing vultures, threatening to roost. *How will I survive this? My strength and hope are gone. What's the point anymore?*

✝

As I write this, my future is awash with uncertainty. I live my life in a dreadful limbo, trying not to dwell on the fact that I have no idea what will become of me. And trying to stave off the near-constant intrusive thoughts and cravings.

I'm so grateful for Garry, who's been such a steady source of support. He keeps assuring me that we'll get through this, saying, "We can sell the house." Or, "I'll get a job as a bus driver," even though he'd just retired after thirty-three years of policing.

Exercise and writing help me cope, though I force myself to do both. Without a vigorous workout, my anxiety disables me. And writing has allowed me to process the trauma that's impacted me for decades. I have so much more self-compassion now. That said, it's also been excruciating. One or two hours per day is all I can manage.

As I write, I have no idea if I'll ever publish this story. Self-doubt is a constant companion. Still, a feisty part of me propels me to persevere. *Keep writing, Beth. Someone might need to read this!* That voice prevails most days, pushing me towards my office, even when I don't think I can bear it.

I'm learning that it's OK if the future remains a mystery.

I've chosen to pursue litigation to win back my disability. This battle may last another twelve months, and there's no guarantee of victory. *But what choice do I have?* I'm nowhere near ready to face the demands of teaching.

Meanwhile, our Grenville lawsuit continues. Our lawyers say that since it's the first of its kind to make it this far in Canada, we're heading into uncharted waters. Loretta has even said that she hopes our case concludes before she retires. Winning the common issues trial was an epic triumph. It validated our pain and forced the former leaders to take accountability. Still, we're by no means finished.

We're now entering the compensation stage with yet another presiding judge, and we've all been tasked with writing impact statements. I've been encouraging everyone involved to tackle this daunting task. Unsurprisingly, it remains too difficult for some. Others got through it with a team of mental health professionals. I continue to be struck by how deeply people were damaged, even if they only attended Grenville for a few months. Decades later, they need therapy and are crippled by self-doubt. They've spent years hating themselves and resorted to substance abuse. They've lost employment opportunities, relationships, or worse. When you intentionally break someone, sometimes they can't be fixed.

This next stage won't be easy. Our common issues trial established general wrongdoing on Grenville's part. Now, to get class members compensated, we have to prove that the damages specific to each person were caused by Grenville's misconduct. If we can't reach a settlement, this may drag on for several more years. As ever, it won't be for the faint of heart.

Chapter 30
Hope

Not every good story ends happily. If the title wasn't a giveaway, here's another spoiler: my story doesn't have a clear-cut, happily-ever-after ending. Fortunately, there is no further carnage in the finale. Just an acknowledgement that recovery is a long journey. And I, for one, am nowhere near the finish line.

I'm currently living in obscurity without income or career. Sometimes, I'm almost without hope. The unending uncertainty often feels unbearable. Worst-case scenarios play out on a loop. Dreams of healing and making a comeback are so dim I can barely access them. Even publishing this story seems like an impossible fantasy.

But there is a flame of hope that still lives inside me. Some days, it is barely flickering. On others, its blaze burns bright. It helps me take stock and look back on my journey with wonder.

I will never regret taking on the lawsuit. Granted, it stirred up a lifetime of complex trauma. But no one can expect deep healing without deep pain. When we began, I only had a vague understanding of how damaging Grenville had been to myself or others. Now, my eyes are wide open. Sometimes I'm overcome with grief, and it occasionally morphs into rage. Doubt and confusion are my close companions. But lately, I sometimes feel an unfamiliar sense of pride pushing my shoulders back. Gratitude and hope are beginning to peer through the clouds more frequently.

Even though I've had my share of pain, I have also been blessed with opportunities. I was the first staff child born at Grenville, and I grew up to represent the rest in court. I became a wife, a mother, and a teacher—things I only dared to dream about growing up. Despite the difficulty of these past few years, I have had the chance to rest, heal, and write. I'm learning it's safe just to exist, without any need to prove my worth. Food is becoming less of a threat, and I feel increasingly comfortable in my own skin. I can now look back at everything I've experienced and feel a growing sense of peace.

Sure, my life is shadowed by doubts. I don't know if my disability benefits will ever be reinstated or if I'll ever teach again. I also don't know if our lawsuit will reach a satisfactory conclusion or if this story will have any kind of positive impact. I guess time, as it always does, will tell. In the meantime, I'll keep walking this path toward healing.

Amidst the pain of uncertainty, I cling to hope.

I hope that other victims of religious abuse may find healing. It is such a long and confusing road to recovery. Until victims understand what happened to them, they can't begin to heal.

This book is my attempt to help build more understanding of the impact of toxic and weaponized religion. The more stories we share, the more I hope survivors will be able to make sense of their trauma. People are breakable. When children are stripped of their self-worth and traumatized in a system of fear, they become adults who can't always cope. Their partners, children, and even colleagues will be impacted. The ripple effects can be staggering.

Therapy is a luxury and can even make things worse. Many survivors I know say they can't find therapists who understand cults or religious abuse. One woman told me that the day her counsellor accused her of fabricating her Grenville memories, she attempted suicide. The pain and isolation are often unbearable. I hope this book will provide readers with the kind of insight I so desperately needed when I was lost.

Furthermore, I hope our lawsuit will set legal precedents and continue to spotlight institutional spiritual abuse. Sadly, Grenville wasn't a one-off. In Canada, we're still reeling from the stories of horrific abuses committed at Native residential schools. For over a century, more than 150,000 Indigenous children were forced to attend boarding schools. The intent was to erase their Indigenous heritage and replace it with Canadian culture and Christian beliefs. Yet, these schools destroyed a lot more than that. Thousands of lives were ruined by physical, sexual, and psychological abuse. Those that survived lived lives tormented by trauma. Even worse, thousands never returned home.

These residential schools were closer in nature to concentration camps. Our nation's history will forever be stained by the cruelty meted out in these institutions of horror. The fact that our churches ran these schools is even more alarming.

In the troubled-teen industry, thousands of youths are still being abused in the name of God. Many therapeutic boarding schools, residential treatment centres, conversion therapy centres, and wilderness programs—most of which are run by religious groups—continue to operate largely unregulated, despite numerous allegations of serious abuse. The fact that their religious status exempts them from government oversight should alarm everyone. Youth don't leave these places unscathed. Like me, they will be scarred for life.

Recently, my heart sank as I read a new CBC headline about exorcisms, violent discipline, and abuse alleged by former students at a private Christian school in Saskatoon. Ailsa Watkinson, a professor at the University of Regina, was quoted saying, "Religion was used to torment, to discriminate. It's cruel. This is torture. Anyone with common sense knows this." (Warick, 2022)

What we need is for common sense to prevail.

I'm not against religion (though I have developed a healthy dose of skepticism). And I understand why millions believe in a higher power. They seek a sense of belonging, purpose, or divine comfort. They want their lives to matter. Believe me, I get it. Sometimes, I even miss it. You don't leave religion without paying a hefty price. For me, one cost of so-called freedom is living with fear of the afterlife. At funerals, preachers proclaim that the dead have gone to a better place. Yet I can't help but think: *Have they? Really?*

For me, the certainty of salvation, Heaven, and Hell is long gone. All I have left are questions.

For instance, if religious freedoms are guaranteed by law, and religious institutions enjoy tax exemptions, is it too much to demand accountability? Why are religious freedoms allowed to cover a multitude of sins? Why are religious leaders free to act with impunity or spread hateful intolerance? I don't understand why those who escape cults have almost zero legal recourse while abusive cult leaders hide behind the religious freedoms built into our constitutions.

I have hope that someday this will change. I envision a future where religious leaders aren't permitted to terrorize, intimidate, or abuse. When religious rhetoric is weaponized, there can be lasting damage. Especially to youth, who don't regard warnings of hellfire as idle threats, or forget the shame of being branded a hopeless sinner. I'm fifty-three at the time of writing, and those accusations still haunt me.

More people must open their eyes to the damage so often inflicted by religion. Don't accept programs and institutions at face value. Take a closer look and question everything. Do their leaders claim to be the sole conduit for God? Do they indulge in acts of cruelty to control members? Do they attempt to break people down? Are their followers living in Hell just to get to Heaven?

Sadly, finding answers to these questions might be nearly impossible unless one infiltrates institutions like an undercover spy. Most churches seem like warm, welcoming communities. From the outside, cults often appear to be a sort of Heaven on Earth. At Grenville, visiting dignitaries, advisers, and even ministry inspectors were always impressed by students and staff. They were never privy to the ugly truth. It doesn't help that followers are usually blind to any abuse. They're taught to suspend independent thought and unlikely to notice the damage being done to them or to those around them.

Sometimes I wonder what might have happened if someone from the outside world had tried to save me from cult life. What if, like a fairy godmother, an aunt had written me letters of support and encouragement?

What if, when I was four years old, she had told me that it wasn't a sin for my parents to love me?

What if she had urged me not to believe the cruel accusations I endured in light sessions? Or not to starve myself to earn my worth?

When I was expelled from Grenville, what if she said that I wasn't responsible for bringing Satan into the school? That I didn't deserve to be treated like a criminal? And what if, when I was fired over a bulimic episode, she insisted I contact a lawyer?

I could play the what-if game forever.

The reality is that even if I'd received support from a beloved relative, it might not have done me much good. I was taught to shun the outside world and everyone in it. I would have distrusted everything an outsider said, as though their words came straight from the fiery pit.

Luckily, I came to my senses on my own. Resolving to escape took nearly three years, but that was the easy part. The work of recovery and deprogramming has taken twenty years and counting.

Here is the heartbreaking truth. When someone's mind is controlled with religious brainwashing, conspiracy theories, or state-controlled news, there isn't much an outsider can say to change their mind. Rampant indoctrination threatens to destabilize us all. Just look at Putin's control of the Russian media during the Ukrainian invasion and slaughter. Or the rise in Christian nationalism and Evangelical extremism that is inextricably linked with a resurgence of bigotry, hate crimes, and worse. I'm frankly becoming terrified for the future of democracy, as I've recently watched millions devote themselves to corrupt charismatic leaders using classic cult tactics to manipulate followers. Many of these devotees are fundamentalist Christians who are convinced that a certain orange felon is God's ordained leader of the USA.

I think we can all agree that mind control is a powerful and dangerous weapon.

Is there an antidote? I don't know. Perhaps all we can do is cultivate compassion and spread awareness. We can open our eyes to harmful indoctrination hurting people in our midst. We can listen and learn from those who have suffered abuse in the name of God. Above all, we must realize that when religious beliefs are weaponized, they can do permanent damage.

Letters of love and compassion to my younger self may not have helped. But then again, they might have made all the difference.

Epilogue

It's widely said that good things come to those who wait. I'm not sure that's always true. Still, the past few years of uncertainty and waiting have begun to pay off.

Since finishing this manuscript, I've finally received some closure. First, after nearly two years without income, I settled out of court with the insurance company that terminated my disability benefits. Soon afterward, our class action lawsuit also reached a settlement. During the days of negotiation, I often cried, feeling such a heavy burden for my peers as we fought for the best possible result. Ultimately, a settlement seemed the most trauma-informed path. The alternative would have meant trials for each class member, and I knew firsthand how traumatizing those would be.

In the end, our lawsuit provided validation, healing, and financial compensation that served a symbolic function in acknowledging the harm so many of us had endured. No amount of money could really suffice, but I'm at peace with the outcome. Our class action has paved the way for similar historical abuse cases. Many barristers across Canada who are representing victims of systemic abuse have already contacted our lawyers for guidance. I'm so proud that our lawsuit is setting valuable legal precedent.

In other news, my mental and neurological health are slowly improving. After the legal battles concluded, I could finally exhale and heal more deeply. I live a quiet life, without the same unrelenting pressure to prove myself or outrun my demons. Little by little, I'm finding my way towards a future of promise and purpose. Thanks to a coach with the last name of Shakespeare (ha!) who texts me daily from England, there's a real possibility that one day I'll be able to say that *I used to have an eating disorder.* These days I rarely binge and I usually feel neutral about my reflection. I'm proud to be a diet-culture dropout. Which, in this new world of injectable weight-loss drugs, I think is pretty badass!

Lastly, I managed to publish this book. Like with the class action, if I'd known how difficult publishing would be, I never would have attempted it. Still, I have no regrets.

I hope, dear reader, that my story has helped you in some way. Maybe it has opened your eyes to the harms of religious abuse. Maybe it has served as a cautionary tale, alerting you to the danger of cults hiding in plain sight. Maybe it has validated your own trauma. Above all, I hope it made an impact. Thank you for braving the journey with me.

Bibliography

Cavanaugh v Haig. Vol 1–9 of Transcripts from Ontario Superior Court of Justice (Sept–October 2019) Court of Appeal No. C68263. https://www.mckenzielake.com/the-grenville-christian-college-class-proceeding

"Community or Cult?" *Chronicle.* WCVB Channel 5. Boston, Massachusetts. Channel V, July 22, 1993.

Court File No. 08-CV-347100CP (Affidavit of Don Farnsworth, 2011, pp. 12–13)

Court File No. 08-CV-347100CP (Affidavit of Ken MacNeil, 2011, pp. 3–6)

Factnet Forum. August-October 2007. http://factnet.org (forum disabled in 2016). Usernames: alwaysonD, bossman, Dignity Quest, dreamtruth, familylove, former gcc girl, gayatgcc, Hobart dishmachine, papillon, purgatory, quietgrl, Tinkerbell84, Tiny, tmw

Grenville Christian College. *Anno Domini.* Brockville, Ontario. 1979/80.

Grenville Christian College. *Anno Domini.* Brockville, Ontario. 1984/85.

Grenville Christian College. *Anno Domini.* Brockville, Ontario. 1986/87.

Haig, J. Alastair. "The 14 Miracles at Grenville Christian College." Brockville, Ontario: Grenville Christian College, 1977

Hassan, Steven. *Combating Cult Mind Control: The #1 Best-selling Guide to Protection, Rescue, and Recovery from Destructive Cults.* 3rd Edition. Newton, MA: Freedom of Mind Press, 2015.

"In the Name of God." *W5.* CTV. Toronto, Ontario. CFTO, 2016.

Johnson, Brian. "Risks Associated with Long-Term Benzodiazepine Use." *American Family Physician* 88, no. 4 (August 15, 2013): 224–6.

Mel McDaniel, post on private Facebook group. May 2021.

McKeehan, Nick. "Do Benzodiazepines Pose a Dementia Risk?" *Cognitive Vitality*, April 12, 2016. https://www.alzdiscovery.org/cognitive-vitality/blog/do-benzodiazepines-pose-a-dementia-risk-yes-no-maybe

Merz, Beverly. "Benzodiazepine use may raise risk of Alzheimer's disease." *Harvard Health Publishing*, September 10, 2014. https://www.health.harvard.edu/blog/benzodiazepine-use-may-raise-risk-alzheimers-disease-201409107397

Sawa, Timothy, Andrew Culbert, Bob McKeown. "New sex abuse allegations target son of former headmaster at now-closed Christian boarding school." CBC News. CBC/Radio-Canada, January 20, 2022. https://www.cbc.ca/news/canada/new-allegations-school-of-secrets-1.6319539

"School of Secrets: New revelations from inside the cult." *The Fifth Estate.* CBC Television. Toronto, Ontario. CBLT-DT, November 11, 2021.

Warick, Jason. "Exorcisms, violent discipline and other abuse alleged former students of private Christian school." CBC News. CBC/Radio-Canada, August 2, 2022. https://www.cbc.ca/news/canada/saskatoon/abuse-alleged-former-students-of-private-christian-school-1.6532329

West, L. J., & Langone, M. D. "Cultism: A conference for scholars and policy makers." *Cultic Studies Journal* 3 (1986): 117–134.

Acknowledgements

I begin by thanking Jacqueline who urged me to write this book in the first place. She believed in me, long before I did.

To my psychologist Dr. Blouin, I would have been lost without you. Thank you for patiently helping me put the pieces of my broken self back together.

Thank you to my husband and children who loved me at my worst during the years I wrote this book. I cherish all the times I'd hear, "You OK?" from the next room. Special thanks to my daughter Victoria, whose literary insight has been wise beyond her years.

To my brother Dan, who generously edited my first draft (all 130,000 words!). Without his encouragement, I might have quit. Thank you to Grace, Dawn, Paul, Loretta, and Wendy who also read my long first draft. Without your positive feedback, I would not have mustered the courage to publish.

Thank you to my parents, who championed this book even though it exposed our family's private painful truths.

To those whose stories are represented in this book, thank you. To my fellow representative plaintiffs, Lisa, Andrew, Richard, and Tim, I am so proud to be in your company. To Mark, Liz, Dawn, Karen, and François, thank you for allowing me to share parts of your stories. To the hundreds of my fellow survivors whose names I didn't mention, thank you for continually inspiring me with your bravery and your vulnerability.

I am especially grateful to our lawyers. The Honourable Russell Raikes and the Honourable Loretta Merritt (who have since been appointed judges of the Superior Court of Justice) along with Sabrina Lombardi were our fearless leaders into battle. I'll never forget your compassion and tireless efforts on our behalf.

Thank you to all the industry experts who helped turn my manuscript into a published book. To Sara Letourneau, thank you for making the process of "killing my darlings" bearable. Thank you to my team at Ingenium Books. Special thanks are owed to Rachael Shenyo who was given the difficult task of copy editing, and who did so rigorously but with great sensitivity. Most of all, I thank my publisher Boni Wagner-Stafford who answered my first DM within minutes and fiercely championed my story from day one.

Finally, I thank my Grandpa Eutsler, who granted me the keys to freedom years before I gathered the courage to use them. I hope this book makes him proud.

About the Author

Beth Granger was the first staff child born at Grenville Christian College, an elite private boarding school in Canada. In truth, it was a cult. After her escape at age thirty-one, she didn't become a drug-addicted street-walker or go straight to Hell, as her cult leaders predicted.

Instead, she earned her Bachelor of Education at Queen's University, got hired after her first teacher interview, married a police officer, and became a mother of two. She also helped spearhead a sixteen-year landmark class action lawsuit against her abusers.

Writing this, her first book, played an essential part in Beth's healing when it became clear that she couldn't outrun her trauma. In addition to complex PTSD, she's been recovering from benzo withdrawal and a lifelong eating disorder.

Beth resides near Ottawa with her family and her three Cavaliers, Harry, Hermione, and Ron. When she isn't writing, you might find her painting, forest bathing, napping, cycling in her Cookie Monster jersey, or singing at the top of her lungs (on stage or behind the wheel).

Beth is dedicated to shedding light on the long-term impact of trauma inflicted by weaponized religion and to helping its survivors heal.

Stay in touch with Beth at www.bethgranger.ca.

You Might Also Enjoy ...

The 49th Protocol

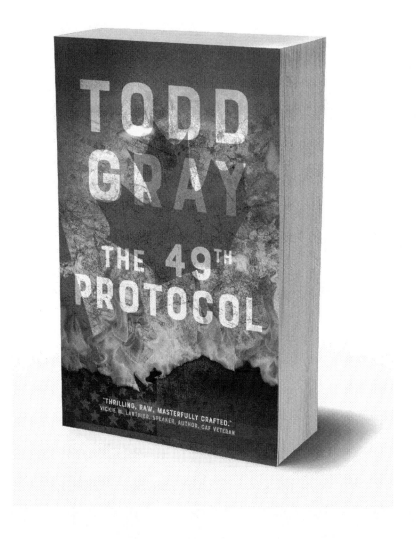

ingeniumbooks.com/49P

12 Elephants and a Dragon:
A Memoir of Survival
and the Kindness of Strangers

ingeniumbooks.com/12ED

Chill:
The Wine Lover's
Introduction to Cannabis

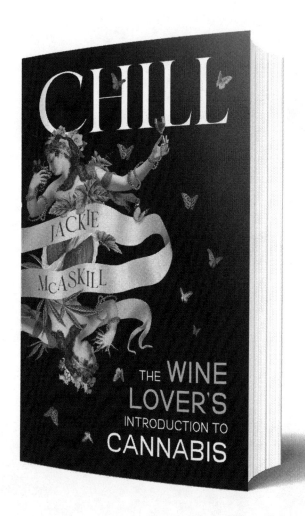

ingeniumbooks.com/CHILL

Choices:
How to Mend or End
a Broken Relationship

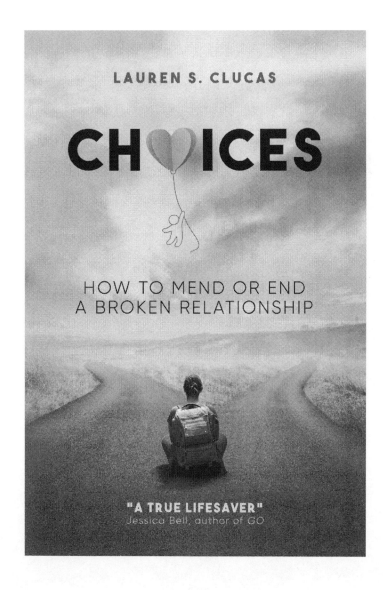

ingeniumbooks.com/CHCS

Mom on Wheels:
The Power of Purpose
for a Parent with Paraplegia

ingeniumbooks.com/as3o

Made in the USA
Columbia, SC
18 February 2025